SUCCESSFUL SCHOOL LEADERSHIP PREPARATION AND DEVELOPMENT

ADVANCES IN EDUCATIONAL ADMINISTRATION

Series Editor: Anthony H. Normore

Recent Volumes:

Volumes 1–5:	Series Editor: Paul W. Thurston
Volumes 6–10:	Series Editor: Richard C. Hunter
Volume 11:	Global Perspectives on Educational Leadership Reform: The Development and Preparation of *Leaders of Learning* and *Learners of Leadership* – Edited by Anthony H. Normore
Volume 12:	Leadership in Education, Corrections and Law Enforcement: A Commitment to Ethics, Equity and Excellence – Edited by Anthony H. Normore and Brian D. Fitch
Volume 13:	Discretionary Behavior and Performance in Educational Organizations: The Missing Link in Educational Leadership and Management – Edited by Ibrahim Duyar and Anthony H. Normore
Volume 14:	Global Leadership for Social Justice: Taking it from the Field to Practice – Edited by Christa Boske and Sarah Diem
Volume 15:	The Management and Leadership of Educational Marketing: Research, Practice and Applications – Edited by Izhar Oplatka and Jane Hemsley-Brown
Volume 16:	Transforming Learning Environments: Strategies to Shape the Next Generation – Edited by Fayneese S. Miller

ADVANCES IN EDUCATIONAL ADMINISTRATION
VOLUME 17

SUCCESSFUL SCHOOL LEADERSHIP PREPARATION AND DEVELOPMENT

EDITED BY

KAREN SANZO
Old Dominion University, Norfolk, VA, USA

STEVE MYRAN
Old Dominion University, Norfolk, VA, USA

ANTHONY H. NORMORE
California Lutheran University, Thousand Oaks, CA, USA

PROPERTY OF
BAKER COLLEGE
Owosso Campus

United Kingdom – North America – Japan
India – Malaysia – China

Emerald Group Publishing Limited
Howard House, Wagon Lane, Bingley BD16 1WA, UK

First edition 2012

Copyright © 2012 Emerald Group Publishing Limited

Reprints and permission service
Contact: permissions@emeraldinsight.com

No part of this book may be reproduced, stored in a retrieval system, transmitted in any form or by any means electronic, mechanical, photocopying, recording or otherwise without either the prior written permission of the publisher or a licence permitting restricted copying issued in the UK by The Copyright Licensing Agency and in the USA by The Copyright Clearance Center. Any opinions expressed in the chapters are those of the authors. Whilst Emerald makes every effort to ensure the quality and accuracy of its content, Emerald makes no representation implied or otherwise, as to the chapters' suitability and application and disclaims any warranties, express or implied, to their use.

British Library Cataloguing in Publication Data
A catalogue record for this book is available from the British Library

ISBN: 978-1-78052-322-4
ISSN: 1479-3660 (Series)

ISOQAR certified Management Systems, awarded to Emerald for adherence to Quality and Environmental standards ISO 9001:2008 and 14001:2004, respectively

Certificate Number 1985
ISO 9001
ISO 14001

INVESTOR IN PEOPLE

CONTENTS

DEDICATION   *vii*

LIST OF CONTRIBUTORS   *ix*

INTRODUCTION   *xiii*

CHAPTER 1 LEADERSHIP PREPARATION PROGRAM EVALUATION: EXPERIENCES AND INSIGHTS
    Ann O'Doherty and Margaret Terry Orr   *1*

CHAPTER 2 THE POWER OF INSTITUTIONAL PARTNERSHIP IN THE DEVELOPMENT OF TURN AROUND SCHOOL LEADERS
    Stephen H. Davis, Ronald J. Leon and Miriam L. Fultz   *25*

CHAPTER 3 PLANNING, CHANGING, AND LEADING A COMMUNITY OF PROFESSIONAL PRACTICE: *LESSONS LEARNED FROM AN INNOVATIVE URBAN SCHOOL LEADERS PREPARATION PROGRAM IN SOUTHERN CALIFORNIA*
    Antonia Issa Lahera and Anthony H. Normore   *49*

CHAPTER 4 CREATING AND SUSTAINING DYNAMIC UNIVERSITY/SCHOOL DISTRICT PARTNERSHIPS FOR THE PREPARATION OF LEARNING-CENTERED SCHOOL LEADERS
    Betty V. Fry, David Collins and Edward Iwanicki   *73*

CHAPTER 5 A RIGOROUS RECRUITMENT AND SELECTION PROCESS OF THE UNIVERSITY OF TEXAS AT AUSTIN PRINCIPALSHIP PROGRAM
    Mark A. Gooden and Richard Gonzales   *97*

CHAPTER 6 LEARNING-CENTERED LEADERSHIP
DEVELOPMENT PROGRAM FOR PRACTICING AND
ASPIRING PRINCIPALS
   Jianping Shen and Van E. Cooley   113

CHAPTER 7 PREPARING AND SUPPORTING
PRINCIPALS IN RURAL SOUTH DAKOTA SCHOOLS
   Jeanne Cowan and Janet Hensley   137

CHAPTER 8 RE-DESIGNING LESSONS,
RE-ENVISIONING PRINCIPALS: DEVELOPING
ENTREPRENEURIAL SCHOOL LEADERSHIP
   Kristy Hebert, Josh Bendickson, Eric W. Liguori,   153
   K. Mark Weaver and Charles Teddlie

CHAPTER 9 LEARNING FROM THE EVOLUTION
OF A UNIVERSITY–DISTRICT PARTNERSHIP
   Karen L. Sanzo and Steve Myran   165

CHAPTER 10 THE RURAL ALASKA PRINCIPAL
PREPARATION AND SUPPORT PROGRAM:
A COMPREHENSIVE APPROACH TO
STRENGTHENING SCHOOL LEADERSHIP
IN RURAL ALASKA
   J. Kelly Tonsmeire, Kathy Blanc, Al Bertani, Susan   183
   Garton, Gary Whiteley, Lexie Domaradzki and Carol Kane

CHAPTER 11 ACCELERATING LEADERSHIP
EXCELLENCE: NYC LEADERSHIP ACADEMY'S
SCHOOL LEADERSHIP COACHING MODEL
   Tierney Temple Fairchild   209

CHAPTER 12 THE INTEGRATION OF PRACTICAL,
COGNITIVE, AND MORAL APPRENTICESHIPS FOR
LEADERSHIP LEARNING: THE EVOLUTION AND
INITIAL IMPACT OF FULL-TIME INTERNSHIPS
   Susan Korach and Maureen Sanders   237

ABOUT THE AUTHORS   265

AUTHOR INDEX   277

SUBJECT INDEX   285

Van Edwin Cooley, Ed.D., was a lifelong learner, advocate for education reform, respected educator, beloved family member and treasured friend. He worked in the field of education for 38 years, serving as a teacher, vice principal, assistant superintendent and superintendent in Indiana, and as an associate professor, professor, department chair and interim dean at Western Michigan University. Dr. Cooley authored or co-authored over 60 scholarly articles and directed or co-directed numerous grants. His memory will live on in the lives that he touched.

LIST OF CONTRIBUTORS

Josh Bendickson	E. J. Ourso College of Business, Louisiana State University, Baton Rouge, LA, USA
Al Bertani	Alaska Staff Development Network (ASDN), Chicago, IL, USA
Kathy Blanc	Alaska Staff Development Network (ASDN), Douglas, AK, USA
David Collins	Southern Regional Education Board, FL, USA
Van E. Cooley	Deceased
Jeanne Cowan	Technology and Innovation in Education (TIE), Rapid City, SD, USA
Stephen H. Davis	California State Polytechnic University, Pomona, CA, USA
Lexie Domaradzki	Reach Education Consulting, Edmonds, WA, USA
Tierney Temple Fairchild	Socratic Solutions, Inc., Charlottesville, VA, USA
Betty V. Fry	Florida Leadership Academy, Florida Turnaround Leaders Program at the Southern Regional Education Board (SREB), Atlanta, Georgia
Miriam L. Fultz	Desertfrost Consulting Group, Inc., Pinon Hills, CA, USA
Susan Garton	University of Alaska Anchorage (UAA), Anchorage, AK, USA
Richard Gonzales	Department of Educational Leadership, University of Connecticut, Storrs, CT, USA

Mark A. Gooden	Educational Administration Department, The University of Texas at Austin, Austin, TX, USA
Kristy Hebert	Advance Innovative Education, Baton Rouge, LA, USA
Janet Hensley	Technology and Innovation in Education (TIE), Rapid City, SD, USA
Antonia Issa Lahera	Graduate Education Division, California State University, Dominguez Hills, Carson, CA, USA
Edward Iwanicki	Neag School of Education, University of Connecticut, Storrs, CT, USA
Carol Kane	Alaska Administrator Coaching Project, Big Lake, AK, USA
Susan Korach	Morgridge College of Education at the University of Denver (DU), Denver, CO, USA
Ronald J. Leon	California State Polytechnic University, Pomona, CA, USA
Eric W. Liguori	Craig School of Business at California State University, Fresno, CA, USA
Steve Myran	Department of Educational Foundations and Leadership, Old Dominion University, Norfolk, VA, USA
Anthony H. Normore	Department of Educational Leadership in the Graduate School of Education at California Lutheran University, Thousand Oaks, CA, USA
Ann O'Doherty	Danforth Educational Leadership Program, Center for Educational Leadership, University of Washington, Seattle, WA, USA
Margaret Terry Orr	Department of Educational Leadership, Bank Street College of Education, New York, NY, USA

List of Contributors

Maureen Sanders	New York City Leadership Academy, New York, NY, USA
Karen L. Sanzo	Department of Educational Foundations and Leadership, College of Education, Old Dominion University, Norfolk, VA, USA
Jianping Shen	Department of Educational Leadership, Research and Technology, Western Michigan University, Kalamazoo, MI, USA
Charles Teddlie	College of Education, Louisiana State University, Baton Rouge, LA, USA
J. Kelly Tonsmeire	Alaska Staff Development Network (ASDN), Douglas, AK, USA
K. Mark Weaver	Mitchell College of Business, University of South Alabama, Mobile, AL, USA
Gary Whiteley	Alaska Administrator Coaching Project, Kenai, AK, USA

INTRODUCTION

The United States Department of Education School Leadership Program funds aspiring and current school leadership preparation programs throughout the United States. These projects represent over 100 million in funding educational leadership development since 2002. In this book we have sought to provide the reader a variety of lessons learned from grants originally awarded in 2008, 2009, and 2010. Within these pages you will learn about the experiences of grantees and how they have worked to provide exemplary preparation for aspiring and current assistant principals and principals in the United States. It is our hope that you will use these chapters to support and strengthen your own programs in order to provide training for our schools' leaders, who, in turn will work to provide high quality educational experiences for our nation's students.

In Chapter 1 O'Doherty and Orr explore the processes used to design and conduct the program evaluation for a multi-site university-based principalship program. The conceptual context of program evaluation is provided, as well as how the comprehensive evaluation was aligned to the goals of the leadership program. The authors also provide lessons learned from their own personal experiences with the evaluation.

Davis, Leon, and Fultz describe in the second chapter the strategies used in establishing the Great Leaders for Great Schools Academy (GLGSA), a high impact and sustainable university-district partnership and the first program to be accredited under California's experimental standards for principal preparation. Chapter contents include descriptions of the key elements of the GLGSA and seven recommendations for those who desire to establish innovative and collaborative approaches to leadership preparation. Issa Lahera and Normore in Chapter 3 examine the process of ongoing planning and changing of an innovative urban school leadership development and preparation program at California State University Dominguez Hills. In this chapter, the authors outline the various components of the USL program and share reflections on the planning and improvement process in our efforts to strengthen and improve the community of professional practice within the program.

In Chapter 4 Fry, Collins, and Iwanicki look at the literature that describes and supports district/university partnerships. They then outline their framework of a successful SLP partnership in Florida and provide insights on "lessons learned" throughout the planning, implementation and evaluation of that partnership to document a road map to a successful district and university partnership.

Gooden and Gonzales discuss in Chapter 5 the recruitment and selection method utilized by the University of Texas at Austin Principalship Program (UTAPP). They have identified in their recruitment process several key components associated with exemplary preparation programs (Darling-Hammond, LaPointe, Meyerson, Orr, & Cohen, 2005). These components include: rigorous recruitment and careful selection of participants, a cohort structure, and an emphasis on powerful authentic learning experiences (Orr, 2006).

Shen and Cooley then discuss the content and process of the Learning-Centered Leadership Development Program for Practicing and Aspiring Principals at Western Michigan University. They discuss the program's focus on seven dimensions of principal leadership associated with student achievement based on an extensive literature review. Shen and Cooley also reflect upon the lessons learned from implementing the program.

The Partnership for Improvement in Rural Leadership and Learning (PIRLL) grant is discussed by Cowan and Hensley in Chapter 7. The project goal was to improve school leadership in rural and remote locations across South Dakota and the grant work that included recruitment and training of aspiring principals as well as capacity-building for practicing principals. This chapter provides an overview of the two key elements used to meet this goal – a customized principal preparation program and on-site mentoring and professional development for practicing principals.

Social entrepreneurs and market-driven organizations are those that hold themselves accountable to both social and financial outcomes; they advance their mission by building focused strategies and sustainable business models that address customer needs and yield competitive advantage. In Chapter 8 Hebert, Bendickson, Liguori, Weaver, and Teddlie showcase this principle in action through the work of a nonprofit in Louisiana, Advance Innovative Education (AIE), which is gaining national attention for its innovative approach to education reform. AIE is improving student outcomes one school at a time by transforming school principals into social entrepreneurs. Its program draws on best practices across sectors and teaches school leaders how to harness market forces to deliver better educational opportunities to children.

Sanzo and Myran offer a synopsis of the development of a USDE SLP funded leadership preparation partnership between a school district and public university. This chapter describes the research and development efforts which involved iterative cycles of design, implementation, reflection and redesign that helped to identify problems of practice and develop meaningful solutions to these identified areas of need. They also describe efforts to cultivate an authentic and purposeful partnership that allowed the program to move beyond the limitations of traditional leadership preparation program.

In Chapter 10 Tonsmeire, Blanc, Bertani, Garton, Whiteley, Domaradzki, and Kane highlight the collaborative efforts of a multitude of partners engaged in four distinct yet interrelated programs designed to build leadership capacity across schools serving rural Alaska.

The Rural Alaska Principal Preparation and Support Program (RAPPS) is a comprehensive system of leadership development programs that develop aspiring leaders, induct and coach new principals, promote the professional learning of practicing principals, and support the school improvement efforts of the state education department. The program is described in detail including unique elements of the program designs including summer institutes, cohort models, distance learning offerings, critical friends conversations, and a festival of ideas.

In Chapter 11, Fairchild discusses the methods and results of the Leadership Academy's coaching model for the 139 principals leading high need schools as part of the U.S. Department of Education's School Leadership Program (SLP) and offers insights into school leadership coaching as a distinct professional practice in education. This chapter highlights the unique school coaching model developed by NYC Leadership Academy (Leadership Academy), a national organization focused on improving student outcomes through effective leadership practice. Using a standards-based, facilitative approach to coaching early-career leaders in high need schools, the Leadership Academy has developed a rigorous process for training and developing a cadre of coaches to provide intensive coaching support to school leaders that focuses on strengthening their leadership performance.

Our last chapter, by Korach and Sanders presents an integrated model of principal preparation featuring full-time internships and inquiry-based coursework. The development of the full-time internship component is the result of an award of a USDE School Leadership Program Grant in 2008 to expand and enhance the Ritchie Program for School Leaders, a collaborative principal preparation program between University of Denver and Denver Public Schools. This chapter describes the evolution of the Ritchie

Program for School Leaders through features and initial impact of full-time internships and offers lessons learned about mentoring aspiring leaders.

Karen Sanzo
Steve Myran
Anthony H. Normore
Editors

CHAPTER 1

LEADERSHIP PREPARATION PROGRAM EVALUATION: EXPERIENCES AND INSIGHTS

Ann O'Doherty and Margaret Terry Orr

ABSTRACT

Through the perspectives of a grant director and external evaluator, this chapter explores processes used and lessons learned to design and conduct ongoing evaluation of a multisite university-based principalship program supported in part by a US Department of Education grant. Using frameworks developed by Guskey (2000) and Kirkpatrick (1998), the authors highlight the conceptual context of program evaluation and describe the process used to develop a comprehensive evaluation plan aligned to program goals. The chapter appendix includes a summary of Developing Evaluation Evidence (Orr, Young, & Rorrer, 2010), a free program evaluation planning resource available at ucea.org.

Leadership preparation program evaluation is gaining momentum as an essential task of program development and operations. The US Department of Education (USDoE) School Leadership Program has moved from its former focus on the number of new leaders produced through grant-funded programs to a current emphasis on comparison of pre and postresults of knowledge and skills and assessment of impact on graduates' careers and schools. Such a shift is essential because well-designed program evaluation has the potential to further link program features to participant outcomes, actual practices of specifically prepared school leaders and school-level outcomes. Thus, a well-designed program evaluation can offer insights into what program components appear effective and identify areas for improvement (Orr, Young, Rorrer, 2010). Yet, scant research exists on how educational leadership preparation programs design and use evaluation research for program improvement (Orr & Barber, 2006).

To fill this gap, we developed a case study of our evaluation research experience with a preparation program supported in part by federal grant funding. We serve as the program director and external evaluator for The University of Texas Collaborative Urban Leadership Program (UTCULP), supported by a USDoE School Leadership Program grant. The USDoE process includes evaluation components; however, our evaluation interests were much broader and deeper than the minimal grant evaluation requirements. We centered our approach to evaluation on the efficacy of each program element as designed and implemented, the influence of different district partners, and the impact of the program experience on graduates' career interest, advancement, and practices as school leaders. Utilizing the grant's external funding, we invested in evaluation systems and resources to review the unique programs implemented in three geographic sites, and serve as a means to improve the quality and effectiveness of candidate leadership preparation. Finally, we selected one program feature – coaching – for in-depth investigation and research.

This case study draws on documentation of the evaluation and program materials, our own reflections, and feedback from program faculty gathered through department meetings and informal meetings. This chapter outlines the conceptual context for the evaluation, describes the program and evaluation goals, details the evaluation process (conceptual, methodological, operational and organizational), offers reflection on lessons learned, and outlines plans for future program evaluation.

CONCEPTUAL CONTEXT

The UTCULP program evaluation was guided by two nested theories of action about evaluation and effective leadership preparation. First, our evaluation work has been based on Kirkpatrick (1998) and Guskey's (2000) models for effective program evaluation. Kirkpatrick conceptualizes the levels of evaluation as a linear chain of effects: assessing participants' reaction, learning, application or transfer, and impact on their organization (Kirkpatrick, 1998). Guskey differentiates organizational outcomes further as the changes that result from participants' learning and the organizational outcomes (Guskey, 2000). Their frameworks guided us to identify evaluation measures for each level of effects.

Using these frameworks, we drew on prior evaluation research and reviews of research on leadership preparation programs and program features (Orr, 2009, 2011; Orr & Orphanos, 2011; Orr & Pounder, 2010) on how to conceptualize the relationship between program design, features, and different levels of program outcomes. We explored research about quality leadership preparation (Darling-Hammond, Meyerson, La Pointe, & Orr, 2010; Frye, O'Neill, & Bottoms, 2006; Jackson & Kelley, 2002), reviews of research on leadership preparation (Orr, 2009) and related studies on impact (Orr, 2009, 2011; Orr & Orphanos, 2011).

With this research, we identified specific program features most likely to influence outcomes. These include rigorous, instructionally focused candidate selection; standards-based curriculum and assessments; active learning strategies; and high quality field-based experiences. Several prior studies have measured graduates' reactions to these features (reflecting Kirkpatrick's level one outcomes), showing that graduates rate these features higher in more well-designed programs than do graduates of more conventional programs (Darling-Hammond et al., 2010; Orr & Barber, 2006). A smaller body of research has assessed what candidates learn (Kirkpatrick's level two outcomes) and related these to program design and features. A few studies did this by comparing assessments of candidates' leadership readiness and perceived availability and adequacy of leadership preparation (Hewitson, 1995; Nicholson & Leary, 2001; Restine, 1997). Orr (2011) compared graduates from different leadership preparation programs on their self-reported learning and found participants' positive ratings of program features were positively correlated with participants' learning ratings.

Studies of how graduates apply what they learned from their programs (Kirkpatrick's level three outcomes) have focused on reports and assessment of leadership practice. In both graduates' self-reports on their practices as school principals (Orphanos & Orr, 2012) and teacher ratings of leadership effectiveness (Korach, Ballenger, & Alford, 2011; Leithwood, Jantzi, Coffin, & Wilson, 1996; Orphanos & Orr, 2012) showed a positive relationship between well-developed program features and effective leadership practices. Other research has linked preparation to graduates' career progress as principals, comparing the likelihood of advancing into a principal position and the length of time for advancement to programs (Fuller & Orr, 2006) and program features (Orr, 2011). A very small, but growing body of research has tried to link leadership preparation and organizational outcomes (Kirkpatrick's fourth level outcome and Guskey's outcomes). The available research includes graduates' reports on school improvement progress (Orr & Orphanos, 2011; Slater et al., 2003) and teacher selection (Fuller, Young, & Baker, 2011) . Some studies have tried to associate program participation to school outcomes, using a direct effects model, without much discernible effects (Haller, Brent, & McNamera, 1997; Vanderhaar, Muñoz, & Rodosky, 2006). In her research review, Orr (2009) argued that an indirect effects model fits better, drawing on the leadership effectiveness research (Leithwood & Jantzi, 1999) as evidence.

Using this research (and a larger body of work reviewed for the *Handbook of Research on Leadership Education*), Orr and others from the UCEA/LTEL-SIG Taskforce on Evaluating Leadership Preparation Programs (Taskforce)[1] developed a conceptual model that mapped out the conceptual pathways and levels of program outcomes, modeled on Kirkpatrick and Guskey (Orr, 2006). From this conceptual model, Orr and others from the Taskforce developed a survey of program graduates which incorporated measures for each outcome level, drawing from available leadership preparation and effectiveness research (Orr, Jackson, & Rorrer, 2009). The survey, which was piloted and refined through several survey administration rounds, was formalized as the School Leadership Preparation and Practice Survey (SLPPS). Introduced in different iterations and improvements since 2003, the SLPPS has been deployed by a wide variety of leadership preparation programs to track graduate outcomes.

To provide further guidance for leadership preparation programs on how to conceptualize and evaluate their programs' impacts, again based on Kirkpatrick and Guskey's levels, Orr, Young and Rorrer developed an evaluation planner, *Developing Evaluation Evidence* (2010). The planner lays out the conceptual pathway as a map and suggests a variety of measures, data collection instruments and sources of data for each level. The planner is based on Orr's (2009) evaluation research review and the Taskforce's conceptual pathway. This planner served to map the components of the UTCULP program evaluation.

The second primary conceptual context for our evaluation was framed by the specific program theory of the UTCULP program. According to Weiss (1998), program theory reflects a program's theories of change, both what the program is expected to achieve and how (Weiss, 1998). The

UTCULP program is founded on a strong social justice orientation and integrates strongly recommended content and pedagogical practices. Leadership preparation experts have recommended that programs prepare candidates to acquire critical social justice knowledge, skills, and dispositions to be able to resist the forces that maintain the status quo in schools and pursue and sustain social justice work in the face of these forces (Capper, Theoharis, & Sebastian, 2006; Theoharis, 2007). Typically, program evaluation work on social justice leadership preparation has been either in the form of case studies (Brown, 2006; Gerstl-Pepin, Killeen, & Hasazi, 2006; Jackson & Kelley, 2002; Ruiz, 2005) or assessment of the effectiveness of selected pedagogical approaches such as the use of project based learning in developing greater sensitivity, insight, and problem solving (Copland, 2001). Two studies have been conducted at the doctoral level: Allen (2006), using focus group interviews and surveys, solicited doctoral student feedback about their learning and application of social justice leadership, while Harris (Harris & Alford, 2003) investigated the extent to which a program's emphasis on social justice leadership changed doctoral candidates' attitudes about social justice leadership. Taken together, these studies suggest that a program emphasis on social justice can yield positive results in terms of social justice orientation and dispositions and may have benefits on leadership practices (reflecting Kirkpatrick's evaluation levels one through three).

A second part of the program's theory of change is to coach candidates as a means of transforming their leadership perspective. The program's inclusion of a coaching component is conceptually based on research on expert problem solving (Leithwood & Steinbach, 1995) that emphasizes leaders' ability to use multi-frame analysis and reflective practice to address complex problems. Experts assert that through cognitive coaching, leaders can develop the capacity for multi-frame analysis, reflection and collaboration in problem solving. While there has been limited research on leadership coaching in preparation programs (Barnett, 1995), some evaluation research exists on executive coaching (Solansky, 2010; Wasylyshyn, Gronsky, & Haas, 2004) that suggests that, when done well, coaching can develop problem solving and reflective skills among candidates.

PROGRAM AND EVALUATION GOALS

The University of Texas Collaborative Urban Leadership Project (UTCULP) has been designed as an unfolding partnership between The

University of Texas at Austin Principalship Program (UTAPP) and school districts located in three urban areas: Dallas Independent School District (ISD), Houston ISD and Austin ISD combined with other Austin-area districts. The primary purpose of UTCULP has been to develop 120 effective, aspiring leaders for secondary schools. Funded in part by the US Department of Education School Leadership Program, UTCULP has five goals:

- Identify the unique needs of each district partner;
- Recruit, identify, select, financially support and prepare at least 120 candidates who have the potential to become effective principals of secondary urban schools;
- Provide ongoing evaluation to ensure candidate growth and program effectiveness;
- Recruit, select, and train a District Site Coordinator and five District Mentors in each partner district; and
- Develop and implement district level strategies to support and retain current effective leaders who can provide follow on and support to future aspiring leaders in the district.

The UTCULP/UTAPP program is aligned with the national Educational Leadership Constituents Council (ELCC) Standards for Advanced Programs in Educational Leadership. UTCULP/UTAPP coursework emphasizes social justice arrived at through data-use and research-informed decisions, collaborative problem solving and deep reflection. Social justice serves as the centerpiece of the program and graduating students must demonstrate the knowledge, skills, and abilities to use data, advocate for traditionally marginalized students and lead change through action. The use of collaborative inquiry models expands leadership notions from those of solitary classroom-based teacher leaders to those approaches associated with school-level collaboration and transformation (Young, O'Doherty, Gooden, & Goodnow, 2011). Extensive reflection serves as a means of learning and as a skill exercised in leadership practice with the assignment of intentionally developed Cognitive Coaches™. While the coursework for the partner districts of Dallas and Houston has been adjusted to reflect the district context, each on-site program is grounded in a social justice orientation and offers a strong coaching component.

Based on Kirkpatrick's evaluation framework, we intentionally aligned the evaluation model to the key learning elements. The evaluation purpose has been to document the project's progress in meeting its goals and assess the impact of the project components on program participants, and the career and school improvement outcomes of program graduates. Given these outcomes, we wanted the evaluation to enable us to determine the overall effectiveness of the program. For the coaching component, we also wanted to determine its benefits for the coaches themselves. Drawing on Weiss's evaluation research guidelines, we designed the evaluation to be able to evaluate the relationship between program features and both graduate and school outcomes, to provide results that can be used to improve program quality. Below is a summary of how these purposes have been operationalized in the design, organization, and implementation of the evaluation.

EXAMINING OUR EVALUATION FOOTPRINT

After receiving grant approval, the two main architects of the grant writing team shifted attention to achieving the goals of the grant. This included setting up meetings with key personnel in our first district partner, Dallas, seeking and hiring a project coordinator, and sharing progress with our incoming UTAPP Director, who would take on the role of principal investigator. Following a spring conference in Washington DC hosted by the USDoE School Leadership Program staff, the on-site team revisited and tightened performance objectives assuring that each objective could be measured with either already available data, or data generated through the grant evaluation process. With the external evaluator, we agreed to deploy the School Leadership Preparation and Practice Survey (SLPPS) the following spring to assess areas for which we lacked available information, particularly in documenting leadership-related candidate characteristics, graduates' ratings of program features, their career experiences, and graduates' ratings of their learning and, if they were school leaders, their leadership practices and school improvement work. Eventually we created a parallel baseline survey of candidate characteristics and initial perceptions of career aspirations and leader practices proficiency.

Conceptualizing the Evaluation

During the second year of the grant, we used the new evaluation planner, *Developing Evaluation Evidence* (Orr et al., 2010), to help us make explicit our primary program evaluation measures in three areas — input (participants' prior experiences and program features), learning outcomes (learning outcomes and career outcomes) and impact (leadership practices, impact on school community, impact on school performance) — and the types of data that we would expect to gather and analyze. The evaluation planner served as both a conceptual framework and data management tool for our evaluation work. Below is a discussion of how we used the evaluation planner both to assess how to use available data for evaluation purposes and to focus our team's planning around how to develop other measures and collect information. For further background, a summary description of the evaluation planner is included in the appendix.

Methodological Issues in Identifying Available Data

After distributing and discussing *Developing Evaluation Evidence* (Orr et al., 2010), we asked members of the on-site grant team (coprincipal investigators, grant director, project director, internal researcher, and professors) to record current data. Team members independently completed the grid provided in the planner to identify which data we already had available or were using to evaluate program inputs, outcomes, and impact. After compiling the information, we were surprised by the findings (Table 1). We had ample data to support preconditions such as prior experiences of our incoming candidates and had deployed the School Leadership Preparation and Practice Survey (SLPPS) to determine program quality features and career outcomes. However, we had limited data to support formal assessment of learning outcomes, and no process in place to evaluate leadership practices and impact on the school community or school performance.

We analyzed the data we had gathered for insight and direction. Our on-site grant team and external evaluator discussed the results and brainstormed additional data sources that would serve as evidence of program learning outcomes and impact. Given UTCULP's emphasis on social justice, we were particularly interested in leadership preparation impact at schools led by program graduates and additionally what influence, if any, could be seen in measured student and/or school performance. After much debate and exploration, we chose to focus on adding more evaluation measures and data collection strategies (Table 2). The following section offers information on data sources, additional areas of focus, and rationale.

Table 1. Result of Initial UTAPP Evaluation Data Review.

Inputs		Outcomes			Impact	
		Learning Outcomes	Career Outcomes	Leadership Practices	Impact on School Community	Impact on School Performance
Participant Prior Experiences	Program Features					
Portfolio rubric results	Program feature survey (SLPPS)	Leadership identity/ problem framing end of program	Career placement rates (SLPPS)			
Assessment center results	Learning outcomes (SLPPS)	Pre/postsurveys of self-reported learning progress				
Leadership identity and problem framing	Internship outcomes (SLPPS)					
GRE scores and GPA averages						

Table 2. Revised UTAPP Evaluation Data Plan.

Inputs		Outcomes			Impact	
Participant Prior Experiences	Program Features	Learning Outcomes	Career Outcomes	Leadership Practices	Impact on School Community	Impact on School Performance
Portfolio rubric results	SLPPS Program Feature Survey	Leadership identity/ problem framing end of program	Career outcomes (SLPPS)	OHI Austin ISD (planned)	OHI (planned)	State Data: Achievement, Attendance, Completion (planned)
Assessment center	SLPPS Learning Outcomes					
Leadership identity and problem framing	SLPPS internship outcomes	Pre/postsurveys learning progress	Career outcomes (State of Texas)	360 survey (planned)	Teacher retention (planned)	Program equity (planned)
GRE scores and GPA averages	*Exit interview*	*Program portfolio ELCC reports State exams (planned)*		*Coach survey*	*Coach focus groups (planned)*	

Added evaluation tools presented in italics.

Initial Evaluation Findings

Our initial examination of available data revealed we had evidence of candidates' prior experiences gathered through an application portfolio. We added our team scoring of candidates during a half-day assessment center to our baseline measures and tracking. From our assessment of our program features, analyzing the SLPPS data for our baseline UTAPP graduates, we learned that UTAPP graduates rated UTAPP higher (5.0) than the national sample (3.9) in having a cohort model (Scale of 1 to 5). This data supported our inclusion of cohorts as a feature of the UTAPP program. When comparing SLPPS survey ratings and our course content, we learned that graduates rated being prepared to lead learning (4.9) well above how well they perceived preparation for management and operations (2.9). We agreed to continue using the SLPPS survey in the future and decided to add a course content analysis to our program evaluation to gather more data on possible gaps and overlaps between and among courses.

To create a pre—post program assessment of candidates' learning outcomes, our team conducted a content analysis, using Stake's strategies for identifying themes and patterns (Stake, 1995), of candidates' application materials on leadership identity and problem framing to a similar end of the program task (Young et al., 2011). To generate formative assessment information, we added a program portfolio to assist in tracking student acquisition of knowledge and skills. Finally, our internal researcher tried unsuccessfully to gather state certification exam passing rate information for our program and other programs across the state for exit score comparisons.[2]

Using the SLPPS career outcome data, we learned that over 66% of our graduate respondents reported serving in school or district level leadership roles as compared to the national sample of 29%. While these data were useful, we lacked evidence concerning how quickly our graduates achieved leadership positions and how our graduates' career paths compared to other programs throughout the state. Most important, we did not know the types of schools our candidates were leading and the impact they were having on these schools.

Finally, our grant funding provided for development and support for coaches for each candidate. However, we did not have a method to measure impact on either the candidates receiving the coaching or on the coaches themselves. Consequently, we determined that we needed additional assessment tools to measure these impacts. Over the course of the next several weeks, our on-site grant team members and external evaluator began to sketch out a more robust evaluation plan (Table 2). We also reviewed our previously approved Institutional Review Board approval for alignment and determined a timeline for implementation. Given the multiple data sources we needed, we assigned some of the data gathering and analysis tasks to our internal researcher and others to the external evaluator.

Operationalizing the Evaluation Work

Given the variety of evaluation tasks we were now adding, our strategy of embedding some of these tasks into the program, drawing from state data sources, and adding new surveys; we concluded there was a need for a coordinated team approach. The program directors managed the formative assessment tasks. The internal researcher was assigned responsibility for obtaining, compiling, and analyzing data available in the state databases to collect data on the roles served by our graduates (and all educators statewide), the length of time between date of certification and obtaining a leadership position, and number of years in each leadership position.

To facilitate an in-depth examination of program features, the external evaluator audited and analyzed program content as documented in course syllabi and assessments aligned to the ELCC standards. This audit sought to determine the coherence of the program content and assessments as a whole. The resulting report highlighted gaps and overlaps and posed questions for program directors to use in program revision work. The external evaluator also created a baseline survey geared to leadership measures in the SLPPS survey, coaches' survey, and interview guides for participants about coaching. To investigate the coaching component further, the external evaluator conducted Skype™ focus groups with interns receiving coaching as well as participants in the coach training. This initial information was used to develop online surveys for coaches and interns.

The external evaluator continues to prepare annual reports, presenting survey and interview findings, and comparing the experiences and outcomes of participants from the grant-funded cohorts and the baseline, non-grant funded cohort. The program director and codirector used the reports for their annual evaluation submitted to the USDoE School Leadership Program, to identify areas for program improvement, and as a basis for further planning and development.

In the future, our program director and internal researcher, supported by graduate research assistants, will draw additional data on the schools served by our graduates (and a comparison group of other principals) on district/campus derived organizational health index/community survey data (if available); student performance as measured by state achievement exams; student attendance; school completion rates; and teacher retention. Such data are collected by the Texas state education department and can be accessed for evaluation research purposes. By using this publicly available data, our internal researcher and graduate research assistants have identified more than 20 schools where our graduates have served as principals for three or more years. A more thorough description of our approach to this line of evaluation is included in the Epilogue below.

Organizing Evaluation Role Relationships

Just as preK-12 schools have experienced greater scrutiny through a more formal approach to accountability, so too have the institutions preparing teachers and leaders for our nation's schools (Frye et al., 2006). But a focus on program evaluation must be much more than compliance with external needs for review; preparation programs have an ethical obligation to determine how best to prepare leaders and measure progress toward intended outcomes (McCarthy, 2001). Program evaluation, like assessments in general, may serve many purposes: "program improvement, accountability, knowledge generation, and political ruses or public relations" (Rossi, Freeman, & Lipsey, 1999, p. 40). When used as a formative tool, program evaluation can inform practices for leadership development improvement (Orr et al., 2010). As more preparation programs move toward the use of formative assessment for the purpose of program improvement, we should expect to see an increase in the number and quality of studies that provide indirect measures of program impact that will support a more nuanced approach to program design in terms of content and delivery of leadership preparation (Orr & Barber, 2006).

The process of moving from collecting some data on candidates before, during, and after the program to having a planned approach to data collection, analysis, and dissemination is a journey. UTAPP's evaluation plan is still a work in progress. Through ongoing scrutiny and maintenance, the program directors intend to use the data we have in a meaningful way – not just collecting and reporting – but actually refining program improvements.

We intentionally used data sources for more than one purpose and gained deeper knowledge about our program outcomes and impact as a result. For example, we collect extensive information on applicants prior to making admission recommendations. The submitted application materials including a graduate essay, letters of reference, and resume are reviewed and scored using a rubric. Selected candidates attend an assessment center. At the assessment center teams of professors, district and campus leaders, and current UTAPP/UTCULP students observe and use a set of rubrics to score each candidate's performance in an interview, learning observation and leadership presentation. Finally, GRE and GPA information are taken into consideration before recommending for admission. While the application and assessment center scores inform selection decisions, we have yet to calibrate whether or not these measures serve as predictors of later career path success. We plan to use this data in different ways to answer such questions as: *Does a high or low score in our selection process in anyway predict who will be selected to serve in campus level leadership roles?* And *Do these scores in anyway predict later effectiveness as a school leader?* If the sample size is robust enough, we propose to use higher order statistical inquiry methods to investigate these questions further.

Developing a systemic approach to program evaluation has caused us to view our data in a more comprehensive way. By organizing and analyzing our data according to the categories proposed by Orr et al., (2010), we have identified gaps in our data and developed a comprehensive plan to fill these gaps. Finally, having a structured approach to evaluation has created opportunities for us to further explore and deepen our knowledge of our preparation programs inputs, outcomes, and outputs.

We adopted a similar systems view for managing our evaluator/director relationship. The evaluation was supported by an overarching evaluation plan, developed by the program director, codirector, and lead evaluator, as well as a close working relationship within this team fostered by other projects. While overall the evaluation plan has been a success, the team experienced some challenges as well. Evaluation tasks divided between the internal researcher and the external evaluator required careful coordination. Some tasks became appreciably more cumbersome due to the external evaluator's geographic distance from the program (New York to Texas) and multiple opportunities to directly observe program operations or conduct focus group interviews were restricted by prohibitive travel costs. Resolving these challenges requires continued coordination and communication.

LESSONS LEARNED: REFLECTIONS

In reflecting on the lessons learned, we have identified a few areas we consider essential for effective collaborative evaluation planning: establish clear goals with flexible processes, communicate frequently, leverage knowledge developed through evaluation, and cocreate all aspects of the evaluation process.

Clear Goals and Flexible Process

As director and external evaluator, first, we shared common assumptions about quality leadership preparation and its evaluation, thus we shared a common focus and interest. Second, we tried to be responsive and flexible throughout the process, to meet changing deadlines and questions. Third, we took the opportunity to build sustainable evaluation systems that could be easily replicated, shifting the evaluation focus over time to new questions while establishing systems to track initial ones.

Communicate Frequently

As a director located in Texas and an external evaluator working in New York, our offices were separated by nearly 1800 miles. To overcome the obstacle of geographic distance and reduce travel costs, we used semiannual conference meetings (AERA & UCEA), annual USDoE meetings and other professional gatherings as a forum for evaluation meetings and relied heavily upon phone and email exchanges to follow up. We also made use of a variety of web-based resources to facilitate planning, communication and data collection, including evaluation planning meetings and focus group interviews conducted through Skype™ conversations and creating a shared document drive (in Google). While web-based tools and resources did not always work well in supporting our work (web-based relationships were difficult to maintain and the shared drive was often unwieldy), such facilitative tools and resources have dramatically improved in recent years and have the potential to improve communication and coordination. We recommend establishing protocols and processes for communication, sharing information, and following up on scheduling changes. At the very least, teams should conduct a monthly check-in (using a web-based alert system) to explore evaluation issues and priorities.

Leverage Knowledge

The tools we used in the evaluation process confirmed some things we suspected and revealed areas for us to address. The SLPPS data gave us solid evidence of what our graduates thought were the strengths and weaknesses of the program. The professors of the school business course and our internship seminar used these findings to revise their courses and more fully address management and finance in the assigned learning experiences. The curriculum audit revealed specific areas of gap and overlap in the syllabi and again, by sharing this data with professors in the program, we shifted course focus areas to more fully align to the ELCC Standards and match course expectations to authentic problems of practice. Finally, the SLPPS data and our efforts in mining the state database gave us solid evidence that the market is hiring our graduates at a much faster rate than the state average or the national sample of other programs. We know we invest more time than most programs in selecting candidates. Now we have evidence for our institution and partners that supports continuation of our rigorous selection process.

Cocreate Along the Way

When we started this process, as the director, I had assumed the thinking, planning and execution of program evaluation would occur in isolation from the evaluation. Working alongside an external evaluator committed to coherent program evaluation quickly turned this into a partnership approach. The term "external" evaluator does not mean "outsider." For example, when we revised the performance objectives, it would have been wiser to have included the external evaluator in that process while we were doing the work — rather than just sending the revisions afterwards. To support the development of this partnership, we recommend writing in several face-to-face meetings with the evaluator with supporting travel funding during the first two years of the grant and at least an annual meeting the final three years. With concentrated time working together in the beginning, we could have mapped out more of the work up front rather than accomplishing tasks and building the evaluation tools along the way. A cocreation approach will enable tapping into the expertise of the evaluator much earlier in the process and much more often.

EPILOGUE – WHERE WE HAVE BEEN AND WHERE WE ARE HEADING

Two years after we began the process of developing an evaluation plan, we are poised on the edge of an exponential increase in useful data about our leadership preparation program (Table 2). We have continued to gather precondition data on all applicants and have the means to review application and assessment center rubric data of those graduates who have been selected for leadership roles by area school districts. Now with four years of program data from three cohorts, we continue to analyze whether program modifications have improved graduates' leadership identity formation and problem framing. This year, we will redeploy the SLPPS graduate survey and analyze the new data for relationships between outcomes and quality program indicators that were documented two years ago. We have also begun to track learning outcomes, using surveys and focus group protocols designed by our external evaluator to track the leadership development benefits of coaching for our interns and their coaches.

Next year, our external evaluator will conduct a follow up review of program syllabi to reassess alignment of courses to program goals, objectives, and standards. Several courses have been redesigned in the past few years, guided in part by the first syllabi review and we anticipate that this second review will spark further refinement and calibration of course and program offerings.

In terms of career outcomes, we have analyzed 10 years of career outcomes for every preparation program in the state, and found that our graduates are hired at a much faster rate than those prepared elsewhere. While we believe that this may be influenced by program quality, it may also be a result of the rigorous selection process. For at least the past 30 years, UTAPP has used an assessment center format or conducted site visits with interested applicants. Requiring candidates to perform leadership tasks similar to those enacted by principals provides a forum for identifying individuals with instructional leadership potential. Indeed, UTCULP's assessment center components have been adopted by partner districts for use in selection of aspiring leaders, assistant principals and principals. Thus, the selection process used to identify potential leaders for our program has also informed the selection process to identify individuals selected to serve as principals and assistant principals.

Finally, as mentioned previously, to evaluate the program's impact on graduates' leadership practices and school outcomes, we have located over 20 graduates currently serving as principals for at least three years at a single school. We are also in the process of identifying schools with matched demographics to serve as comparison sites for follow up analyses of our program's impact on graduates' leadership practices.

Through the Texas state education databases, our team has access to longitudinal data for all publically supported schools and local education agencies, including charter schools and districts, operating in the state. This data will allow for comparisons between schools as well as between groups of graduate-led and comparison program-led sites on a variety of factors including: demographic characteristics of schools and districts, student academic performance, completion rates, college readiness, attendance, spending levels, percentages and academic achievement for students served through bilingual, special education, English Speakers of Other Languages, and gifted and talented programs.

Once the UTCULP/UTAPP graduate-led and comparison sites have been identified, the program director and staff will begin analysis of these publically available data sources and simultaneously seek permission to field surveys to collect leadership practice perceptions of teachers, supervisors, and other key stakeholders at both UTCULP/UTAPP graduate-led and comparison sites. This site-specific survey data will be augmented with the state database reports on student academic performance, completion rates, college readiness levels, and student attendance. We anticipate this two-pronged analysis will reveal differences, if any, between and among performance indicators and/or perceptions of leadership practice at schools led by our graduates compared to those led by graduates of other preparation programs.

The evaluation process has impacted us individually and developed our ability to learn and function as a team. This inquiry approach has offered confirming information, compelling surprises and additional questions to answer. We look forward to continuing to develop ways to measure growth and identify areas for program improvement.

NOTES

1. For a history of the taskforce, see (Kottkamp & Rusch, 2009; Orr, 2008).
2. As of this printing, the Texas attorney general has determined that state certification exam scores by preparation program cannot be released even if individual results are masked.

REFERENCES

Allen, L. A. (2006). The moral life of schools revisited: Preparing educational leaders to "build a new social order" for social justice and democratic community. *International Journal of Urban Educational Leadership*, *1*, 1–13.

Barnett, B. G. (1995). Developing reflection and expertise: Can mentors make the difference? *Journal of Educational Administration, 33*(5), 45.

Brown, K. M. (2006). Leadership for social justice and equity: Evaluating a transformative framework and andragogy. *Educational Administration Quarterly, 42*(5), 700–745.

Capper, C. A., Theoharis, G., & Sebastian, J. (2006). Toward a framework for preparing leaders for social justice. *Journal of Educational Administration, 44*(3), 209.

Copland, M. A. (2001). The reform of administrator preparation at Stanford: An analytic description. *Journal of school leadership, 11*(4), 335–366.

Darling-Hammond, L., Meyerson, D., La Pointe, M. M., & Orr, M. T. (2010). *Preparing principals for a changing world*. San Francisco, CA: Jossey-Bass.

Frye, B., O'Neill, K., & Bottoms, G. (2006). *Schools can't wait: Accelerating the redesign of university principal preparation programs*. Atlanta: Southern Regional Educational Board.

Fuller, E., & Orr, M. T. (2006). *Texas leadership preparation programs and their graduates' school leadership advancement: A trend comparison of institutional outcomes, 1995–2005*. Paper presented at the University Council of Educational Administration, San Antonio, TX.

Fuller, E., Young, M. D., & Baker, B. D. (2011). Do principal preparation programs influence student achievement through the building of teacher-team qualifications by the principal? An exploratory analysis. *Educational Administration Quarterly, 47*(1), 173–216.

Gerstl-Pepin, C., Killeen, K., & Hasazi, S. (2006). Utilizing an "ethic of care" in leadership preparation. *Journal of Educational Administration, 44*(3), 250.

Guskey, T. R. (2000). *Evaluating professional development*. Thousand Oaks, CA: Corwin Press.

Haller, E. J., Brent, B. O., & McNamera, J. H. (1997). Does graduate training in educational administration improve America's schools? *Phi Delta Kappan, 79*, 222–227.

Harris, S. & Alford, B. (2003). A study of doctoral students' changing attitudes toward social justice issues. Paper presented at the University Council of Educational Administration Annual Conference in Portland, OR.

Hewitson, M. T. (1995). The preparation of beginning principals in Queensland: An overview of findings. *Journal of Educational Administration, 33*(2), 20.

Jackson, B. L., & Kelley, C. (2002). Exceptional and innovative programs in educational leadership. *Educational Administration Quarterly, 38*(2), 192–212.

Kirkpatrick, D. L. (1998). *Evaluating training programs: The four levels* (2nd ed.). San Francisco, CA: Berrett-Koehler.

Korach, S., Ballenger, J., & Alford, B. (2011). Linking principal preparation to teaching and learning: Lessons learned through a multiple case study. *The International Journal of Educational Leadership Preparation, 6*(4), ISSN 2155-9635.

Kottkamp, R. B., & Rusch, E. A. (2009). The landscape of scholarship on the education of school leaders, 1985–2006. In M. D. Young, G. M. Crow, J. Murphy & R. T. Ogawa (Eds.), *Handbook of research on the education of school leaders* (pp. 23–85). New York, NY: Routledge.

Leithwood, K., & Jantzi, D. (1999). Transformational school leadership effects: A replication. *School Effectiveness and School Improvement, 10*(4), 451–479.

Leithwood, K., Jantzi, D., Coffin, G., & Wilson, P. (1996). Preparing school leaders: What works? *Journal of School Leadership, 6*(3), 316–342.

Leithwood, K., & Steinbach, R. (1995). *Expert problem-solving: Evidence form school and district leaders*. Albany, NY: State University of New York Press.

McCarthy, M. M. (2001). Challenges facing educational leadership programs: Our future is now. *TEA-SIG Newsletter, 8*(1), 1,4.
Nicholson, B., & Leary. (2001). Appalachian principals assess the efficacy and appropriateness of their training. *Planning and Changing, 32*(3/4), 199–213.
Orphanos, S., & Orr, M. T. (2012). Learning leadership matters: The influence of innovative school leadership preparation on teachers' experiences and outcomes. *Educational Management, Administration & Leadership*, forthcoming.
Orr, M. T. (2006). Research on leadership education as a reform strategy. *Journal of research on leadership education, 1*(1), 1–5.
Orr, M. T. (2008). *UCEA/LTEL-SIG Taskforce on Evaluation Leadership Preparation Programs (ELPP) Updates*. Paper presented at the American Educational Research Association, New York, NY.
Orr, M. T. (2011). Pipeline to preparation to advancement: Graduates' Experiences In, Through, and Beyond Leadership Preparation. *Educational Administration Quarterly, 47*(1), 114–172.
Orr, M. T., & Barber, M. E. (2006). Collaborative leadership preparation: A comparative study of innovative programs and practices. *Journal of School Leadership, 16*(6), 709–739.
Orr, M. T., & Barber, M. E. (2009). Program evaluation in leadership preparation and related fields. In M. D. Young & G. Crow (Eds.), *Handbook of research on the education of school leaders*. New York, NY: Routledge.
Orr, M. T., Jackson, K., & Rorrer, A. (2009). Following up graduates: Development of the school leadership preparation and practice survey and a shared research process. *UCEA Review, 50*(2), 29–35.
Orr, M. T., & Orphanos, S. (2011). How preparation impacts school leaders and their school improvement: Comparing exemplary and conventionally prepared principals. *Educational administration quarterly, 47*, 18–70.
Orr, M. T., & Pounder, D. G. (2010). Teaching and preparing school leaders. In S. Conley & B. S. Cooper (Eds.), *Finding, preparing, and supporting school leaders: Critical issues, useful solutions*. Lanham, MD: Rowman Littlefield.
Orr, M. T., Young, M. D., & Rorrer, A. (2010). *Developing evaluation evidence*. Austin, TX: University Council of Educational Administration and National Center for the Evaluation of Educational Leadership Preparation and Practice.
Restine, L. N. (1997). Learning and development in the context(s) of leadership preparation. *Peabody Journal of Education, 72*(2), 117–130.
Rossi, P. H., Freeman, H. E., & Lipsey, M. W. (1999). *Evaluation, A systematic approach* (6th ed.). Thousand Oaks, CA: Sage.
Ruiz, R. d. J. (2005). *Linguistically and culturally diverse school leaders: A qualitative study of principal pre-service preparation*. Unpublished Ed.D., University of Houston, TX.
Slater, C. L., McGhee, M. W., Capt, R. L., Alvarez, I., Topete, C., & Iturbe, E. (2003). A comparison of the views of educational administration students in the USA and Mexico. *International Journal of Leadership in Education, 6*(1), 35–55.
Solansky, S. T. (2010). The evaluation of two key leadership development program components: Leadership skills assessment and leadership mentoring. *The Leadership Quarterly, 21*(4), 675–681.
Stake, R. E. (1995). *The art of case study research*. Thousand Oaks, CA: Sage.
Theoharis, G. (2007). Social justice educational leaders and resistance: Toward a theory of social justice leadership. *Educational Administration Quarterly, 43*(2), 221–258.

Vanderhaar, J. E., Muñoz, M. A., & Rodosky, R. J. (2006). Leadership as accountability for learning: The effects of school poverty, teacher experience, previous achievement, and principal preparation programs on student achievement. *Journal of Personnel Evaluation in Education, 19*(1-2), 17.

Wasylyshyn, K. R., Gronsky, B., & Haas, W. (2004). Emotional competence: Preliminary results of a coaching program commissioned by Rohm and Haas Company. *HR: Human Resource Planning, 27*(4), 7.

Weiss, C. H. (1998). *Evaluation: Methods for studying programs and policies* (2nd ed.). Upper Saddle River, NJ: Prentice Hall.

Young, M. D., O'Doherty, A., Gooden, M. A., & Goodnow, E. J. (2011). Measuring change in leadership identify and problem-framing. *Journal of School Leadership, 21*(5), 704–734.

APPENDIX

About the evaluation planner

The evaluation planner asks programs to identify their primary measures and sources of data for candidate preconditions, program quality features, learning outcomes, career advancement outcomes, leadership practice, leadership impact on school practices, and leadership impact on student and school performance (see http://www.ucea.org/educational-leadership-prepara/). Each of these categories with possible measures has been summarized below.

Preconditions are candidate characteristics that a preparation program intentionally selects for in candidates, and can include demographic data such as gender, race, and language, and prior accomplishments such as leadership roles already served and years of teaching experience, and/or results of standardized assessments. This information can be collected through an application or student survey.

Quality of the program features are measures of the extent to which the program has core features associated with exemplary programs: an articulated theory of action, coherent curriculum, integrated field-based learning, supportive structures such as coaching and mentoring, and ongoing assessment of candidate progress (Darling-Hammond et al., 2010). Measurement includes documentation of the presence of the program components and measurement of the relative strength of program features through candidate perceptual data, using a survey such as the School Leadership Preparation and Practice Survey (SLPPS).

Learning outcomes may be measured through both formative and summative evidence. This includes assignment and course grades and state licensure assessment. In addition, effective principal preparation programs align performance assessments with authentic problems of practice (Frye et al., 2006), and can be either formative or summative.

Career advancement outcomes include tracking the types of positions graduates assume, the length of time between program completion and advancement into leadership positions, and how long graduates remain in leadership posts. This data can be gathered through self-reports from graduates and state data systems, if available and accessible.

Leadership practices assessments offer insight into how graduates enact the many roles of an educational leader. This can be ascertained through graduate perceptual surveys and 360-degree feedback surveys of teachers, parents, supervisors, and students.

Impact on schools To discover program impact on school and student outcomes, program personnel may identify the schools where graduates serve as leaders and gather data on student achievement, teacher retention, program equity, and other measures of school and student performance.

CHAPTER 2

THE POWER OF INSTITUTIONAL PARTNERSHIP IN THE DEVELOPMENT OF TURN AROUND SCHOOL LEADERS

Stephen H. Davis, Ronald J. Leon and Miriam L. Fultz

ABSTRACT

In this chapter, we describe the strategies used in establishing the Great Leaders for Great Schools Academy (GLGSA), a high impact and sustainable university–district partnership and the first program to be accredited under California's experimental standards for principal preparation. The partnership has evolved into a robust professional learning community dedicated to the task of preparing practice-ready *school leaders with the knowledge, skills, and dispositions needed to turn around low performing schools in the Pomona Unified School District. Chapter contents also include descriptions of the key elements of the GLGSA and seven recommendations for those who desire to establish innovative and collaborative approaches to leadership preparation.*

INTRODUCTION

What does a mutually supportive and effective relationship between a university educational administration department and public school district look like? How can two institutions that traditionally operate within vastly different educational environments and organizational contexts work in partnership to bring theory and practice together to build an innovative, dynamic, and powerful academic program designed to prepare school leaders who are equipped to turn around underperforming schools?

In this chapter, we respond to these questions by describing how educational administration faculty members at California State Polytechnic University, Pomona (Cal Poly), leaders from the Pomona Unified School District (PUSD), and an external evaluator from the Desertfrost Consulting Group, Inc. (DFCG) worked together to create the first nontraditional administrator preparation program to be fully accredited through California's Experimental Program Standards. This is the story of a strong interagency collaboration that is based on a shared vision, a willingness to challenge the status quo, mutual trust, and an enduring focus on maintaining fidelity to the principles of empirical inquiry.

We begin this chapter by describing seven key elements that distinguish the Great Leaders for Great Schools Academy (GLGSA) from traditional administrative credential programs. Second, we provide seven recommendations on how to build or strengthen university–local district partnerships and how such relationships can be sustained and nurtured. Finally, we discuss important lessons learned from this partnership that can help others forge strong interagency collaborations in building powerful and innovative school leadership preparation programs.

THE KEY ELEMENTS OF THE GREAT LEADERS FOR GREAT SCHOOLS ACADEMY

Funded by a $2.5 million leadership development grant from the US Department of Education (USDE), the primary goal of the GLGSA is to assist the PUSD with meeting both state and federal standards for student achievement by preparing a cadre of highly skilled and practice-ready school leaders. Over the five-year funding period the program will prepare 30 credentialed administrators (in annual cohorts of six) who can facilitate the organizational reforms and systems needed to ensure that every child succeeds academically. With 25 of its 42 schools failing to meet state achievement growth standards, the district determined that it would need 30 highly trained school leaders who could fill anticipated principal vacancies over the course of the five-year grant period. The district's interest was on the quality, not quantity of newly credentialed administrators – and particularly on preparing new leaders who had a long-term commitment to turning around low performing schools in the PUSD.

In terms of program-level outcomes, the GLGSA aims to produce graduates who will exhibit both theoretical and practical knowledge regarding effective teaching and learning processes for ethnically diverse and socioeconomically disadvantaged children, the implementation of effective organizational systems and processes in low performing urban schools, and effective leadership behaviors and management strategies. In addition, graduates will be able to apply knowledge of important political, legal, ethical, technological, and financial aspects associated with public schools toward school improvement activities, building school–community relationships, and ensuring the academic success of diverse learners.

The program consists of two categories of activities that span 24 months for each cohort group: a 12-month Tier I Administrative Credential Program (Year One) and a 12-month professional support and retention program that includes one-on-one executive coaching and continued cohort support (Year Two). In the sections that follow we describe these categories and their related activities in greater detail.

Operational and policy oversight of the GLGSA is provided by the GLGSA Planning Team, which is composed of PUSD leaders, Cal Poly Pomona faculty, and an external evaluator. The Planning Team is a vibrant and essential part of this successful partnership. The PUSD representatives provide critical perspectives about the district-relevant work that continuously informs GLGSA program components and learning activities. In addition to the PUSD Chief Academic Officer, other school district members of the Planning Team include a lead PUSD principal (who has also served as a mentor principal) and a recently retired PUSD Administrative Director of Elementary Education who provides coaching and direct support to both graduates and candidates. Her contributions to the success of the GLGSA are invaluable due to her deep understanding of district systems, procedures, goals, and the expectations for administrators. In addition, she personally knows most district and site level administrative employees.

The PUSD Planning Team members bring a wealth of practical knowledge about past and current efforts made by the PUSD to raise student achievement and to promote leadership development. They also continuously inform the implementation of the GLGSA by keeping Cal Poly faculty members informed about important district plans, issues, changes, and events. Their continual input has allowed the GLGSA to strategically adapt to emerging needs and changing conditions over the years.

The GLGSA differs from most traditional administrator preparation programs in six important ways:

1. A full-time administrative apprenticeship and principal mentoring.
2. A PUSD context specific, thematically integrated, and problem-based curriculum.
3. A cohort-based community of learners.
4. A rigorous candidate nomination and selection process.
5. A multi-method assessment and evaluation approach that aligns candidate learning with program outcomes.
6. A year of intensive executive coaching that is provided to newly employed graduates who work as PUSD administrators and ongoing support for graduates awaiting employment in the PUSD.

Full-Time Administrative Apprenticeship

For four months during the winter and spring quarters of their first year in the GLGSA, candidates are released from their teaching duties to serve as full-time administrative apprentices at school sites other than their teaching assignments. The USDE leadership development grant reimburses the district for the cost of hiring substitute teachers. Unlike traditional Tier I programs that limit candidate exposure to the real world of administrative practice through part-time and after-hours fieldwork activities, the GLGSA apprenticeship immerses candidates in the daily (and minute by minute) challenges of administrative practice. The program draws upon the principles of experiential learning theory to provide learning activities framed around authentic, real-world problems and events (Fenwick, 2003; Kolb, 1984). During the apprenticeship, candidates experience the daily rhythms and complexities of administrative work. In addition, they receive ongoing and immediate feedback regarding the quality of their performance and formative assistance in the development of key administrative skills. The quality of the apprenticeship experience is ultimately a product of the synergistic effects of workplace characteristics, structured skill development activities, and effective mentoring. When carefully and appropriately aligned, these factors stimulate powerful and long-lasting transformational learning experiences (Mezirow, 1991).

The Role of Mentor Principals

In January of each year, mentor principals are carefully selected by the GLGSA Planning Team on the basis of their success in advancing student learning at their schools, the length of experience as a school principal, their expressed interest in working closely with a mentee, and their ability to promote positive interpersonal relationships. Before the apprenticeship period begins, a Cal Poly Pomona faculty member provides the mentor principals with training on key mentoring strategies, apprenticeship goals and outcomes, and the methods used to assess apprentice performance. Throughout the apprenticeship, mentors and Cal Poly Pomona faculty meet regularly to discuss mentoring activities, candidate progress, and participate in problem-solving and planning activities. One month prior to the first week of the apprenticeship, each candidate meets with his/her mentor principal to begin planning for the development of a school-wide change initiative (SWCI) assignment – the capstone activity for the state credentialing component of the GLGSA. For this activity, candidates must synthesize important theories, concepts, and skills from their coursework into a strategic school improvement plan with a focus on teaching and learning. Mentors also assess their apprentice's administrative skills and performance at the beginning and at the end of the apprenticeship using a version of the PUSD Leadership Stages Rubric (described later in this chapter). This is the same rubric that forms the basis for the mentor principal's assessment of mentee progress in relationship to the apprenticeship outcomes, and it also serves as the major conceptual framework for PUSD operations and reform initiatives.

Context Specific, Thematically Integrated, and Problem-Based Curriculum

Unlike the one-size-fits-all, subject-content-based curriculum common to most traditional principal preparation programs, the GLGSA curriculum was designed to meet the specific educational and organizational needs of the PUSD. The GLGSA curriculum focuses first on understanding problems of practice and then enriches that knowledge by introducing key theories and concepts in education. This approach differs significantly from the traditional approach that begins with understanding theory and its subsequent relevance to practice. The GLGSA curriculum was deeply influenced by Kolb's (1984) model of the experiential learning cycle, in which the learner's concrete experience(s) lead to personal reflection and subsequently to the development of abstract concepts and their application in new situations.

In order to implement this experiential learning model, the GLGSA Planning Team determined that a problem-based curriculum was needed. Rather than present domains of content knowledge in discrete and disconnected courses (e.g., school law, personnel, leadership, finance, operations), the professor and the students bring real school problems and issues to a weekly seminar session. In these sessions, theories and concepts from the various content domains within educational administration are applied to candidate experiences as administrative apprentices. This approach stimulates discussion and analysis and deepens the students' understanding of effective (and multiple) ways to address problems of practice. Often, a problem-based case study or a recent news story is used to investigate more deeply important problems of practice (e.g., special education, teacher employment, campus safety) or to augment apprenticeship experiences. Problems and issues discussed in the weekly sessions also relate to the field in general (e.g., federal or state policy issues such as Race to the Top, charter schools, teacher evaluation), to the candidate's own professional experience, to situations at the candidate's school site, or to issues within the PUSD.

The problem-based learning approach aims to prepare candidates to think from an administrator's perspective, grapple with problems that parallel those encountered in the real world, develop concrete problem solving, decision-making, and conflict resolution skills, and increase capacity for self-reflection. This approach tends to sacrifice breadth of content coverage for depth and quality of inquiry and analysis. Nevertheless, for beginning administrators, a certain amount of content knowledge is required in order to move confidently and with competence into the profession.

To provide the content that may be missed through the PBL-based curriculum, students participate in a series of six content modules (two per quarter) that focus on specific tasks and skills needed to lead PUSD schools (e.g., budgeting, using data, special needs students, supporting EL learners, evaluating teachers using PUSD assessment tools). PUSD division or program leaders with expertise in a particular domain of school administration develop and teach the modules in collaboration with a PUSD faculty member. As a result, candidates receive practical instruction based on core administrative tasks that relate to the field in general and also grounded in the key management practices and systems of the PUSD. To facilitate the community of learners and the transition from teaching to administrative work, GLGSA graduates are also invited to attend these modules.

A Cohort-Based Community of Learners

For the GLGSA, the cohort approach represents much more than a strategy for grouping and organizing students – it is a form of pedagogy designed to stimulate transformative and collaborative learning (DuFour, 2004; Mezirow, 1991). Through the integration of their individual experiences and skills, guided discourse, and collective inquiry, cohort members and the professor teach to and learn from each other. The professor introduces new ideas, provides supporting theories and materials, and encourages the students to challenge longstanding assumptions and worldviews. Most importantly, the professor establishes a climate of emotional and intellectual safety, trust, and mutual respect. Literally, what is shared with the cohort *stays* with the cohort. Judgmental and scornful criticisms of individual feelings and perspectives are not permitted. Cohort members operate by the norm that an idea – not the person – may be subject to criticism.

As with any group of people who are brought together for the first time, and who had no prior professional relationship, the process of developing a safe and highly collaborative learning community unfolds over time. The first academic quarter serves largely to reorient students to graduate studies, while the second, third, and fourth quarters increasingly build a "community of learners" through a series of highly interactive group assignments and discourse structured to support individual apprenticeship projects and experiences. To sustain the PLC, in the years following graduation from the GLGSA, students are provided with ongoing group and individual coaching by program and district leaders. Of course, the ultimate success of the cohort as a learning community begins with the group's confidence and trust in the professor (or group leader), who must reorient his/her role from being a "sage on the stage" to a "guide on the side." Rather than establishing a dependency on the professor for new knowledge, the GLGSA strives to build knowledge through collective inquiry, hands on experience, and discourse, guided by the professor. We found it especially important to explain and continually reinforce the "logic" of the GLGSA as it pertains to the implementation of a professional learning community (PLC).

The cohort model also serves another function – ongoing professional networking and support. Our evaluation evidence indicates that the

GLGSA had a positive and profound impact on the first two cohorts, and we anticipate a similar result for subsequent cohorts. Graduates from cohorts one and two maintain e-mail and telephone communication and frequently attend GLGSA events. Graduates uniformly describe the exceptional *esprit de corps* that developed over the course of their GLGSA experience. To quote one graduate, "We are our own best professional resource." By the end of the five-year grant-funding period, our intent is to have a self-perpetuating learning community that functions independent of the GLGSA.

Rigorous Recruitment and Selection

The GLGSA is focused on training leaders who are certain about their administrative career aspirations and who have demonstrated a broad commitment to their schools beyond their immediate classroom assignments. Hence, the GLGSA only admits highly talented teachers who are identified and nominated by school principals and district office officials on the basis of their instructional skills and leadership potential. Nominees admitted to the program are high performing educators who clearly possess the goal of becoming school and/or school district administrators.

The candidate selection process begins with a letter of nomination by a school principal followed by a letter of interest from the candidate and a final endorsement by the superintendent. A thorough review of candidates' academic and professional background is made by Cal Poly faculty members, along with a simulated classroom observation, an in-basket problem-solving activity, and one-on-one interviews. These data provide additional insights into the instructional and leadership abilities of candidates and support the GLGSA program emphasis on developing highly skilled instructional leaders.

Next, a selection score is created for each applicant. Each requirement is weighted by importance. We recognize that each candidate will possess a variety of knowledge, skills, dispositions, and experiences. Therefore, we do not expect that every candidate will meet each criterion with equal levels of skill and experience. We consider the attributes of each candidate holistically and place particular emphasis on emergent leadership, instructional expertise, an orientation of service to the school and profession, breadth of experience, evidence of collegiality and collaboration, and an unwavering passion for educating children.

A Multi-Method Assessment and Evaluation Approach

Beginning with the development of the grant proposal submitted to the USDE, assessment and program evaluation methodology served as the framework for thinking about the flow and logic of the work, the guiding rationale for what needs to be accomplished, a vehicle to focus human behavior (e.g., teaching and learning), and as a way to determine if what was intended was accomplished. Hence, assessment and evaluation are more than mechanisms for ensuring that candidates who graduate from the program have attained the necessary knowledge, skills, and abilities needed to function successfully as educational leaders in the PUSD.

Under the guidance of the GLGSA external evaluator, program components (e.g., PBL curriculum, fieldwork) were aligned with the GLGSA goals, short-term outcomes, and the key evaluation questions that guide all assessment, data analyses, and evaluative decisions. At the beginning, mid-point, and end of their first year, candidates complete several assessment tools that are used to determine the degree to which they exhibit the program candidate outcomes. These assessments include the Leadership Practices Inventory (LPI), the California Critical Thinking Skills Test (CCTST), the Problem-Solving Inventory (PSI), the Multidimensional Emotional Intelligence Assessment (MEIA), the Leadership Skills Assessment (administered by the National Association of Secondary School Principals), the School Leadership Practices and Preparation Survey (SLPPS), and the California Professional Administrative Credential Exam (CPACE). To assess the impact of postgraduation executive coaching, graduates also complete many of these assessment tools at the end of their second year in the GLGSA (i.e., the second year of GLGSA participation begins once they secure employment as an administrator in the PUSD).

Together, the assessment data provide a comprehensive, valid, and reliable portrait of each candidate's professional, cognitive, and emotional characteristics, skills, and attributes. In addition, the data illuminate how well the various elements and activities of the GLGSA are doing in terms of addressing key program goals. Most importantly, the assessment tools are used to promote self-reflection and serve as benchmarks for the candidates' professional growth and development. The assessment results are shared with the cohort at the end of Year One (i.e., each individual candidate receives a portfolio of his/her personal results).

As described above, assessment and evaluation permeates all aspects of the GLGSA. Although the GLGSA is an academic program, it is also a research project (based upon funder criteria and the criteria contained within the California Experimental Program Standards that are used for Tier I program accreditation purposes). As such, we must effectively prepare school leaders within a carefully articulated research framework that requires us to *plan, do, assess, analyze, evaluate, report to stakeholders, and use evidence to refine the GLGSA*. Several GLGSA short-term outcomes focus on developing a model of urban school administrator preparation and communicating successful GLGSA practices to the profession at large (and policy makers). In this sense, a key purpose of the GLGSA is not only to transform school leaders, but also to transform the profession.

To date, our understanding of how well the GLGSA prepares leaders who can turn around underperforming schools is very limited. Only three cohorts of six students each have graduated from the GLGSA. One graduate is entering his fourth years as an elementary principal, one is entering his second year as a middle school assistant principal, and five are entering their first year as assistant principals in various elementary, middle, and high schools. That only seven of the 18 are academy graduates are currently employed as school administrators is a direct consequence of California's ongoing education budget crisis. As with the majority of the state's school districts, the PUSD has had to confront budgetary shortfalls for each of the past four years and as a result, has reduced the number of assistant principal positions throughout the district. These constraints have prevented the GLGSA from gathering longitudinal data regarding the performance of its graduates or regarding the effectiveness of our evaluation and assessment strategy. Nevertheless, the program is prepared to gather and analyze longitudinal performance data as the demand for leadership positions unfolds in the PUSD. On a positive note, the administrative vacancies that have become available over the past three years have gone to GLGSA graduates.

Executive Coaching

If selected as a PUSD administrator during the five-year duration of the grant-funding cycle, GLGSA graduates receive one year of one-on-one executive coaching (i.e., during Year Two). The purpose of coaching is threefold, (1) to continue the development and refinement of leadership skills within the context of the GLGSA graduate's job, (2) to provide a supportive and smooth transition from classroom teacher to administrator, and (3) to increase the likelihood that GLGSA graduates will remain in PUSD administrative positions (Speck & Krovetz, 1996). A recently retired

PUSD district office administrator serves as the executive coach to graduates hired as administrators and as teacher leaders by the PUSD. This individual served the district for over 38 years in the capacity of teacher, principal, and assistant superintendent. Moreover, as a principal her schools were among the most successful in the PUSD in terms of student achievement. She was recommended for the coaching role by the district's Chief Academic officer and supported by the superintendent. The executive coach's duties and activities are carefully monitored and supported by a Cal Poly EADM faculty member who has extensive experience as a district superintendent and as an executive coach.

RECOMMENDATIONS FOR ESTABLISHING UNIVERSITY–PUBLIC SCHOOL DISTRICT PARTNERSHIPS

As a result of our experiences, we have developed *seven recommendations* for others who seek to establish and maintain a durable relationship between university educational administration departments and public school districts. The seven recommendations fall within two categories, (1) establishing a relationship, and (2) maintaining a relationship. The following three recommendations fall under the category of establishing a relationship: (1) ensure support and buy-in from the district, (2) identify and establish mutual needs and interests, and (3) involve an external evaluator from the very start of building a partnership. Four recommendations fall under the category of maintaining a relationship: (4) reaffirm program goals early in the program implementation process and revisit them often to keep on track, (5) anchor the program in the actual needs and issues of schools and districts, (6) ground program implementation in the district's goals and objectives (usually formalized in a district's strategic plan), and (7) use evaluation evidence to inform program refinements and district planning.

Recommendation One: Ensure Support and Buy-in from the District

Soon after deciding to apply for the USDE School Leadership grant, the EADM faculty focused on procuring a school district partner who met the USDE eligibility requirements. We identified several prospective districts within a few miles of the Cal Poly Pomona campus. Our most immediate neighbor, the PUSD, was the perfect match. In addition, the PUSD and Cal

Poly shared a history of education-focused partnerships. Like many districts in the Inland Empire region of Southern California, the PUSD has large numbers of students who are classified as low-income, limited English proficient, and English language learners. With a number of schools located under the shadow of Program Improvement (PI) status as mandated by the California Department of Education, the PUSD was perilously close to suffering the imposition of state sanctions in the spring of 2008. Other challenges included a devastating state budget crisis that continues in 2012 and has caused an annual ritual of teacher and administrator layoffs. As we began the planning process, the Cal Poly faculty members wondered, "Is this the right time to introduce yet another reform initiative? How would the district respond to an invitation to serve as a partner? Would teachers be interested in participating in a new and untested administrative credential program? Will there be administrative jobs available for our graduates?

From the PUSD perspective, time was short and the stakes were high. The District needed an infusion of talented leaders who would have an immediate impact on improving the academic achievement of all children and who could take bold actions to move schools and the district out of PI status. A newly hired superintendent had a mandate from the PUSD Board of Trustees to move away from an emphasis on the acquisition of property and technology and to focus on the improvement of student learning and achievement. Thus, Cal Poly faculty members were cautiously optimistic that the district leaders would see the benefit of partnering with the university on a project that could assist the district with meeting this mandate.

Early Discussions and Meetings – A Courtship Begins
Following an exchange of emails and phone calls, Cal Poly faculty members requested a meeting with the superintendent of the PUSD (Dr. Thelma Melendez de Santa Ana) and her Administrative Cabinet. During her superintendency, Dr. Melendez had earned a reputation for being a dynamic and forward-thinking leader focused on enhancing student achievement. Following her departure to assume a high level position in the USDE, her successor, Richard Martinez, continued this direction and provided strong support for the program. However, during our initial meeting with the district we were hopeful that Dr. Melendez would agree to explore the possibility of partnering with Cal Poly Pomona. We also knew that the process of securing a firm commitment might take several meetings and a very compelling argument.

We first met over lunch at a local restaurant (neutral territory) with Dr. Melendez and members of her cabinet (Deputy Superintendent, Chief

Academic Officer, and the Directors of Professional Development and Elementary and Secondary Education). From the start, we knew that their support and buy-in was critical to securing the USDE funding. For this first meeting, our primary goal was to provide an overview of the USDE eligibility criteria and to share our initial thoughts regarding program design and the nature of a possible collaboration between the PUSD and Cal Poly Pomona. Because we understood that several past projects between Cal Poly and PUSD had not been fully realized, we were aware of the need to tactfully *sell* the idea and our commitment to district officials, all of whom came to the meeting with full plates and some degree of skepticism regarding whether those from the "ivory tower" could deliver the kind of practical results the district desired.

We provided a rough outline of the primary program goals and related objectives and activities. Rather than talking *at them,* we focused on talking *with them.* Our remarks were brief and to the point (i.e., we kept our professorial inclinations in check). In addition, we purposely asked many questions and tried to initiate a conversation that focused on the needs and interests of the PUSD rather than on those of Cal Poly Pomona. Our orientation was one of service to the PUSD and the facilitation of an initiative designed to address district needs. We wanted the PUSD to see Cal Poly as a useful resource and not as a bastion of *know it all* academics or researchers. Granted, while this approach may seem overly cautious, we were acutely aware of the longstanding perception that higher education faculty and PreK-12 practitioners live in separate worlds.

Initial reactions from the PUSD were guarded but positive (e.g., "looks like a good idea; we may be interested; let's see how it goes"). After the meeting, we sensed that we had successfully *planted the seed* with the Superintendent and her leadership team. However, given the short deadline for submission of a fully developed and comprehensive proposal to the USDE, we remained acutely aware that more interaction was needed in order to move forward, we needed to continue our focus on building the buy-in and support of the PUSD leadership team.

Recommendation Two: Identify and Establish Mutual Needs and Interests: Timing Can Make a Difference

We later learned of the fortuitous timing of our initial meeting with district officials. Given its ongoing challenges in meeting state and federal academic performance standards, the PUSD was faced with the prospect of implementing mandated sanctions. In addition, the district was initiating system-wide commitments to accelerate student achievement through the adoption and implementation of three district reform initiatives: The Six Essentials, Balanced Scorecard, and a Principal Leadership Stages Rubric based upon the Six Essentials. These initiatives were designed to provide teachers and administrators with a clear vision and mission, goals, and performance standards aimed toward the enhancement of learning and teaching. In essence, the district was reforming its approach to the development of instructional leadership (i.e., building a cadre of instructional leaders with teaching and learning as the center of their work). Our proposal to help them identify and train future administrators was a perfect match for the new direction of the PUSD.

Motivation of the Potential Partners
The primary motivation for the Cal Poly faculty members was to develop and test a better way to prepare school leaders that was firmly rooted in principles of adult and experiential learning theories. For the PUSD, the focus rested on developing a cadre of school leaders who possessed the knowledge, skills, and abilities needed to turnaround low performing schools in the district. Cal Poly's credibility was undoubtedly enhanced by the fact that one of its educational administration faculty members had been providing Superintendent Melendez with personalized executive coaching under the sponsorship of a nonprofit professional development and consultancy organization. Together, we determined that the motivations of the PUSD and CPP faculty were strongly aligned. Cal Poly could provide the *fuel* for the proposed program through its faculty expertise, grant funding, and grant oversight, while the PUSD could provide the *engine* (e.g., the context for the program, candidates, and district resources). Within a period of days, both potential partners clearly understood that their shared motivation was to create a program that prepared and supported a new generation of practice-ready leaders who could turnaround low performing schools in the PUSD. Both institutions realized that they needed each other to achieve this vision.

Proposal Development and the Evaluation Perspective
We began the proposal development process with a substantial understanding of the district's needs and priorities as well as a clear idea of the major elements of the administrator preparation program. Given the extremely tight turnaround from the release of the USDE request for proposals (RFP) to the submission deadline, Cal Poly and the PUSD worked

quickly to craft a thoughtful, innovative, and collaborative proposal in the period of one month.

The proposal development process was both reciprocal and iterative as the team simultaneously crafted the elements of the GLGSA and addressed USDE grant program requirements. Respected and trusted leaders from the PUSD (i.e., the Deputy Superintendent and the Director of Professional Development) served as the district liaisons. Within a period of days, Cal Poly and PUSD "stakeholders" quickly came to respect the insights, experiences, and judgments of the other. With a common purpose, a "can-do" spirit, a focus on submitting a winning proposal, and the willingness to collaborate without pride of authorship, the proposal was submitted in May of 2008.

These qualities exist today and demonstrate the importance of garnering buy-in and support by focusing on mutual needs and interests from day one. The GLGSA Planning Team currently functions as a powerful PLC, in part due to this early emphasis on buy-in, support, and mutual trust. Today, their level of involvement is equally strong and influential.

Recommendation Three: Involve a Professional External Evaluator from the Start

We cannot overemphasize the importance of involving a professional external evaluator from the very beginning of the program planning process – even before the goals and activities have been established. For the GLGSA, the evaluator served as a vital and equal member of the proposal development process. When we began our work on the proposal, we made a significant strategic error by waiting to address the evaluation requirement until the proposal was nearly complete. As we later learned, this was a common approach used by many grant applicants. We engaged the evaluator with only two weeks to go before the proposal submission deadline, and quickly learned that the proposal did not show the alignment of key goals with the activities (objectives), the questions that would focus the evaluation (evaluation questions), or the intended results (outcomes). With the evaluator, whose focus rested on developing a solid evaluation and program design, we worked furiously to align program components. In addition to the professional evaluator, we also engaged the services of a professional grant writer with a track record of writing successful USDE proposals. Her knowledge of USDE proposal development and submission protocols was invaluable. Moreover, she was instrumental in synthesizing the various ideas expressed by Planning Team members into one coherent "voice."

Had we engaged our evaluator from the very beginning, we would have greatly reduced the amount of time and effort needed to develop the proposal. We now understand that the full and ongoing engagement of the evaluator is far more important to the success of a complex project such as the GLGSA than simply hiring someone to write the evaluation section while remaining disconnected from program implementation activities. From the development of the proposal to our current stage in the program implementation cycle, the GLGSA external evaluator has become an essential member of the team and of the learning community. Like a "critical friend," she coaches, facilitates, and constantly encourages planning team members to think deeply and logically while always keeping the GLGSA goal in mind. If we can't answer her most basic and enduring questions ("when and how will you know"), we know we have more work to do together.

Reflections and Insights on Establishing Institutional Partnerships

Establishing a durable partnership requires a judicious alignment of contextual factors (e.g., organizational, policy, and community dynamics) and stakeholder interests, values, and skills. Initial elements in such a partnership include, (a) the willingness to listen to others with an open mind, (b) the identification of mutual needs and interests, (c) personal and professional respect, (d) patience and a degree of tolerance for ambiguity, and (e) credibility gained through personal investment and follow through. By paying attention to these elements, a solid foundation is established for other key aspects of establishing a partnership, including the buy-in and enthusiastic support among partners, establishing mutual trust, and building a shared vision. In working with PUSD, this meant helping the district address its top priorities, building the district's internal capacity to train and support future administrators, and creating a durable partnership with Cal Poly that added significant value to its reform efforts. At the same time, engaging the services of a professional external evaluator early was critical, especially in terms of developing an empirically supported action plan (evaluation plan) that all stakeholders "owned" for themselves during all aspects of program planning, implementation, assessment, and evaluation. We now understand that by planning with the "end in mind," the process of program development and implementation is likely to be more rational, coherent, comprehensive, purposeful, and (most importantly) effective.

Once the initial working of building a partnership had been accomplished, we turned to the question of what needed to be done in order to *maintain* a deep and sustainable partnership. In the next section, we present four recommendations for moving beyond an initial agreement and into a robust, mature, and long-term partnership. We also describe how the partnership has evolved from the early days to the present.

Soon after we received the grant award we realized that the process of establishing the partnership may be easier than sustaining the partnership. As stakeholders inevitably come and go and as institutional priorities change, we knew that maintaining the partnership would require a collective attention to detail and periodic reinforcement of the partners' mutual commitment. Our questions now became: How do we fully realize (e.g., institutionalize) the partnership? How do we make it last? What obstacles will we face? Will we be able to work at the same level of passion? We knew that only time would tell.

Recommendation Four: Reaffirm Program Goals among Partners Early and Revisit Often

The successful implementation of the GLGSA meant that Cal Poly and the PUSD needed to move to a deeper level of communication and collaboration as the partnership evolved over time. First and foremost, we reaffirmed that the goal of the GLGSA was to develop a cadre of talented new leaders who could take bold actions to turn around low performing schools in the district and who could help to stimulate a district-wide culture of leadership excellence. This is an important point. A key rationale for developing the GLGSA was not only its potential to train 30 school leaders over five years, but also the potential to stimulate a district-wide culture of high expectations (grounded in exceptional leadership skills) that would influence the practices of *all* administrators, regardless of whether they participated in the GLGSA. Essentially, the GLGSA provided another mechanism for the PUSD to transform a system-wide leadership reform within the district.

The question then became: How can we ensure the long-term success of this effort? The GLGSA Planning Team developed several strategies to focus the team's efforts. First, the team aspired to develop and implement a durable partnership between the PUSD and Cal Poly that extended beyond the activities of the GLGSA. The GLGSA Planning Team not only wanted to prepare students to meet state credential requirements, but also to build an ongoing system of professional development and support that included Cal Poly faculty members, PUSD leaders, and the cohort members themselves in an extended PLC. The rationale was that a PLC would accelerate the positive impact of GLGSA graduates on schools, promote the retention of the GLGSA graduates within the district, and expand to include administrators who were not GLGSA graduates. Second, the team aspired to shape an administrator preparation program around important and empirically grounded principles of adult learning (e.g., Knowles's, 2005, theory of andragogy) and experiential learning. Finally, the team determined that the program would be grounded in the professional standards and initiatives of the PUSD (and most importantly, the PUSD Six Essentials).

As a consequence of California's withering fiscal crisis, over the past three years the PUSD was forced to reduce administrative positions across its schools and within the district office. Thus, finding administrative placements (typically assistant principalships) for GLGSA graduates became unexpectedly challenging. To date, of the 18 GLGSA graduates (e.g., three cohorts), only seven have been hired as school administrators (one principal, six assistant principals). However, eight of the other eleven graduates have been placed in various teacher leadership positions (e.g., school site specialists and resource teachers) as they await PUSD administrative vacancies. To ensure that these GLGSA graduates continue to nurture their administrative knowledge and skills and to address their evolving professional needs, we continue to provide them with quarterly group coaching sessions, various scholarly materials and updates, and access to a GLGSA social networking site. In some cases, GLGSA graduates with special skills are invited to address current cohort class sessions. Facilitated by the GLGSA Planning Team, this process ensures that the GLGSA will produce 30 practice-ready school leaders who will be poised to assume leadership positions within the district as administrative positions arise within and beyond the five-year funding period of the grant.

Recommendation Five: Anchor the Program in the Actual Issues of Schools and Districts

As we began the implementation of the GLGSA, we focused on grounding the activities of the candidates in authentic and "real-world" learning activities. From the beginning, the GLGSA Planning Team agreed that the timeworn didactic model of teaching and learning was not our intent (i.e., where professors lecture and students listen and where the domains of knowledge in the field are treated as discrete and separate from each other). Informed by a sizeable body of research and scholarly work in areas such as problem-based learning, thematically integrated curriculum, adult learning, and experiential learning, Cal Poly faculty members carefully identified the best ideas from the literature and worked with PUSD partners to fashion a leadership development program that would provide rigorous and authentic learning experiences and which would result in a shorter time between program completion and employment in a PUSD school leadership position. The strong and collaborative partnership between PUSD and Cal Poly enables the GLGSA to quickly adapt to changing district needs, emerging research, and changing policy initiatives.

Now, we continuously infuse district initiatives and needs into the weekly seminars based upon feedback from the district and from advances in the field of educational administration. For example, a classroom observation protocol content module was added to the curriculum to address an increased emphasis on this activity by the district.

Recommendation Six: Ground Program Implementation Strategies Upon District Goals and Objectives

Early in her tenure, Superintendent Melendez worked with the school board, community, employee groups, and other stakeholders to develop a framework for district reform titled the *Six Essentials*. These professional standards have become the driving force behind PUSD planning, professional development programs, operations, and assessments. The *Six Essentials* include the following categories, (1) *Responsive Instruction* — to ensure that each child experiences powerful teaching and learning, (2) *Student Work and Data* — to assess learning, (3) *Aligned Resources* — to support and assure student learning, (4) *Family and Community* — to support student learning, (5) *Shared Leadership* — to sustain a collaborative culture, and (6) *Professional Development* — to improve instruction.

Based on the Essentials, the district also developed the *Principal Leadership Stages Rubric*. The district uses this tool to establish principal goals for the year, to specify areas of future professional development, and to assess principal accomplishment and success in meeting each of the goals. The rubric is aligned with the California Professional Standards for

Education Leaders (CPSELs), the 2008 Interstate School Leaders Licensure Consortium (ISSLC) Standards, and the work of the Mid-continent Research for Education and Learning's (McREL) on Balanced Leadership (Waters, Marzano, & McNulty, 2003).

The rubric describes 67 administrative practices with designations that include, (1) practice that is directed toward the standard, (2) practice that approaches the standard, (3) practice that meets the standard, and (4) practice that exemplifies the standard. This rubric serves as the foundation for GLGSA course content, practicum activities, mentoring, and coaching. A few of the outcomes were modified given that the GLGSA focuses on aspiring school leaders rather than existing leaders. During the first and final weeks of the apprenticeship, the mentor principals use the modified rubric to assess apprentice performance while the candidates use the same tool to self-assess their performance.

Recommendation Seven: Use Evaluation Evidence to Inform Program Refinements and District Planning

Earlier, we noted the importance of beginning with the end in mind – a principle that holds true for proposal and program implementation. Similarly, our evaluation approach and the use of evaluation tools and methodology are especially important threads in the complex tapestry of relationships that comprise this strong interagency partnership. The development of a comprehensive program evaluation plan by the GLGSA Planning Team, facilitated by the GLGSA external evaluator, provided both partners with a clear roadmap from which to plan program activities, to assess outcomes, to evaluate progress toward achieving the goal, and to hold each other accountable for implementing and improving plan elements.

However, an evaluation plan must contain information that is useful and relevant to the major stakeholders. To this end, the external evaluator facilitated a process to assist the GLGSA Planning Team in developing focal research questions that were important to key stakeholders and that would be used to guide program implementation activities and assess program effectiveness. The GLGSA evaluation plan also illuminates the data that the PUSD can use to sharpen and revise its leadership development strategies, leadership recruitment and selection policies, leadership performance/competence assessments, and information regarding how core values and principles (e.g., The Six Essentials, PUSD Leadership Stages

Rubric) are operationalized through the behaviors and practices of school leaders.

To summarize, in this section we described seven recommendations for those who desire to build innovative principal preparation programs that are grounded upon strong and sustainable interagency collaboration. These included:

1. Ensure Support and Buy-in from the District
2. Identify and Establish Mutual Needs and Interests: Timing Can Make a Difference
3. Involve a Professional External Evaluator from the Start
4. Reaffirm Program Goals among Partners Early and Revisit Often
5. Anchor the Program in the Actual Issues of Schools and Districts
6. Ground Program Implementation Strategies Upon District Goals and Objectives
7. Use Evaluation Evidence to Inform Program Refinements and District Planning

Together these recommendations underscore the importance of building a set of common goals, trusting relationships, and a commitment to sustain mutual engagement in the work. Finally, sponsoring graduate programs must be willing to share the "intellectual agency" with partner school districts by acknowledging the importance and credibility of practitioners' perspectives in the preparation of school leaders.

MAINTAINING AND NURTURING A UNIVERSITY-DISTRICT PARTNERSHIP

Maintaining the PUSD–Cal Poly partnership requires fidelity to common *values* and the integrity with which those values are embodied in the partnership. From the very beginning of the partnership, one constant is the ongoing communication between members of the GLGSA Planning Team. The team spends a significant amount of time together listening, emailing, learning, establishing goals and outcomes, evaluating the assessment data, and solving problems. The result is a climate of mutual respect and shared commitment that is greatly valued and serves as solid base for the entire program. Furthermore, *all* major decisions about the program or candidates occur with the input and buy-in of the team members. Because the PUSD is a large suburban school district with urban characteristics, Cal Poly faculty members must work closely with the district to insure effective communication across many stakeholders, including site principals who recommend candidates, mentor principals who work with the GLGSA candidates during their apprenticeship, and with district leaders and department heads.

The importance of establishing strong and sustainable interagency collaboration in the development and implementation of innovative and robust principal preparation programs is supported by Darling-Hammond, LaPointe, Meyerson, Orr, and Cohen (2007, p. 64). In their investigation of eight exemplary principal preparation programs, these researchers concluded that, "The programs we studied were distinguished by the willingness of central actors within both districts and universities to establish policies facilitating cross-sector collaborations." Moreover, the authors noted that,

> Collaborations between organizations can prepare principals for specific district and regional contexts and can develop a stronger and more committed leadership pool. Partnerships expand the resource pool available to programs for offering both quality coursework and quality field placements. In addition, collaborations between universities and districts increase the likelihood that leaders receive relevant and consistent support and professional development once they have completed their credential program. (p. 64)

FINAL REFLECTIONS AND COMMENTS

With the goal of developing 30 practice-ready school leaders and a comprehensive assessment and evaluation approach to gauge progress toward the achievement of this goal, the partnership between Cal Poly and the PUSD began as a dynamic and results oriented collaboration. From the start, the proposed project was not about imposing a university or federal policy agenda. Rather, we focused on meeting the district's need for future leaders while addressing the university's need to reach out and positively impact the field of K-12 education. During our first three years of operation we have committed ourselves to practicing flexibility; listening well; reflecting often; questioning assumptions, and aligning district, learning, and program outcomes.

We are pleased with the success of our first three cohorts and continue to use the multiple forms of assessment data to gain valuable feedback and to generate new ideas. We work to not only add value to the PUSD, but also to generate knowledge about innovative approaches to leadership development that can inform universities, school districts, and policy makers. At the end of the day, successful programs and schools require effective leadership that is grounded in the collective commitment, focus, and contributions of all stakeholders – the efforts of any one person are not enough. The success of the GLGSA partnership can be attributed to the qualities and attributes of the dedicated people who work with a common purpose and dedication to achieving the goals of the program.

The GLGSA is one of a growing number of innovative principal preparation programs in America that is based upon robust interagency collaboration. Nevertheless, it is a *small batch* program framed around the particular contexts and needs of one school district and one university provider. As such, we acknowledge that our approach may be of limited value to programs that serve multiple districts or geographical regions. Therefore, the key findings from our work may be less relevant in terms of scalability than replicability.

We also believe that the future of principal preparation rests with the transition away from "one-size-fits-all" program design to more context sensitive strategies that more effectively match curriculum, pedagogy, and local school district needs (Fry, O'Neill, & Bottoms, 2006). Although we have yet to gather sufficient data to draw valid conclusions regarding the efficacy of our particular rendition of a collaborative and problem-based program model, our theory of action rests on the assumption that the convergence of theory and practice is best served when universities and school districts engage mutually in the design, implementation, and evaluation of programs. A viable example of this theory was described by Cheney, Davis, Garrett, and Holleran (2010) in their research on the Urban Educational Leadership Program (UELP) at the University of Illinois, Chicago. Developed to provide highly skilled principals for the Chicago city schools, since its inception in 2001 the UELP has established an impressive track record of preparing principals capable of leading change in low performing urban schools.

Ultimately, the success of any interagency collaboration to prepare principals depends upon the vision, determination, and political skills of university program leaders. We clearly found this to be true, as did Darling-Hammond et al. (2007) in their analysis of exemplary preparation programs. Moreover, practitioners have ample reason to doubt the intentions or relevance of university academics. Davis (2008, p. 84) noted that, "Researchers and practitioners reside in vastly different professional worlds characterized by deep suspicions and enduring feelings of mistrust for the intentions and abilities of the other." Davis also contends that the nature of work in the university contrasts dramatically with work in the field. In light of such divergent professional orientations and workplace dynamics, it is particularly incumbent upon university program faculty members to actively reach out to local school districts in the spirit of collegiality, and not paternalistically.

In most parts of the country the marketplace is well saturated with credentialed school administrators and school districts have ample opportunities to hire candidates from a broad range of programs. It is our position that the effort to build collaborative relationships is stimulated when higher education actively reaches out to local school districts with innovative ideas, a sincere commitment to work in partnership, and a measure of humility.

ACKNOWLEDGMENT

The Great Leaders for Great Schools Academy is supported by US Department of Education (USDE) Grant, PR#U363A080106, awarded to California State Polytechnic University, Pomona.

REFERENCES

Cheney, G. R., Davis, J., Garrett, K., & Holleran, J. (2010). *A new approach to principal preparation*. Fort Worth, TX: Rainwater Charitable Foundation.

Darling-Hammond, L., LaPointe, M., Meyerson, D., Orr, M. T., & Cohen, C. (2007). *Preparing leaders for a changing world: Lessons from exemplary leadership development programs*. Stanford, CA: Stanford Educational Leadership Institute.

Davis, S. H. (2008). *Research and practice in education: The search for common ground*. Lanham, MD: Rowman & Littlefield Education.

DuFour, R. (2004). Schools as learning communities. *Educational Leadership, 61*(8), 6–11.

Fenwick, T. J. (2003). *Learning through experience: Troubling orthodoxies and intersecting questions*. Malabar, FL: Krieger Publishing Company.

Fry, B., O'Neill, K., & Bottoms, G. (2006). *Schools can't wait: Accelerating the redesign of university principal preparation programs*. Atlanta, GA: Southern Regional Education Board.

Knowles, M. S., Holton, E. F., & Swanson, R. A. (2005). *The adult learner* (6th ed.). Boston, MA: Elsevier.

Kolb, D. A. (1984). *Experiential learning: Experience as the source of learning and development*. Englewood Cliffs, New Jersey: Prentice Hall.

Mezirow, J. (1991). *Transformative dimensions of adult learning*. San Francisco, CA: Jossey-Bass.

Speck, M., & Krovetz, M. (1996). Developing executive peer coaching experiences for school administrators. *ERS Spectrum, 14*(1), 37–42.

Waters, T., Marzano, R. J., & McNulty, B. (2003). *Balanced leadership: What 30 years of research tells us about the effect of leadership on student achievement*. Aurora, CO: Mid-continent Research for Education and Learning.

CHAPTER 3

PLANNING, CHANGING, AND LEADING A COMMUNITY OF PROFESSIONAL PRACTICE: *LESSONS LEARNED FROM AN INNOVATIVE URBAN SCHOOL LEADERS PREPARATION PROGRAM IN SOUTHERN CALIFORNIA*

Antonia Issa Lahera and Anthony H. Normore

ABSTRACT

This chapter examines the process of ongoing planning and changing of an innovative urban school leadership development and preparation program at California State University Dominguez Hills. Currently in its fourth consecutive year, the five-year Urban School Leaders (USL) program is the result of a partnership with Local Districts 5, 6, 7, and 8 within Los Angeles Unified School District (LAUSD) and California State University Dominguez Hills (CSUDH). The program is intended to prepare, place, and retain leaders for high needs schools and provide staff development to these leaders with the ultimate outcome resulting in student achievement gains. LAUSD Local Districts 5–8 are contiguous and in close proximity to CSUDH. These districts encompass some of Los Angeles' poorest neighborhoods, including East LA, South LA, South Central LA, and the Harbor area. In this chapter, we outline the various components of the USL program and share reflections on the planning and improvement process in our efforts to strengthen and improve the community of professional practice within the program.

Effective educational leadership development and preparation has become increasingly imperative for large urban school districts in the current education reform environment. A plethora of educational researchers (e.g., Levine, 2005; Tucker & Codding, 2002) has relentlessly expressed the need "to focus on the effective development and preparation of educational leaders in order to build congruity and connectedness between the worlds of educational leadership theory and practice" (Bruner, Greenlee, & Somers Hill, 2007, p. 1). Long criticized for a wide range of transgressions (Levine, 2005) many programs offer little connection between the preparation programs' curriculum and actual school leaders' daily job realities. Further, "Essential cultural, ethnic, gender, and linguistic issues in school communities are frequently missing from course consideration and clinical experiences are occasionally insipid, unstructured, and sometimes even absent" (Herrity & Glassman, 1999, cited in Bruner et al., 2007, p. 1). Other researchers note that leadership development programs will better address future challenges when comprehensive structures, systems, and holistic learning opportunities are in place to support an organizational *culture* to build capacity and sustain leadership over time (Fulmer & Goldsmith, 2000; Miller, Caldwell, & Lawson, 2001; Simmons, 2006). Culture influences every aspect of a school's activities, including the levels of collegial and collaborative interaction, communication among participants, organizational commitment, and motivation (Tierney, 2006).

In response to the need for effective leadership programs, some school districts and universities have established partnerships, coalitions, and networks (see Brooks, Harvard, Tatum, & Patrick, 2010). These collaborative partnerships deliver programs that develop emerging leaders, commonly referred to as *growing theirown* (Giber, Carter, & Goldsmith, 2000; Hix, Wall, & Frieler, 2003, cited in Normore, 2007). In order to *grow their own* leaders, school districts and their partner organizations must have a passion and understanding for growing the *right* leaders. The intent of leadership development and preparation "is to produce leaders" (Milstein, 1992, p. 10) that have the requisite knowledge, dispositions, and skills to lead contemporary schools competently and effectively (Institute for Educational Leadership, 2000; Kelley & Peterson, 2000).

According to Browne-Ferrigno (2007) and other researchers (e.g., Fullan, 2003; Murphy, 2002, 2005; Waters, Marzano, & McNulty, 2003), new performance expectations for school site leaders in the United States, as reiterated in administrator standards established by the Council for Chief State School Officers (CCSSO, 1996) and individual states, "have modified the long-standing perception of a principal as a school manager to a perspective of learner-centered leaders who focus on high levels of learning for all students" (Browne-Ferrigno, 2007, p. 1). Subsequently, many university-based preparation programs have redesigned their delivery formats, aligned their curricula to new professional standards (e.g., ISLLC, ELCC), and updated their performance assessments for graduate students (Jackson & Kelley, 2002; Murphy & Forsyth, 1999). Further, the Southern Regional Education Board (SREB) continues to call upon educational leadership departments "to awaken from their complacency, reject the status quo, and respond to appeals and criticisms from the field by identifying new content that addresses what principals need to know in order to do their jobs and by devising instructional processes that ensure principals master essential knowledge and skills" (Fry, O'Neil, & Bottoms, 2006, p. 11).

The purpose of this chapter is to broaden the inquiry on leadership development. In response to educational leadership reform movement coupled with criticisms of leadership preparation programs, the author(s) discuss the efforts of one holistic, changing, and innovative educational leadership development program designed for preparing more effective school leaders in southern California. Known as *Urban School Leaders (USL)* the program is housed at California State University Dominguez Hills (CSUDH) and made possible through a partnership between CSUDH's educational administration program, the Associated Administrators of Los Angeles (AALA), and Local Districts (LD) 5, 6, 7, and 8 within Los Angeles Unified School District (LAUSD). Insights gained from the efforts of designing and/or redesigning the USL program may be instructive to other programs that are in the process of reforming leadership preparation. Currently in its fourth year the five-year program is funded through a grant from The US Department of Education, School Leadership Program, Office of Innovation and Improvement.

The chapter is organized into the following sections: (1) Review of literature, (2) Program context, (3) Program design, (4) Key elements of program, (5) Program changes, and (6) Lessons learned. Final thoughts, reflections and implications are also presented.

REVIEW OF LITERATURE

We preface this chapter by cataloguing certain salient themes gleaned from a review of literature on leadership development, preparation and training programs. These themes are: (1) Criticisms of educational leadership development programs, (2) Responses to the criticisms, (3) Program delivery and structures, (4) Cohort model, and (5) University and school district partnerships. The balance of the literature review is devoted to a discussion of each of these themes in turn.

Criticisms of Educational Leadership Development Programs

The criticisms of educational leadership preparation programs are numerous and have a broad range including: candidate recruitment and selection processes (Normore, 2007); a profound lack of agreement on the inadequate and inappropriate program content for training programs that indiscriminately adopt practices untested and uninformed by educational values and purposes (Clark, 1988); a seemingly endemic unwillingness on the part of the professoriate to address the content issue (McCarthy, Kuh, Newell, & Iacona (1988); inadequate attention to diversity and social justice (Jean-Marie, Normore, & Brooks, 2009; Preiss, Grogan, Sherman, & Beatty, 2007); mediocre pedagogical strategies employed (Levine, 2005; McCarthy, 1999; Murphy, 2006; NCEEA, 1987); the separation of the practice and theory (Bruner et al., 2007); a weak clinical program and a lack of attention to leadership skills (Bruner et al., 2007; Jean-Marie et al., 2009); the concomitant failure to address outcomes (Haller, Brent, & McNamara, 1997); and program effectiveness (Murphy, 2006).

For too many leadership preparation programs, parochialism exists that "anybody is better than nobody" (see Jacobson, 1990). Two problems are affiliated with this parochialism: first, and as noted by Murphy (2006) "the catchment area for most programs is quite local and within a 25–50 mile radius of the university," and second, "since nearly all entering students are functioning as teachers or administrators, questions continue to rise whether students are exposed to new ideas and/or are receptive to alternative views that clash with accepted local norms" (2006, cited in Jean-Marie & Normore, 2010, p. 8).

Responding to the Critics

Critics have indicated that many educational leadership preparation programs are disconnected from the realities of today's schools (Farkas, Johnson, Duffett, Foleno, & Folley, 2001). According to Bruner et al. (2007),

> ... as programs struggle to redefine themselves they are continually challenged to address age-old criticisms of academia by spotlighting how to blend theory and practice ... .More corporate skills in marketing, sales, and considerable self-promotion are necessary to change past perceptions as many programs are making great headway blending theory and practice through course assignments, practitioner partnerships in course instruction and program development, as well as through expanded experiences and timeframes around field experiences. (p. 17)

Fundamental shifts in the thinking of graduate programs in educational leadership have created a need to think differently about the profession of school leadership and the education of school leaders (Brooks et al., 2010, Murphy, 2005, 2006). Jackson and Kelly (2002) identified several practices of exceptional and innovative programs in educational leadership including: the use of problem-based learning; the use of cohort models; meaningful and substantive field-based experiences; cutting-edge technology; and collaborative partnerships. Murphy (2006) further reiterated these and other recommendations that interested stakeholders are responding to including: new views of politics, governance, and organization; new views of internal and external collaborative partnerships, interdisciplinary content, and delivery systems; new views of technology; and new views of learning and teaching. Murphy further claims that these call for quite different understandings of school leadership and redesigned models of developing school leaders (2006). To be prepared to provide effective leadership for learning that leads to improvement in student performance researchers have indicated that preparation and professional development must be redesigned (see Brooks et al., 2010; Browne-Ferigno, 2007; Bruner et al., 2007; Grogan & Andrews, 2002; Jean-Marie & Normore, 2010; Preiss et al., 2007).

Program Delivery Structures and Components

Each educational leadership preparation program is unique and many contain similar elements. Preiss et al. (2007) claim that most programs are "university-based and organized around courses that prepare students for administrative licensure within a degree program" ... and in some cases, "students who already have master's degrees are able to gain licensure by taking a certain set of courses" (p. 3). Most programs include components of practice including internships or field-based learning experiences, and are commonly divided into two distinct components: instructional leadership coursework and internships (Hess & Kelly, 2005; Jackson & Kelley, 2002, cited in Preiss et al., 2007, p. 3). Many programs emphasize case studies as part of coursework, problems-based learning (PBL), and hands-on learning experiences (Jackson & Kelly, 2002; McCarthy, 1999; Milstein & Krueger, 1997). Programs often range in length from one to three years and require 18–36 credit hours for completion (Goldring & Sims, 2005; Hess & Kelly, 2005; Jackson & Kelley, 2002) with an average class or program size between 10 and 25 students (Whitaker & Barnett, 1999). Further, portfolios or other methods of authentic assessment are now typical within the educational leadership preparation arena (Clark & Clark, 1997; Hess & Kelly, 2005; Milstein & Krueger, 1997).

Online course offerings and weekend class meetings that can also be web assisted are viewed as effective ways to better accommodate working professionals (Goldring & Sims, 2005; Hughes, 2005; Jackson & Kelley, 2002). Exceptional and innovative educational leadership programs incorporate the use of contemporary instructional technologies into their delivery. Other features tailored to the working professional include summer institutes or other intensive, time-condensed workshops (Jackson & Kelley, 2002). By a considerable margin, the most studied delivery mechanism is what is generally described as "a cohort" model (Barnett & Muse, 1993, p. 401).

Cohort Models of Leadership Preparation

A cohort is defined as "a group of students who begin and complete a program of studies together, engaging in a common set of courses, activities, and/or learning experiences" (Barnett & Muse, 1993, p. 401). The use of cohorts in leadership preparation programs is growing in popularity because it is believed "to be both responsive to 'consumer' needs and to address some of the criticisms of leadership preparation of the past"

(Preis et al., 2007, p. 5). Most estimates today claim that over 50% of leadership preparation programs use the cohort model (Barnett, Basom, Yerkes, & Norris, 2000). Cohort models are often characterized by their common external features such as a standard size and a common schedule (Barnett & Muse, 1993; Jean-Marie & Normore, 2010). In defining a cohort-oriented leadership preparation program, proponents argue that the cohort is "more than a structure for delivery of a program .... Instead, they think of it in terms of a learning model for adult students" (Norris, Barnett, Basom, & Yerkes, 1996, cited in Preis et al., 2007, p. 7). These same proponents further assert that the success of the model is impacted by the degree to which faculty embrace the program at their university and are effective in working with adult learners (Browne-Ferrigno & Muth, 2003). In support of other research (e.g., Diller, 2004; McCabe, Ricciardi, & Jamison, 2000), Preis and colleagues claim that "Since adult learners are self-directed and have strong internal motivation, it is argued that cohort models engage them in a meaningful way" (p. 5).

According to Browne-Ferrigno (2007) and others (e.g., Browne-Ferrigno & Muth, 2003; Bruner et al., 2007) "a community created by the closed-cohort structure and maintained through purposeful group-development activities is perceived to strengthen curriculum integration and team teaching" (2007, p. 4). Further, it builds trust relationships, creates safe learning environments, enhances professional learning, expands collegial networks and fosters the development of reflective abilities, professional behaviors, and interpersonal relationships (Horn, 2001; Jackson & Kelly, 2002; Leithwood, Jantzi, & Coffin, 1995). One recurring criticism of the cohort model is that "no conclusive scientific research exists to substantiate a positive impact on the leadership abilities of the cohort participants versus non-cohort participants" (Barnett et al., 2000, cited in Preis et al., 2007, p. 11).

Use of Powerful Partnerships between School Districts and Universities

The literature is replete with studies conducted on the positive impact of well-established partnerships between schools and universities (Barnett, 2005; Brooks et al., 2010; Goldring & Sims, 2005; Sherman, 2006). Preiss et al. (2007) reiterate how partnerships "have the potential to bridge the gap between theory and practice that has often been a criticism of educational leadership preparation offered by universities" and "offer more options for program delivery" (p. 17). Further research confirms that effective and successful partnerships involve multilevel collaboration and cooperation of each participating organization (Grogan & Roberson, 2002; Whitaker & Barnett, 1999). Many successful university-school district partnerships have had development and reconstitution committees where constituents were well represented and had input on the structure and expectations for the partnership (Goldring & Sims, 2005). In addition, to be successful, "all partners must share a commitment to the partnership and respect what the other partner has to contribute" (Whitaker & Barnett, 1999, cited in Preiss et al., 2007, p. 16).

Strong collaboration between schools and universities open up opportunities for collaborative delivery models (Brooks et al., 2010). For instance, practicing administrators can lead seminars or team-teach with university faculty (Aiken, 2001; Clark & Clark, 1997; Milstein & Krueger, 1997). Effective veteran administrators are also incorporated into program design by serving as mentors for those in leadership preparation (Aiken, 2001; Whitaker & Barnett, 1999). In addition, a number of university programs offer courses on-site within school districts or teach the entire program on-site (Grogan & Roberson, 2002; Jackson & Kelley, 2002; Whitaker, King, & Vogel, 2004) thereby allowing the partner districts "to have as much say in determining what gets taught, how, and when, as the university faculty has" (Preis et al., 2007, p. 17).

The balance of this chapter is dedicated to the examination of efforts of the *USL* program personnel at SCMU and how the program has responded to the call for reform of leadership preparation programs and the education for more effective school leaders.

URBAN SCHOOL LEADERS PROGRAM: CONTEXT

CSUDH and LAUSD's LD 5, 6, 7, and 8 designed and implemented the *USL* program in 2008. The program is intended to develop, prepare and retain effective aspiring and practicing USL to transform underperforming schools and improve student achievement. CSUDH is a four-year urban public institution located in the South Bay region of Greater Metropolitan Los Angeles. The campus is one of the most ethnically diverse in the southern region of California, reflecting the demographics of the surrounding communities. The vision of CSUDH's School of Education is to maintain a model of collaborative urban educational excellence that is recognized for preparing teachers, administrators, counselors, and other specialists who work effectively with a variety of learners from diverse backgrounds.

CSUDH and LAUSD have a long history of collaboration, including a 2002 School Leadership grant, which recruited and trained 205 ethnically diverse participants and placed 73% in administrative or quasi-leadership positions. While the 2002 project succeeded in helping participants earn their administrative credential and master's degree, we learned that aspiring leaders needed additional support to complete LAUSD's rigorous one- to two-year process to become eligible and be placed as principals and assistant principals.

The USL program serves LAUSD LD 5, 6, 7, and 8 — all which are contiguous and nearest in proximity to CSUDH. These LDs encompass some of Los Angeles' poorest neighborhoods, including East LA, South LA, South Central LA, and the Harbor area. There are 300,921 students in 282 Title 1 schools. The student ethnic majority in all districts is Hispanic, ranging from 62% in LD 8 to 98% in LD 6. The second largest student ethnic group is African-American, which averages approximately 20% in LD 7 and 8. English Learners comprise approximately 22% (LD 8) to 48% (LD 5–6) of the students. The Association of Administrators Los Angeles (AALA) is the union representing administrators in LAUSD. AALA brings a rich knowledge of the leadership challenges and political realities within this large urban district. A profile of these districts is seen in Table 1.

Table 1. Profile of Local Districts 5, 6, 7, and 8.

	District 5	District 6	District 7	District 8	Total
Student population					
No. of students	89,702	60,775	71,667	78,777	300,921
Free/reduced lunch (%)	83	81	81	68	78
Major ethnicity	94% Hispanic	99% Hispanic	78% Hispanic	62% Hispanic	83%
			21% Black	23% Black	12%
Schools					
No. of schools	89	48	63	82	282
Title 1 schools (%)	100	100	100	100	100
Program Impr. schools	59 (66%)	28 (58%)	44 (70%)	32 (39%)	163 (58%)
Certificated staff					
No. of teachers	4,587	3,001	3,655	3,943	15,186
Highly qualified teachers (%)	89	87	83	98	89
No. of school administrators	204	121	161	174	660

A survey of district superintendents by the Association of California School Administrators found that 90% reported a lack of qualified candidates for high school principal positions, 84% for middle schools, and 73% for elementary schools. LAUSD has embarked on a school-building project to relieve overcrowding, which will add 132 schools — 70 of them in LD 5–8, requiring more than 200 principals and assistant principals. Also, LAUSD is reconfiguring its high schools into small learning communities, which requires additional assistant principals. Compounding the shortage is the imminent retirement of administrators, as noted in a study that found more than half of LAUSD school administrators were age 50 or older as of the 2005–2006 school year, and predicted large-scale retirements of administrators in the coming years (Jakubowski & Leidner, 2007).

Urban School Leadership Program Design

The five-year USL program is a partnership program with LAUSD and intended to prepare leaders for high need schools, place aspiring leaders in high need schools, retain leaders in schools for two or more years, and provide staff development to leaders with the ultimate outcome resulting in student achievement gains. USL expands the emphasis on participants' reflection on their core values and dispositions while fostering and promoting diversity, equity and excellence in order to improve interpersonal and professional practice. In support of research, this emphasis supports a shift from "tolerating diversity" to a "transformational commitment to equity" (Nuri-Robins, Lindsey, Terrell, & Lindsey, 2007). Prominent researchers and commentators have long pressed for equity in our schools (Darling-Hammond, French, & Garcia-Lopez, 2002; Kozol, 2005; Theoharis, 2007). The USL program is committed to the development of leaders who advocate for equitable opportunity and practice so that every child has an equal chance to improve academic achievement.

Principles that guide the USL program focus on the need to recruit qualified school-leader candidates (Hess & Kelly, 2007; Murphy, 2001; Spillane, 2005), especially those who are culturally, economically, and/or linguistically diverse (Barth, 2002), as well as assistant principals and principals with less than five years experience, to meet the leadership needs of underperforming schools. The program is intended to provide high-quality training and support that prepares participants to attain credentials, degrees, or skills needed for school leadership positions. As a result of the program, it is anticipated that participants are placed and retained in school leadership positions in order to increase student achievement in underperforming schools.

USL Program Model

The movement to reform educational leadership programs has led to the examination and redesign of preparation programs (SREB, 2005). Representing research-based findings (e.g., SREB, 2005), particular emphases are placed on the collaborative partnership between the USL program and LAUSD LDs 5, 6, 7, and 8. Further, a cohort model design (Jackson & Kelley, 2002) for initial certification is emphasized where systemic changes are ongoing in university curricula, internships, and state certification and licensure procedures for educational leaders. According to these researchers, the advantages of this model include powerful "social and interpersonal relationships, increased contact with faculty members, better integration into the university, clearer program structure and course sequencing, higher program completion rates, greater cohesiveness, and the development of professional networks" (Jackson & Kelley, 2002, cited in Brooks et al., 2010, p. 421). In designing the USL program, we researched best practices in response to Fry et al. (2006). These researchers assert "the need to identify new content that addresses what principals need to know in order to do their jobs and by devising instructional processes that ensure principals master essential knowledge and skills" (p. 11). Further, we recognize that the extensive leadership needs in LAUSD require that USL provide training and support for three distinct groups: (1) *Aspiring leaders* who need certification, (2) *Aspiring leaders* who have graduated from the USL program, but in an economic climate devoid of administrative openings, these leaders continue to increase their skills while awaiting administrative positions, and (3) *Sitting Administrators* who comprise what is known as the USL's *Principals' Academy*. The goal is to retain their positions for an increased length of time as well as to increase their leadership skills that support teachers so that it results in improved student achievement. All participants of all three groups are involved in the *Leadership Learning Community (LLC)*, a professional network of aspiring and practicing school leaders which offers three major professional development activities each year: August and January urban leadership conferences, and summer seminar series.

EXAMINING KEY ELEMENTS OF USL PROGRAM

The following section examines the essential key elements that comprise the USL program.

Incentives

The USL program includes incentives for participants that provide motivation and commitment. Local Districts in LAUSD need incentives to support availability of participants during the workday for various experiences including an incentive to attend activities, and stay up-to-date on research. For candidates in their preparation program, the USL encompasses a wide range of research-based activities and program delivery strategies that are intended to prepare candidates for California's Administrative Services Credential.

Individual Induction Plan

As part of the USL leadership program, building or system administrators must work with beginning leader candidates to develop an individualized induction plan that will define the responsibilities for the beginning leader candidate's residency program. The IIP provides the beginning leader candidate with substantial responsibility that increases over time and complexity and involves direct interaction with appropriate staff, students, parents, and community leaders (see Alliance for Excellent Education, 2004; Kardos, Johnson, Peske, Kauffman, & Liu, 2001). The USL IIP evaluates candidates leadership needs based on a battery of web-based self-assessments including: *Emotional Intelligence* (Goleman, Boyatzis, & McKee, 2002); *Temperament* (Keirsey & Bates, 1984); *Cultural Proficiency* (Nuri-Robins et al., 2007) *Leadership Skills* (Kearney, 2005). Keeping with the research, principals, and other school leaders must extend their roles beyond performance evaluation to include instructional support – and not just help with classroom management (Youngs, 2002).

Curriculum Content

Created as part of the regular educational administration program USL is based on national policy standards including Interstate School Leaders

Licensure Consortium (ISLLC, see Green, 2008), the National Council for Accreditation of Teacher Education (NCATE), Educational Leaders Constituent Council (ELCC) and the California Professional Standards for Educational Leaders (CPSELS). The program encompasses four full semester courses (i.e., Pre-Assessment/Induction for School Leadership; Post-Assessment; Shadowing, Fieldwork and Internship; and Fieldwork and Internship). Candidates also complete six intensive five-week content courses with each content course aligned to specific ISLLC/ELCC standards (i.e., *Visionary Leadership*; *Instructional Leadership for Teaching and Learning*; *Organizational Leadership and Resource Management*; *Collaborative and Responsive Leadership for All Students*; *Ethics and Educational Leadership*; and *Political, Social, Economic, Legal and Cultural Leadership*). The curriculum is focused on problem-based instructional strategies which according to Lortie (1998) can "increase awareness of whether further knowledge is needed, particularly when groups studying cases find gaps in the knowledge base" (p. 8) of fields which inform the preparation and development of educational leaders.

In response to research that suggests the integration of contemporary instructional technologies in content delivery (Hughes, McLeod, Brahier, Dikkers, & Whiteside, 2005), the USL program is delivered in a blended hybrid format via Blackboard technology, face-to-face interaction, and field experiences. As asserted by Hughes (2005) (cited in Brooks et al., 2010, p. 422) instructional technologies "... help leaders develop and appreciation of what it means to lead in a rapidly changing world of technological advance."

Field-Based Project

Beyond the coursework, students conduct a Field-Based Project based on a theory of action and designed to provide leadership experience at their school sites (i.e., internship component). The Field-Based Project involves the candidate's leadership ability to work with other adults on the site (i.e., teachers, counselors, coaches, etc.) who in turn assesses student-learning needs. It requires participants to collect continuous improvement and outcome data to more clearly demonstrate how their efforts contributed to improvement of student achievement. According to Jackson and Kelley (2002), field experiences are intended to be meaningful and substantive and integrated into other educational experiences in order for relevant learning and growth. The USL Field-Based Project is designed to help students practice course concepts and skills that teachers will need as administrators to meet the goal of improving student outcomes (e.g., behavior, climate, attendance, as well as achievement) and holding themselves accountable for the improvement every step of the way over the course of one year (Browne-Ferrigno, 2007).

Leadership Learning Community

All USL participants are members of the LLC – a professional network and learning community (Dufour, 2004) in which members and groups interact collegially, encourage and support each other. Some activities are intended for all learning community members, while others are intended for specific groups. A corollary purpose of the LLC is to maintain a high level of commitment in continuing to seek an administrative position and improve leadership skills identified as key by LAUSD partners. The LLC activities have featured well-known speakers such as Tavis Smiley, Mike Schmoker, Carl Cohn, and a professional book club study group. The LLC continues to offer professional experiences, speaker seminars, and learning opportunities about job seeking and interviewing skill development. In addition, they serve as informational and motivation connection to current research, trends, and leadership topics. The LLC is also intended to serve as a component of problem solving via collaboration. Following research by Lortie (1998), and led by professors in the program the participants engage in a myriad of professional activities that involve "acquiring and improving skills that are eminently practical in the practice of administration including the ability to win confidence of informants, developing interviewing and observational skills, and not least of all, learning to sift through and separate significant from trivial facts" (p. 8).

Supervision of Instruction

Supervision of Instruction is a series of practicum workshops. This training also has an implementation project where the participants use data to identify instructional needs, implement what they have learned and use outcome data to determine the project's effectiveness (Dufour, 2004; IEL, 2000; Jackson & Kelley, 2002). These workshops are designed for teams of aspiring leaders (Group 2), and current leaders (Group 3) from the same school. The team design has three purposes: to improve aspiring leaders' skills; to connect aspiring leaders with current administrators for networking purposes; and to involve grant participants in a site-based practicum of workshop skills and knowledge.

Master Schedule Training and Coaching Training: Principals Academy

As part of the *Principals Academy*, current administrators (Group 3) participate in training for effective master schedule planning in order to meet student needs. These hands-on workshops provide opportunities for the administrators to get their "hands" into this work usually reserved for counselors or other members of the administrative team. These same administrators participate in Coaching Training. The goal for the Principals' Academy continues to be improvement of leadership skills as measured by the NASSP 360. The Academy consists of three yearlong courses or workshops: *Essential Elements of Effective Instruction (EEEI)*, *Master Schedule Training* (10 sessions), and *Coaching Training* (an 18 month program). Participants must take all three courses.

Biannual USL Conference

The purpose of the USL conferences is to build community, help develop commitment to urban education, inspire a culture of change in LAUSD, as well as culmination and induction of new members. Various USL participants present research. Speakers have included television personality Tavis Smiley, prominent author-researcher Mike Schmoker, well-known educator and former Superintendent of schools for Long Beach Unified School District, Carl Cohn, and local Superintendent of LAUSD Ramon Cortines. It has also featured Kyla Wahlstrom who shared findings from the 2010 Wallace Report study titled *Investigating the Links to Improved Student Learning*, and the new LAUSD Deputy Superintendent, and LAUSD Chief Academic Officer.

EVALUATING PROGRESS: FORMAL AND INFORMAL ASSESSMENTS

The goal for the *Aspiring Leaders Seeking Certification* is that a diverse group of experienced teachers will complete the California Preliminary

Administrative Services Credential. These students will complete coursework for the Preliminary Credential and conduct a Field-Based Project designed to provide leadership experience at their school sites. A new element was added to the Field-Based Project for 2010–2011. Requirements have been fine tuned so that students will not only work with colleagues to address a student-learning need, but will be required to collect continuous improvement and outcome data to more clearly demonstrate how their efforts contributed to improvement of student achievement. In 2009–2010, LAUSD created a new category of schools, the Public School Choice (PSC) schools, consisting of both low performing Title 1 schools and new schools. These PSC schools offer opportunities for aspiring leaders to become administrators. However, the work of these schools requires "turnaround" leadership. The revision of the Field-Based Project is designed to help students practice those concepts and skills needed for teachers to coalesce around the goal of improving student outcomes (i.e., behavior, climate, attendance, and achievement) and holding themselves accountable for the improvement every step of the way. In response to suggestions from our Project Monitor, we plan to require that Field-Based Project reports include: (1) the number and percent of students served at the site, (2) the number and percent of teachers at a grade level participating, (3) a pre–post assessment of student achievement (or other outcomes), (4) a link between FBP activities and predicted outcomes on the California Standards Tests used for Accountability purposes, and (5) a participant reflection on which leadership skills were improved as a result of the project and in which areas they would like continued support.

The goal for our *Aspiring Leaders Awaiting Placement* involves LAUSD-Priority Skills leadership training though a yearlong EEEI workshop and school practicum accompanied by LLC activities. The original USL program activities were designed to prepare aspiring leaders to pass the LAUSD administrative exam. That exam was suspended in 2008–2009 and has not yet been reinstated. In 2009–2010, the Aspiring Leaders Seeking Placement group consisted of former administrators reassigned to the classroom as well as aspiring leaders who failed the LAUSD exam. Activities for this group consisted of creating a LLC designed to keep morale high so they will continue to seek leadership positions, and improve leadership skills identified as key by the LAUSD partners. The 2009–2010 skill development identified as high priority by LAUSD was a Response to Intervention (RTI) workshop.

With the realization that for 2011–2012, and perhaps indefinitely, that the USL will no longer be preparing the "Aspiring-Awaiting" group for an administrative exam, and that those in the "holding pattern" will increase due to continued LAUSD administrative reassignments and budget cuts, USL personnel needed to create a more structured program for the Aspiring-Awaiting group. In 2011–2012, the goals for Group 2 continue to be placement in an administrative position. However, the program will focus on several major activities including job seeking and interview skills, district-identified leadership training, and professional networking. These activities are designed both to keep the candidates job-ready and to maintain morale during discouraging times. LLC will continue to offer speakers and study groups, but will include job seeking and interviewing skills. LAUSD continues to want leaders to implement RTI. The RTI workshop evaluations indicated that participants felt they understood RTI concepts but had no deep understanding of the most important component, *Good First Teaching*. In 2010–2011, to support not only RTI initiatives, but also to improve aspiring leaders' skills in teacher evaluation and supervising school turnaround, the program provides a series of practicum workshops in the EEEI. The EEEI workshops are designed for teams of aspiring leaders, current leaders and teachers from the same school. The team design has three purposes: (1) to improve aspiring leaders' skills, (2) to connect aspiring leaders with current administrators for networking purposes, and (3) to involve both teachers and USL grant participants in a site-based practicum of workshop skills and knowledge.

There were few Group 3 (sitting administrators) last year because of LAUSD reassignments and budget cuts. As a service to LAUSD and to strengthen the partnership, the USL program offered leadership training in both RTI and Master Schedule Development to LASUD administrators. These activities were used to recruit experienced administrators for *USL* training in the current year. In 2009–2010 there was a Group 4 of new administrators seeking the Tier 2 administrative credential and were provided with training in either "coaching" or "leading staff development." In 2010–2011, the Principals' Academy was developed as a more systematic staff development program intended to improve leadership skills. To reiterate an earlier point, the goal for the *Principals' Academy* continues to be improvement of leadership skills as measured by the NASSP 360 so that leaders are retained in their positions and have an effect on student achievement.

Leverage Points/Change Process Description

At the end of each course all students take a course survey that asks them to respond to course content, and instruction. In the summer, fall, and spring, USL faculty members and adjunct instructors assemble during an organized USL leadership retreat to review student responses, debrief classroom experiences, and revise and refine the curriculum based on these data. In addition, in the summer of 2010, a student focus group came together to provide input based on these data. A number of revisions, assignments, and requirements were put into place based on this cumulative input.

Further, a series of meetings was held with the Chief Academic Officer of LAUSD to clearly understand the current goals and the strategic blueprint for the district. Additional meetings were held with the USL Management team which consists of LD 5, 6, 7, and 8. They provided input on additional offerings we might consider for administrators. This not only includes strategies and skills, but also includes resources that are currently used in the district.

LESSONS LEARNED: FINAL THOUGHTS, REFLECTIONS, AND IMPLICATIONS

As we revisit the literature, examine and re-conceive the USL leadership preparation and development program our collective endeavor is intended to ultimately improve education and continue to learn lessons. Based on regular feedback from students on all content course surveys, the program exit survey and student focus groups, the USL course curriculum content has been re-examined in light of NCATE and ISLLC/ELCC standards incorporating critical tasks for academic rigor and field-base tasks for relevance to urban schools. A leadership retreat is held each semester with all educational leadership faculty and adjunct instructors who engage in professional discourse and dialogue around the predominant theories that drive our program – transformational and distributed leadership. Further, program personnel recognize that successful completion of an educational leadership program and passage of licensure examinations makes one eligible to serve as an assistant principal and subsequently a principal. However, becoming a successful school leader requires important dispositions and skills including "the integration of new knowledge into authentic practice, reflection about school leadership issues, and confidence to take calculated risks" (Browne-Ferrigno, 2007, p. 21).

Program personnel continually discover that more quantitative data are needed for formative evaluation. As a result a series of regularly administered measures for every activity, workshop, and event is developed. The goal is to create a system for administration, data collection and analysis that operates seamlessly and in "real time." Program personnel have also learned that training coaches is a very complex endeavor and takes longer than what was originally scheduled in the first year of the program. Further, we learned that having outside trainers to support our efforts makes for a more rigorous and richer experience. Using a 360 pre–post measure of leadership skill development with a group of busy and geographically scattered participants posed a formidable challenge. We decreased the number of needed raters from 6 to 3 for the NASSP 360 which provides leaders with feedback about their leadership skills.

We need to continually revise the USL program based on the economic climate and needs of LAUSD LD. As with other programs in educational leadership (e.g., Brooks et al., 2010; Browne-Ferrigno, 2007; Bruner, et al., 2007, Preiss, et al., 2007) we have found that keeping up with the rapidly changing expectations and demands placed on school sites and the needs of our students have given us an opportunity to reflect on our leadership development and preparation program. We struggle to change and adapt our program to prepare leaders for our urban schools and that are highly accountable for student performance. We have begun to examine program effectiveness data in search of answers to evaluation questions, respond to project goals/objectives/benchmarks, and serve to monitor project progress over the five-year period. Several evaluation questions include:

- To what extent does the Tier 1 and 2 credential programs meet the California standards for high-quality school leadership preparation programs?
- What do USL participants learn and are they able to apply their learning in underperforming urban schools?
- To what extent does student performance and achievement improve at participating principals' schools as a result of USL learning activities?
- Does the USL project result in increased retention of school leaders in target schools?

The USL program is an evolving quest to change, improve, and adjust while still maintaining rigor within the curriculum. The challenge for us is staying abreast of the ongoing changing demands while at the same time meeting and exceeding NCATE, national and state leadership standards, and addressing LAUSD LD 5–8 educational leadership needs in an economic recession period with budgetary shortfalls. As a collective endeavor of theoretical and clinical expertise, we continue to revisit and dialogue about course content and delivery in relation to standards, research/evidence-based practices, relevant field experiences, and expectations of school leaders. This process informs the USL program design and/or redesign while simultaneously making us aware that there will be times when we must pause to evaluate our progress. Similar to other leadership preparation programs, USL program must deal with "the realities of accountability placed upon schools that will be led by younger, more inexperienced teachers and provide the necessary programmatic changes to ensure that novice leaders have the skills and support system necessary to succeed" (Bruner et al., 2007, p. 20).

Building and maintaining partnerships with school districts and programmatic change that reflect leadership and student demands requires extensive time and effort, flexibility and creativity to assure meaningful dialogue among all stakeholders in order to better serve our students needs in the LAUSD region. The making of an effective educational leader is an ongoing learning process and often stimulated through active-learning experiences in schools and guided reflections about these experiences. In turn, the leadership and learning continuously improves the community of professional practice (Matthews & Crow, 2003; Wenger, 1998). If we are to be "the change that we seek" and survive in the current plethora of reforms, then it is incumbent upon us to monitor, recognize, embrace, and address program challenges and conflicts and respond accordingly. Keeping with the spirit of staying proactive in connecting the worlds of research and practice will essentially determine the future direction of the USL program. It is our belief that educational leaders will continue to serve a critical role in molding the future of generations of children to come.

REFERENCES

Aiken, J. A. (2001). Supporting and sustaining school principals through a state-wide new principals' institute. *Planning and Changing*, 32(3/4), 144–163.

Alliance for Excellent Education. (2004). *Tapping the potential: Retaining and developing high-quality new teachers.* Washington, DC: Alliance of Excellent Education.

Barnett, B. G. (2005). Transferring learning from the classroom to the workplace: challenges and implications for educational leadership preparation. *Educational Considerations*, 32(2), 6–16.

Barnett, B. G., Basom, M. R., Yerkes, D. M., & Norris, C. J. (2000). Cohorts in educational leadership programs: benefits, difficulties, and the potential for developing school leaders. *Educational Administration Quarterly*, 36(2), 255–282.

Barnett, B. G., & Muse, I. D. (1993). Cohort groups in educational administration: promises and challenges. *Journal of School Leadership*, 3, 400–415.

Barth, R. (2002). The culture builder. *Educational Leadership, 59*(8), 6–11.
Brooks, J. S., Havard, T., Tatum, K., & Patrick, L. (2010). It takes more than a village: inviting partners and complexity in educational leadership preparation reform. *Journal of Research on Leadership Education, 5*(12). Retrieved from http://www.ucea.org/storage/JRLE/pdf/Fall_2010_Special_Issue/12_4_Brooks_et_al.pdf
Browne-Ferrigno, T. (2007). Developing school leaders: practitioner growth during an advanced leadership development program for principals and administrator-trained teachers. *Journal of Research on Leadership Education, 2*(3). Retrieved from http://www.ucea.org/storage/JRLE/pdf/vol2_issue3_2007/BrowneFerrignoArticle.pdf
Browne-Ferrigno, T., & Muth, R. (2003). Effects of cohorts on learners. *Journal of School Ledership, 13*, 621–643.
Bruner, D. Y., Greenlee, B. J., & Somers Hill, M. (2007). The reality of leadership preparation in a rapidly changing context: best practices vs reality. *Journal of Research on Leadership Education, 2*(2). Retrieved from http://www.ucea.org/Storage/JRLE/pdf/vol2_issue2_2007/Bruneretal.pdf
Clark, D. C., & Clark, S. N. (1997). Addressing dilemmas inherent in educational leadership preparation programs through collaborative restructuring. *Peabody Journal of Education, 72*(2), 21–41.
Clark, D. L. (1988, June). *Charge to the study group of the National Policy Board for Educational Administration.* Unpublished Manuscript.
Council of Chief State School Officers (CCSSO). (1996). *Interstate school leaders licensure consortium: Standards for school leaders.* Washington, DC: CCSSO.
Darling-Hammond, L., French, J., & Garcia-Lopez, S. P. (2002). *Learning to teach for social justice.* New York, NY: Teachers College Press.
Diller, P. F. (2004). *Duquesne University IDPEL cohorts: A laboratory for leadership.* Unpublished doctoral dissertation. Pittsburgh, PA: Duquesne University.
DuFour, R. (2004). *Whatever it takes: How professional learning communities respond when kids don't learn.* Washington, DC: National Educational Service.
Farkas, S., Johnson, J., Duffett, A., Foleno, T., & Folley, P. (2001, November). *Trying to stay ahead of the game: Superintendents and principals talk about school leadership.* New York, NY: Public Agenda.
Fry, B., O'Neill, K., & Bottoms, G. (2006). *Schools can't wait: Accelerating the redesign of university principal preparation programs.* Atlanta, GA: SREB.
Fullan, M. (2003). *The moral imperative of school leadership.* Thousand Oaks, CA: Corwin Press.
Fulmer, R., & Goldsmith, M. (2000). Future leadership development. *Executive Excellence, 17*(12), 18.
Giber, D., Carter, L., & Goldsmith, M. (2000). *Linkage Inc.'s best practices in leadership development.* San Francisco, CA: Jossey-Bass.
Goldring, E., & Sims, P. (2005). Modeling creative and courageous school leadership through district-university-community partnerships. *Educational Policy, 19*(1), 223–249.
Goleman, D., Boyatzis, R. E., & McKee, A. (2002). *Primal leadership: Realizing the power of emotional intelligence.* Boston, MA: Harvard Business School Press.
Green, R. L. (2008). *Practicing the art of leadership: A problem-based approach to implementing the ISLLC standards* (3rd ed.). Upper Saddle River, NJ: Prentice Hall.
Grogan, M., & Andrews, R. (2002). Defining preparation and professional development for the future. *Educational Administration Quarterly, 38*(2), 233–256.

Grogan, M., & Roberson, S. (2002). Developing a new generation of educational leaders by capitalizing on partnerships. *International Journal of Educational Management, 16*(7), 314–318.

Haller, E. J., Brent, B. O., & McNamara, J. H. (1997). Does graduate training in educational administration improve America's schools? *Phi Delta Kappan, 79*(3), 222–227.

Herrity, V. A., & Glasman, N. S. (1999). Training administrators for culturally and linguistically diverse school populations: opinions of expert practitioners. *Journal of School Leadership, 9*(4), 235–253.

Hess, F. M., & Kelly, A. P. (2005). An innovative look, a recalcitrant reality: the politics of principal preparation reform. *Educational Policy, 19*(1), 2005.

Hess, F. M., & Kelly, A. P. (2007). Learning to lead: what gets taught in principal-preparation programs. *The Teachers College Record, 109*(1), 244–274.

Hix, B., Wall, S., & Frieler, J. (2003). From the ground up: growing your own principals. *Principal Leadership (High School Ed.), 3*(6), 22–25.

Horn, R. A. (2001). Promoting social justice and caring in schools and communities: the unrealized potential of the cohort model. *Journal of School Leadership, 11*, 313–334.

Hughes, J. E., McLeod, S., Brahier, B., Dikkers, A. G., & Whiteside, A. (2005). School technology leadership: theory to practice. *Academic Exchange, 9*(20), 51–55.

Hughes, R. C. (2005). Creating a new approach to principal leadership. *Principal, 84*(5), 34–39.

Institute for Educational Leadership. (2000, October). *Leadership for student learning: Reinventing the principalship.* Washington, DC: Institute for Educational Leadership.

Jackson, B. L., & Kelley, C. (2002). Exceptional and innovative programs in educational leadership. *Educational Administration Quarterly, 38*(2), 192–212.

Jacobson, S. L. (1990). Reflections on the third wave of reform: rethinking administrator preparation. In S. L. Jacobson & A. Conway (Eds.), *Educational leadership in an age of reform* (pp. 30–44). New York, NY: Longman.

Jakubowski, T. G., & Leidner, D. (2007). The CSUN/LAUSD collaborative: a model university/school district in the preparation of new school administrators. In A. H. Normore (Ed.), *Teaching leaders to lead teachers* (pp. 57–74). Bingley, UK: Emerald Group Publishing Limited.

Jean-Marie, G., & Normore, A. H. (2010). *Educational leadership preparation: Innovative and interdisciplinary approaches to the Ed.D and graduate education.* New York, NY: Palgrave Macmillan.

Jean-Marie, G., Normore, A. H., & Brooks, J. (June, 2009). Leadership for social justice: preparing 21st century school leaders for a new social order. *Journal of Research on Leadership Education, 4*(1). Available [online]: http://www.ucea.org/jrle-v5_i1/

Kardos, S. M., Johnson, S. M., Peske, H. G., Kauffman, D., & Liu, E. (2001). Counting on colleagues: new teachers encounter the professional cultures of their schools. *Educational Administration Quarterly, 37*(2), 250–290.

Kearney, K. (2005). Guiding improvements in principal performance. *Leadership, 35*(1), 184.

Keirsey, D., & Bates, M. (1984). *Please understand me: Character and temperament types.* Del Mar, CA: Prometheus Nemesis Book Company.

Kelley, C., & Peterson, K. (2000, November). The work of principals and their preparation: Addressing critical needs for the 21st century. Paper presented at the annual meeting of the University Council for Educational Administration, Albuquerque, NM.

Kozol, J. (2005). *The shame of the nation: The restoration of Apartheid schooling in America.* New York, NY: Crown Publishing Group.

Leithwood, K., Jantzi, D., & Coffin, G. (1995). *Preparing school leaders: What works.* Toronto: Ontario Institute for Studies in Education.

Levine, A. (2005). *Educating school leaders.* Washington, DC: The Education Schools Project.

Lortie, D. (1998). Teaching educational administration: reflections on our craft. *Journal of Cases in Educational Leadership Summer, 1*(1), 1–10.

Matthews, L. J., & Crow, G. M. (2003). *Being and becoming a principal: Role conceptions for contemporary principals and assistant principals.* Boston, MA: Allyn and Bacon.

McCabe, D. H., Ricciardi, D., & Jamison, M. G. (2000). Listening to principals as customers: Administrators evaluate practice-based preparation. *Planning and Changing, 31*(3/4), 206–225.

McCarthy, M. M. (1999). How are school leaders prepared? Trends and future directions. *Educational Horizons, 77*(2), 74–81.

McCarthy, M. M., Kuh, G. D., Newell, L. J., & Iacona, C. M. (1988). *Under scrutiny: The educational administration professoriate.* Columbia, MO: The University Council for Educational Administration.

Miller, L., Caldwell, K., & Lawson, L. (2001). The leadership investment: how the world's best organizations gain strategic advantage through leadership development. *HRMagazine, 46*(2), 152–153.

Milstein, M. M. (1992, October–November). *The Danforth Program for the Preparation of School Principals (DPPSP) six years later: what we have learned.* Paper presented at the annual meeting of the University Council for Educational Administration, Minneapolis, MN.

Milstein, M. M., & Krueger, J. A. (1997). Improving educational administration preparation programs: what we have learned over the past decade. *Peabody Journal of Education, 72*(2), 100–106.

Murphy, J. (2001). The changing face of leadership preparation. *School Administrator, 58*(10), 14–17.

Murphy, J. (2002). Reculturing the profession of educational leadership: new blueprints. *Educational Administration Quarterly, 38*(2), 178–191.

Murphy, J. (2005, February). Uncovering the foundations of ISLLC Standards and addressing concerns in the academic community. *Educational Administration Quarterly, 41*(1), 154–191.

Murphy, J. (2006). *Preparing school leaders: Defining a research and action agenda.* Lanham, MD: Rowman & Littlefield Education.

Murphy, J., & Forsyth, P. B. (Eds.). (1999). *Educational administration: A decade of reform.* Thousand Oaks, CA: Corwin Press.

National Commission on Excellence in Educational Administration. (1987). *Leaders for America's schools.* Tempe, AZ: University Council for Educational Administration.

Normore, A. H. (2007). A continuum approach for developing school leaders in a large urban school district. *Journal of Research on Leadership Education, 2*(3). Retrieved from http://www.ucea.org/storage/JRLE/pdf/vol2_issue3_2007/NormoreArticle.pdf

Norris, C., Barnett, B., Basom, M., & Yerkes, D. (1996). The cohort: A vehicle for building transformational leadership skills. *Planning and Changing, 27*(3/4), 145–164.

Nuri-Robins, K., Lindsey, D. B., Terrell, R. D., & Lindsey, R. B. (2007). Cultural proficiency: tools for secondary school administrators. *Principal Leadership, 8*(1), 16–227.
Preiss, S., Grogan, M., Sherman, W., & Beaty, D. (2007). What the research and literature say about the delivery of educational leadership programs in the United States. *Journal of Research on Leadership Education, 2*(2). Retrieved from http://www.ucea.org/Storage/JRLE/pdf/vol2_issue2_2007/Preisetal.pdf
Sherman, W. H. (2006). Transforming the preparation of educational leaders: a case for ethical district-university partnerships. *International Journal of Educational Reform, 15*(3), 309–330.
Simmons, J. (2006). *Breaking through: Transforming urban school districts, Columbia University*. New York, NY: Teachers College Press.
Southern Regional Educational Board. (2005). *SREBs leadership curriculum modules: Engaging leaders in solving real school problems*. Atlanta, GA: Southern Regional Educational Board.
Spillane, J. P. (2005). Distributed leadership. *The Educational Forum, 69*(2), 143–150.
Theoharis, G. (2007). Social justice educational leaders and resistance: toward a theory of social justice leadership. *Educational Administration Quarterly, 43*(2), 221.
Tierney, W. G. (2006, April). The changing nature of organizational leadership and culture in academic work. *Journal of Research on Leadership Education, 1*(1). Retrieved from http://www.ucea.org/JRLE/issue.php
Tucker, M., & Codding, J. (2002). *The principal challenge: Leading and managing schools in an era of accountability*. San Francisco, CA: Jossey-Bass.
Waters, T., Marzano, R. J., & McNulty, B. (2003). *Balanced leadership: What 30 years of research tells us about the effect of leadership on student achievement*. Aurora, CO: Mid-Continent Research for Education and Learning.
Wenger, E. (1998). *Communities of practice: Learning, meaning, and identity*. New York, NY: Cambridge University Press.
Whitaker, K. S., & Barnett, B. G. (1999). A partnership model linking K-12 school districts and leadership preparation programs. *Planning and Changing, 30*(3/4), 126–143.
Whitaker, K. S., King, R., & Vogel, L. R. (2004). School district-university partnerships: graduate student perceptions of the strengths and weaknesses of a reformed leadership development program. *Planning and Changing, 35*(3/4), 209–222.
Youngs, P. (2002). *State and district policy related to mentoring and new teacher induction in Connecticut*. New York, NY: National Commission on Teaching and America's Future.

CHAPTER 4

CREATING AND SUSTAINING DYNAMIC UNIVERSITY/SCHOOL DISTRICT PARTNERSHIPS FOR THE PREPARATION OF LEARNING-CENTERED SCHOOL LEADERS

Betty V. Fry, David Collins and Edward Iwanicki

ABSTRACT

The impact of an effective principal on the quality of teaching and learning has been clearly established. Logically, the next question to be answered is: How can we best prepare principals to lead the improvement of instructional practices and outcomes for students? Partnerships between school districts and universities have shown the capacity to be an effective means of preparing principals, and much has been confirmed about how those partnerships should be structured in order to benefit both partners. This document looks briefly at the literature that describes and supports these partnerships, outlines the framework of a successful partnership in Florida, and provides insightful "lessons learned" throughout the planning, implementation, and evaluation of that partnership.

Since both organizations realize important benefits, constructing a district/university partnership should be easy. However, differences in the professional cultures of the two organizations as well as differences in the demands and constraints they each face make it a challenging task. From finding the right university partner to planning the collaborative work in detail; what was learned in the Florida partnership is described in straightforward terms. In this way, the document provides a road map to a successful district and university partnership.

INTRODUCTION

Over the past decade, significant advances have been made to better understand the role of the principal in improving student achievement and what principals need to know and be able to do to lead such efforts. With respect to the role of the principal, the most important finding is that principals do make a difference in the quality of teaching and student learning in schools. Research has shown that

> Leadership is second only to classroom instruction among all school-related factors that contribute to what students learn at school ... The total (direct and indirect) effects of leadership on student learning account for about a quarter of total school effects. (Leithwood, Seashore Louis, Anderson, and Wahlstrom, 2004, p. 5)

Knowing that principals are capable of making such a difference has focused more attention on understanding how principals should be prepared for the role of instructional leader (Hale & Moorman, 2003). The literature that resulted from this increased attention on principal preparation has confirmed that meaningful and productive university/district partnerships are effective in preparing principals as learning-centered school leaders (Davis, Darling-Hammond, Meyerson, & LaPointe, 2005; Whitaker, 2006; Darling-Hammond, LaPointe, Meyerson, Orr, & Cohen, 2007). Real partnerships between school districts and local universities have produced significant benefits for both partners. Darling-Hammond et al. (2007) found that:

> Although district/university partnerships take effort, their benefits include expanded resources, a more embedded, hence powerful, intervention for developing practice, and reciprocal institutional improvement that produces better programs and stronger leaders. (p. 21)

While the literature is quite clear as to the benefits that accrue to each partner, only limited progress has been made in redesigning principal preparation programs to be more learning-centered and to include meaningful and productive university/school district partnerships. Often this lack of progress is attributed to the difference in cultures between universities and school districts. While differences exist, they are not insurmountable. To overcome them requires collaboration at each phase: design, planning, execution, monitoring, and evaluation. When partners work through each aspect of creating a strong principal preparation program jointly, with a shared vision of what they want the program to do, the partnership produces the kind of leaders schools need.

PURPOSE

This document has been developed for those who are ready to embark on the journey of developing a meaningful and productive university/district partnership for the preparation of school leaders who have the competencies necessary to improve school and student performance. It is intended to guide the broad brush planning of such a partnership and to highlight the lessons learned from a recent partnership of several Florida school districts and a state university offering a state approved master's degree program in educational leadership that leads to initial licensure. In this document we provide a brief overview of the research literature that supported this collaborative work in Florida, a description of the program produced by that partnership, and share lessons learned during the implementation of the program.

LITERATURE ON UNIVERSITY/DISTRICT PARTNERSHIPS

Understanding the Benefits

Partnerships require effort. Effort expended should produce desirable outcomes; else it is a waste of district and university resources. But, what are those outcomes? Orr, King, and LaPointe (2010) identified a short list of what each partner gains from the collaboration. Districts get better prepared leader candidates – candidates with a greater readiness for that first job as a principal, candidates who have a smoother transition into an initial position, candidates who are able to begin immediately to make the differences in teaching and learning that the district desires. Districts also learn more about leadership. In designing the program, district leaders reflect on what principals need to know and be able to do in order to ensure the schools they lead achieve the priority goals set by the district and what experiences might best produce that knowledge and skill. Universities learn what their "customers" need and want in a principal preparation program. They attain an inside look at the leadership needs of their local school districts – a perspective that might otherwise not be available to them. Both partners enhance their leadership capacity as they move to the cutting edge of principal preparation and wrestle with the real issues of getting people ready for this most important role.

Committing to a Partnership

A strong commitment is the foundation for developing a meaningful and productive university/district partnership for the preparation of learning-centered school leaders. When partners make this level of commitment, they follow through on critical policy initiatives such as supporting participants with stipends and tuition waivers, increasing the relevance of the preparation curriculum, enhancing field experiences, and streamlining the hiring process to get the strongest candidates into the neediest schools (Darling-Hammond et al., 2007).

Key features of an effective partnership include (a) a joint commitment by the university and school district to prepare highly qualified learning-centered school leaders, (b) collaboration and shared decision-making in planning the preparation program, (c) allocation of significant resources by the university and school district for the implementation of the program, and (d) joint accountability for the success of the program and its graduates.

Strong commitment by both partners is important in generating positive actions, but it is also important in overcoming obstacles. In forming university/district partnerships, the issue of the difference in cultures between the two organizations is often raised as a significant obstacle. It has been noted that

> Educational practitioners work in cultures that value action and application of experience-based knowledge, whereas university professors work in cultures that value reflection, analysis, and research-based knowledge. The activity-reflectivity dichotomy between P-12 systems and postsecondary institutions spans a continuum from a focus on *localized, practical concerns and activities* by school districts to *emphasis on research and scholarship* at universities. (Browne-Ferrigno & Barber, 2010, p. 1)

Often the inability of universities and school districts to form meaningful and productive partnerships is attributed to these differences in culture. Yet these differences can be overcome if each partner makes an effort to understand and respect the pressures and demands that are part of the other partner's professional culture (Orr et al., 2010). For districts, this may take the form of understanding that universities have requirements for accreditation that may constrain aspects of their work. University leaders may recognize that districts operate under accountability pressures that drive them to look for practical, relevant assignments and learning experiences for their prospective principals.

Orr et al. (2010) also noted that while it is preferable to form truly collaborative university/district partnerships for the preparation of school leaders, there are other arrangements whereby universities and school districts can work together initially in preparing school leaders that may lead to stronger partnerships at some later time. The arrangements listed below have potential for developing into partnerships over time.

- *Independent but cooperative relationships* where the university and school district are both committed to quality leadership preparation but they have not constructed a collaborative program based on a shared mission statement and common objectives. This type of affiliation involves cooperation on logistical aspects, but may not include collaboratively planned content or shared priorities.
- *Contractually developed partnerships* where the school district has established priorities in the mission statement and objectives of its preparation program to which the university agrees. These partnerships align content and learning experiences with district requirements, but produce little ongoing dialogue or experimentation.
- *Emergent collaboration* where one or more universities have input into the development of the mission statement, objectives, and design of the school district's preparation program. Then a commitment to work with a particular university emerges through this process. This arrangement allows for districts and universities to explore the fit between their respective missions and needs prior to formalizing a sustained partnership.

Involving Key Leaders

Goldring and Sims (2005) found that three types of leaders need to be involved in making a commitment to form a university/district partnership for the preparation of school leaders. These include "top-level leaders, frontline leaders, and internal networkers, also known as bridge leaders" (p. 231). The top-level leaders include the superintendent and other key senior administrators in the school district, the dean of the school or college of education and other interested senior university officials, a key state department of education representative, and the senior executives of other organizations involved in the partnership such as a foundation or broader community network that may be contributing financially to the partnership. When the top-level leaders commit to the partnership, they generate excitement and enthusiasm around the promise the partnership holds for both organizations. They possess the authority to create processes to support planning, decision-making, resource allocation, and the ongoing work of the partnership. They can also set clear expectations for those from within each organization who will be responsible for planning and implementing the partnership.

Frontline leaders are those who will actually perform the work of designing the preparation program. They understand the needs, capacities, and constraints of their respective organizations and, therefore, can speak authoritatively on what might work and what will not. These frontline leaders serve as the champions of the partnership as they develop and communicate the specifics of the partnership's mission, vision, and strategies to various constituencies.

Bridge leaders are often overlooked when committing to partnerships even though they serve a valuable function.

Bridge leaders know how to connect people and how to build bridges to new ideas and practices. They often serve as coaches, mentors, internal consultants, and thinking partners (Wheatley, 2002). The bridger moves freely among the [key organizations in the partnership] and is viewed as legitimate by each organization (Goldring & Sims, 2005, p. 233).

Also, the bridge leaders are adept at resolving conflicts that may emerge as the university/district partnership is constructed and later, as it begins the work of preparing principals. As noted previously, forming a university/district partnership involves bringing together people from different cultures to design a new and better program for the preparation of school leaders. In this type of collaborative process, conflicts will arise. For example, what university professors may value in the preparation process may not be valued or perceived as feasible by practicing principals. In such situations the bridge leader(s) work up front and behind the scenes with both parties, and sometime with top-level leaders, to resolve the impasse and move the work of the design team forward. While it is clear that a bridge leader or leaders need to be included on the design team when committing to a partnership, it is not always easy to identify an individual who can assume this critical role effectively. Looking back at projects within an organization that required collaboration across departments or units may be a way to identify those who have fulfilled this role previously.

All three of these roles may, at times, function as a "champion" for the program. The champion role was identified by Milstein (1993) through his examination of how universities and school districts participating in the Danforth Foundation Network formed effective relationships for the preparation of school leaders. Program champions are necessary to move the process forward. Changing the status quo requires finding individuals who are firm believers in the new program and can communicate these beliefs. Champions have the commitment and energy around which others can coalesce. These individuals have the vision to see results can be better for program graduates, school districts, and the university, if the changes are implemented. They also must have the skills necessary to guide the effort through the thorny thickets of university and school district bureaucracies and the status to get others to join them.

THE FLASII PROGRAM

In this section we provide an overview of our US Department of Education School Leadership Program (SLP). We then outline lessons learned from our partnership efforts and the implementation of this collaborative model as well as a checklist for use by districts and universities that are at the critical initial stage of partnership formation.

The Florida Leadership Academy for Schools of Innovation and Improvement (FLASII) is a partnership initiative of the Florida Department of Education, Southern Regional Education Board (SREB), University of North Florida and the school districts of Duval, Escambia, Gadsden, Highlands, Madison, and Orange counties. These districts represent a mix of urban and rural contexts within the state, and all are classified as high need as defined by the US Department of Education's criteria. The partnership's mission is to increase the supply of highly qualified principals who are able to lead continuous improvement efforts for student achievement in high-need districts and schools across the state. To accomplish this mission, FLASII worked diligently toward these objectives:

– Develop and test a replicable leadership academy model for preparation and professional development of both aspiring and current school

leaders that builds their capacities to lead continuous improvement of low-achieving schools.
- Recruit, train, certify, and retain new school leaders who can work with teachers, parents and others to bring about improvement in high-need schools.
- Provide professional development and coaching for current principals and assistant principals to support them in implementing proven practices that are linked to increased student achievement.

The FLASII was designed through a structure that provided strong support from the highest levels of policymakers and educational leaders while leaving the detailed planning and day-to-day management tasks to a smaller group of educators who were selected to both represent the perspectives of all partners and bring to bear significant levels of practical expertise and experience. This structure is illustrated in Fig. 1.

The Academy Oversight and Design Model (Fig. 1) has been used to support our partnership efforts as we move forward with the design and implementation of our program. Since its inception in fall 2008 with the award of a grant to SREB from the US Department of Education's SLP and special funding from the Florida Department of Education, the FLASII has made substantial progress toward achieving each of the three goals.

- The program model, with enhancements based on the lessons learned in its initial implementation as an SLP model, is currently being scaled to five additional urban and suburban districts as a major component of the state's Race to the Top initiative, through a state contract with SREB.
- Twenty-four candidates have successfully completed the FLASII aspiring principal preparation program and qualified for state licensure in educational leadership. Evaluative measures administered during Year 3 show the following:
  o Participants reported greater ability on each of 13 SREB-identified critical success factors of effective school leadership in 2011 than they perceived themselves having before participating in the FLASII program.
  o University faculty, mentor principals, district staff, and candidates perceive the program as being of high quality and worthy of statewide scaling.
  o District administrators think candidates are being well trained; the mentoring and practicum components of the program are comprehensive;

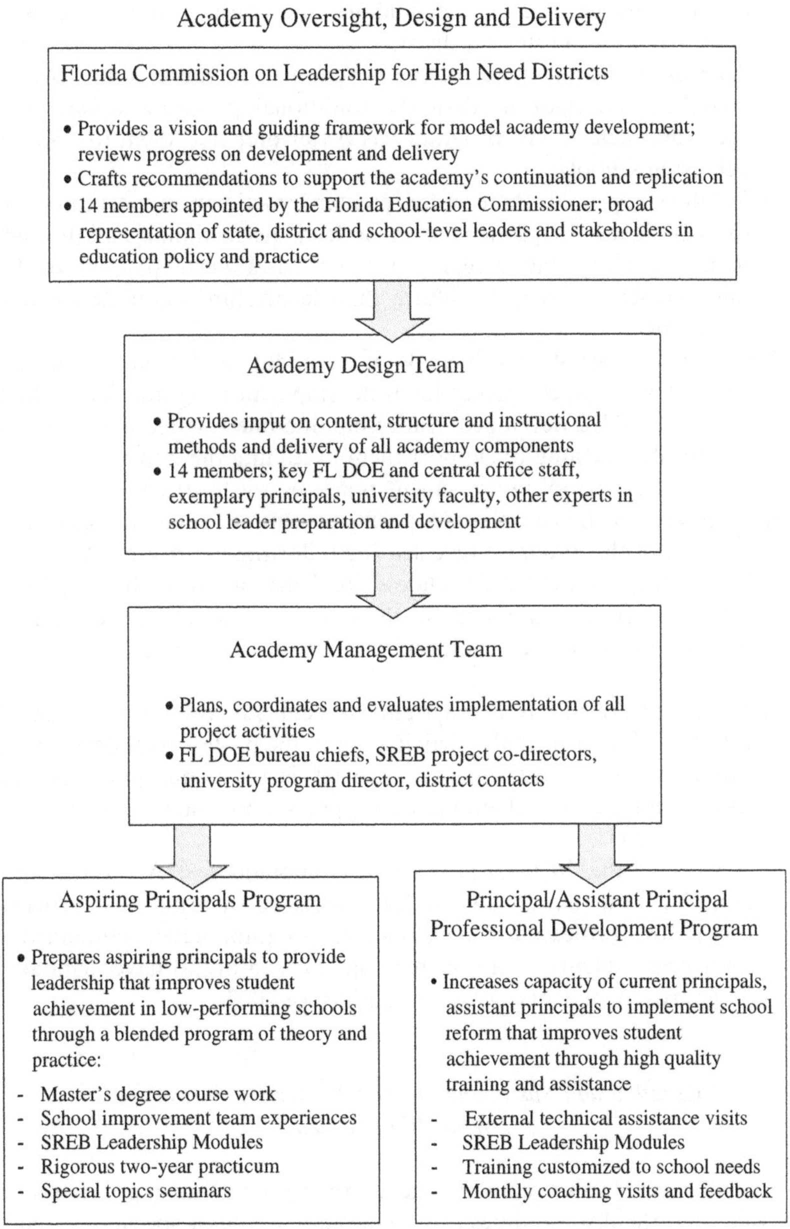

Academy Oversight, Design and Delivery

Florida Commission on Leadership for High Need Districts

- Provides a vision and guiding framework for model academy development; reviews progress on development and delivery
- Crafts recommendations to support the academy's continuation and replication
- 14 members appointed by the Florida Education Commissioner; broad representation of state, district and school-level leaders and stakeholders in education policy and practice

Academy Design Team

- Provides input on content, structure and instructional methods and delivery of all academy components
- 14 members; key FL DOE and central office staff, exemplary principals, university faculty, other experts in school leader preparation and development

Academy Management Team

- Plans, coordinates and evaluates implementation of all project activities
- FL DOE bureau chiefs, SREB project co-directors, university program director, district contacts

Aspiring Principals Program

- Prepares aspiring principals to provide leadership that improves student achievement in low-performing schools through a blended program of theory and practice:
  - Master's degree course work
  - School improvement team experiences
  - SREB Leadership Modules
  - Rigorous two-year practicum
  - Special topics seminars

Principal/Assistant Principal Professional Development Program

- Increases capacity of current principals, assistant principals to implement school reform that improves student achievement through high quality training and assistance
  - External technical assistance visits
  - SREB Leadership Modules
  - Training customized to school needs
  - Monthly coaching visits and feedback

Fig. 1. Academy Oversight and Design Model.

and they would give these candidates first consideration for assistant principal positions in their districts.
- Aspiring principals perceive the program to be more comprehensive, complex, and rigorous than the traditional programs found in the state, and believe this program has better prepared them to lead low-achieving schools.
- Mentors reported there were greater practicum opportunities for the candidates to participate in or lead instructional walkthroughs, handle grading and assessment issues, and participate in or lead improvements in school culture than leadership candidates in other programs.

• Principals and assistant principals of 22 middle and high schools have completed a three-year professional development program that included a series of SREB-developed leadership modules, semiannual retreats, and monthly coaching to support them in leading the implementation of research-based school improvement practices and instructional interventions linked to increased student achievement. Evaluative measures of the impact of this program revealed the following improvements:
- The principals rated their schools' implementation of the 19 effective school practices emphasized in the training either at the beginning or middle level of implementation, with all showing some progress since 2008.
- Results of the SREB Teacher and Student Surveys indicated that the schools led by principals participating in the professional development program have substantially improved instructional practices, academic supports, social emotional supports, and students' home activities since 2008.
- Results of the 2010–2011 Florida Comprehensive Assessment Test (FCAT) show that 36% (8 of 22) schools led by principals participating in the professional development program have maintained or improved students' scores in reading; 23% (5 of 22) have maintained or improved students' scores in math since 2007.

Creating and Sustaining District/University Partnerships: What We Learned

A dynamic partnership between the university or other type of training provider and the district(s) desiring to develop a pool of specially prepared principals is essential to ensure that all aspects of the preparation program are aligned to cutting-edge theory and research as well as the practical role, tasks and needs of principals. The guiding framework for the FLASII Aspiring Principal Program incorporated the best practices gleaned from the literature on such partnerships as well as the lessons learned from SREB's 20+ years of on-the-ground work in school improvement and leadership development.

In creating an effective district/university partnership to develop and test the FLASII model, the first order of business was identifying a university with a *will* to collaborate for change and a *commitment* to allocate the necessary resources of time, money, staffing, and other resources. *Will* was defined as dissatisfaction with the current program in terms of preparing aspirants to become effective leaders of low performing schools, a sense of urgency to take action that would alleviate or improve the situation, and a shared vision of the ideal program the partners hoped to create.

Lesson Learned: Finding a university partner with the requisite *will* and *resources* to become a partner in designing a special-purpose leadership academy can be difficult.

Although the FLASII project secured a commitment from a major state university in the early stages of planning, that commitment did not remain in place and it took negotiating with three other universities before a viable partner was secured. Understanding the obstacles a university must face when forming this type of partnership can make the negotiations easier. Many educational leadership programs have a limited number of faculty and their ranks are further reduced during summer terms when full employment is not feasible. These limitations make it difficult or impossible for some universities to provide courses in the desired sequence and timeframe. If the program requires a full slate of courses during the summer term or that courses be offered in a sequence other than what the university has planned, this may be problematic. However, if the program can guarantee a specific number of participants, this obstacle may be less of a problem. Because educational leadership departments are typically stretched thin in terms of full-time faculty, department chairs are reluctant to obligate faculty to the additional work of tailoring courses and supervising an extra cohort during the practicum or internship. There are many practitioners who possess expertise in leadership, but constraints imposed by accreditation and state program approval requirements regarding faculty credentials make them cautious about hiring practitioners to teach courses.

It is very important that an agreement with the university partner be reached early in the process. Delays in securing a university partner lead to delays in advertising the program and recruiting aspiring principals. A delay shortens the time available for designing curriculum components, getting candidates admitted to graduate school, selecting and training mentor principals and a host of other essential pre-training activities.

Lesson Learned: High-ranking district and university administrators such as the superintendent, school board chair, and the university president, vice president or provost, education dean and leadership program director should be engaged in the decision to become partners in creating a special principal preparation program.

The partnership should not move forward until there is (1) evidence of joint commitment to the program's purpose, design framework and expected outcomes, and (2) a signed memorandum of understanding that outlines each party's commitment to perform certain necessary responsibilities, provide specific resources and work as equal partners for the achievement of agreed upon outcomes. Both partners should come away with a clear understanding that all aspects of the program – from recruitment and selection of candidates to course content, to field-based experiences, to assessment of candidates – will be a collaborative effort.

University/district partnerships should be confirmed by the signing of a memorandum of understanding *at least one year prior to the scheduled date for beginning delivery of the specialized program* in order for necessary joint program design, candidate selection and admission and course tailoring to be completed in a timely manner. Meetings of the primary signers of the memorandum of understanding should be convened on a monthly basis during the planning year and throughout the first year of implementation of the partnership program, moving to a quarterly schedule thereafter if development and implementation are on schedule.

Lesson Learned: Planning and coordination must be structured, scheduled and assigned, in order to sustain full involvement of both partners and accomplish goals.

A design team comprised of primary stakeholders — including current principals, teacher leaders, university faculty, central office administrators, and other individuals with special expertise in school leadership and school improvement — should be created immediately upon the signing of the memorandum of understanding to refine the program model and its curriculum in ways that meet district's needs for improved school and student performance, while continuing to meet state standards for program approval. The role and responsibilities of the design team and how it will accomplish its work should be defined, described in writing and shared with its members and other stakeholders.

Because of the complex nature of the planning effort, a consultant or a district or university employee with expertise and experience in project management should be included as a design team member to help structure and manage the team's work. The design team's efforts should produce a high-level project management plan that includes the basic elements of effective project management. These include a clear, agreed upon statement of the scope of the project, key requirements (the things the program must have or do), a risk assessment, a timeframe and an estimate of the funds required to create and sustain the partnership.

The design team should conduct ongoing meetings on a quarterly schedule to review and evaluate progress on program development and implementation and recommend midcourse adjustments as necessary to ensure program effectiveness. A quarterly written report of progress and existing challenges to program development and implementation should be prepared and forwarded to the district superintendent and university administrators who signed the memorandum of understanding. When challenges beyond the design team's scope of authority and responsibility arise, a meeting with key university and district administrators should be convened to explore viable solutions.

The English proverb, *"everybody's business is nobody's business"* holds true in the case of the university/district partnership. Unless individuals are given a specific, clear task within the design team, everyone will believe that someone else is responsible and essential tasks will be neglected. To assure tasks are accomplished, a central office person with experience and passion for leadership training and development should be selected and assigned a defined portion of his/her duty time to work closely with the university program director in providing oversight of the project management plan and day-to-day planning, coordination, resourcing, and formative evaluation of academy development and implementation. This person should have access to the superintendent and should establish a regular time each month to report to the superintendent regarding the program's progress and challenges.

The university program director also should have some significant part of his/her workload assigned to providing planning, coordination and evaluation for the special program.

In addition to taking a leading role on the design team, implementing the special program entails myriad tasks and issues of candidate selection and admission; scheduling the customized courses, staffing, and registration; planning and oversight of a long-term embedded practicum; and extra recordkeeping chores beyond those of the regular educational leadership programs offered by the university.

Lesson Learned: Aligning the university/district designed preparation program with current district leadership initiatives is essential to creating a coherent, effective, and efficient system of principal preparation and development.

Candidates want to see a clear pathway for their advancement to the assistant principal position and on to the principalship. Failure to align a new principal preparation program with existing district leadership initiatives results in a waste of scarce state and district resources, redundant requirements for candidates, and missed opportunities to maximize their readiness for the job. Candidates become frustrated when they have to participate in training that is a repeat of what they have learned in their university preparation program and put together yet another portfolio of evidence to demonstrate that they have met entry-level leadership standards. Resources the district spends on providing the collaborative program's graduates a repetitive program would be better spent on one that advances their knowledge, skills and behaviors beyond the entry level.

The design team and the district leadership training director must work together to align the special preparation program with existing programs and needs of the district and local schools so that candidates experience a seamless system of induction and continuing professional development that moves them from novice principal to expert practitioner. The special preparation program can be a catalyst for the district to review policies and begin developing a coherent, efficient principal succession system.

Lesson Learned: University faculty and staff buy-in and ongoing engagement must be planned and nurtured.

The entire university program faculty should participate in a well-planned, jointly presented orientation to the partnership effort and be allowed to raise issues and provide input for its development and implementation. This might best be achieved through a special retreat where key representatives of the partnership (such as district superintendent, provost, dean, or department chair) make presentations about its purpose, requirements, and benefits and the faculty has a chance to meet and interact with members of the design team. Subsequently, all involved faculty members should be requested to sign a memorandum of agreement to engage in collaborative planning and implementation of enhancements to course content, assignments, and assessments that are in keeping with the expected program outcomes. If members of the faculty are unwilling to sign the agreement or participate as stipulated in the agreement, the program director should have the opportunity to select qualified persons from other colleges, universities and local school districts to serve as faculty for the special program.

The relationship of the design team and the faculty should be well thought out and carefully explained so that both groups understand how they will work together. University faculty highly value their academic freedom and are not known for seeking or being extremely open to input from others about what and how they will teach. This relationship can become a point of contention if not well defined and respectful of what each group brings to the program design and implementation process.

The expectations for engaging university faculty in tailoring courses to academy goals and objectives and the types of recognition and rewards they will receive for this work should be discussed early in the process of forming a university–district partnership. Faculty who tailor courses, develop and present special seminars or spend extra time advising and coaching candidates during the practicum deserve to be recognized and rewarded in meaningful ways.

This is a challenging issue, since the traditional university system of performance evaluation, promotion, and tenure places little value on this work. Stipends alone proved to be an ineffective incentive for engaging some, including those striving for tenure and seasoned professors at the top of the ranks. Including a well-planned research agenda in the memorandum of understanding that addresses problems and issues of interest to the district and provides opportunities for university faculty to engage in meaningful research and publication, coupled with a stipend, might be a stronger incentive.

Beyond the program faculty, there are other university administrators and personnel in key positions whose cooperation and good will are essential to the special program's implementation, from start to finish. This includes a key person within the registrar's office who can assist candidates and program staff with problems related to course enrollment; someone in the controller's office who has power over decisions about such issues as third-party invoices, late tuition fees, and other issues of student and program finance, and last but not least, an understanding administrative assistant in both the university educational leadership department and the district central office who are untiring in their efforts to assist communication and dissemination of information, help keep data and records straight, provide information for the right person to talk with about a problem and facilitate meeting arrangements.

Lesson Learned: The university and district partners should be located within reasonable driving distance from each other.

While this recommendation might seem unnecessarily restrictive or a frivolous basis for a university/district partnership, having the partners located hundreds of miles apart can have adverse impacts on program design, resources and participation. Even when the university courses are delivered online and use of communication technologies supports ongoing interactions among stakeholders, many other program management and delivery issues make it necessary for district and university administrators and staffs as well as design team members and the aspiring principal cohort to meet together. If these various groups are located in distant regions of the state face-to-face meetings will require substantial amounts of time and resources to be spent on travel and the interpersonal relationships necessary for effective collaboration among partners might not be fully developed.

Distance can also require more resources in order to maintain program quality and meet the needs of participants. For example, convening seminars for the aspiring principal cohort and providing them individual coaching at their practicum sites will require more coaching staff, more money for coaches' travel, and more time away from teaching and family responsibilities for cohort members. Cohort members appreciate the fact that they don't have to travel to campus when courses are delivered online, but they still express a strong desire to meet and interact with program staff and their instructors in person, especially at the beginning of the program and before starting each course.

For most of the meetings that we have found necessary to convene – excluding quarterly weekend seminars for aspiring principals – the business at hand can be completed in a time range of two to five hours. Limiting the distance between partners to no more than a two-hour travel time will make it possible for participants to leave their homes or workplaces at 8:00 a.m. and arrive on time for a 10:00 a.m. meeting. Adjourning the meeting by 3:00 p.m. makes it possible for them to return home by 5:00 p.m., thus avoiding the expense of airline tickets and overnight hotel accommodations.

Lesson Learned: Turnover among district and university contacts must be anticipated and strategies implemented to mitigate the impact of losing key stakeholders.

You will want to avoid losing momentum in the event a design team member leaves the project. Planning for such an eventuality is as important as getting the right people on the team originally. The individuals who are chosen to serve on the design team are likely to be the type of high-performers who are upwardly mobile, either through promotion within their current organization or leaving their position for a higher level job in another organization. For these and other reasons, it is important to plan in advance for what you will do if a critical stakeholder is no longer part of the program. There are four things that can be done to mitigate the loss of key players: (1) know who will appoint a replacement and contact that person as soon as it is confirmed that a member of the team will no longer be able to fulfill his or her responsibilities; (2) know what those responsibilities are (you may have to explain them to the person who will appoint a replacement); (3) arrange for a transition period during which knowledge transfer can take place between the outgoing person and the replacement; and (4) identify someone who can take over those responsibilities on a temporary basis if a replacement is delayed.

When a replacement is identified, you will want to get that person up to speed as quickly as possible. Save copies of any initial orientation materials so the newcomer will get the same explanation of the program and its objectives and structure as others received. Assign a member of the team as the "go to" person whom the new team member can contact with questions.

Lesson Learned: District leadership plays a critical role in recruiting and selecting the right candidates.

To make the greatest impact on student achievement, the most promising candidates need to be chosen for the new principal preparation program. One of the most common criticisms of the typical graduate program in educational leadership is that the participants are self-selected. This strategy does not guarantee a pool of principal candidates with the right set of characteristics and experiences. Using district leadership to identify and recommend the candidates provides at least three benefits over self-selection: (1) District leaders have firsthand knowledge of how potential candidates have performed on key responsibilities, primarily instructional, and leadership responsibilities; (2) they understand the role for which the program will prepare its participants and they are able to use that understanding to assess potential candidates; and (3) by recommending them, the district leadership makes an initial investment in the potential participants' success and they are more likely to be supportive of the candidates' work in the program.

Lesson Learned: A communication plan must be developed (and followed) to ensure all stakeholders stay committed to the program.

Those who are asked to work on the development of a partnership to prepare principals are likely to be busy people with many competing responsibilities. The communication plan should make it easier (not harder) for team members to stay in touch with the progress that is being made and to keep the lines of communication open between the partnering organizations. Key elements of a good communication plan are:

- Each communication has a clear purpose. Don't create communications that aren't needed, but plan for and meet all valid communication needs.
- The "who, when, and how" are spelled out in advance. For example, if your communication plan includes a weekly status report to senior

leadership of both partners, it should be predetermined who will draft the report, who will review it prior to its being sent, who will send it, when it will be sent, and what form will be used to communicate the report (electronic, hard copy, or presentation).
- Communications are consistent. This means a certain communication always comes from the same person. There is a consistent structure or form to all program communication (right down to an official font for all program communications and a consistent header on program documents). If there is a schedule (i.e., the status report is sent on Fridays) then it is always followed.
- It should eliminate redundancies or mixed messages that might confuse district or university participants.
- If a response is required, the original communication should clearly identify that, including who is to respond, where the response is to be sent, what is needed in the response, and any appropriate deadline.
- Communications that will be shared with others should make that point clear to the recipients so they know they are responsible for forwarding it.
- The plan should ensure that key messages about the program and its implementation reach the top-level leaders as needed.
- The communication plan is written out and approved. If the plan changes, then it should be rewritten to reflect those changes so that it is always current.

Lesson Learned: Planning with stakeholders is iterative and must go beyond a broad brush concept to include a detailed project management plan that is approved by all and used by program leaders to direct and monitor the work of implementation.

Top-level leaders of both organizations will want to see a plan before granting final approval to the partnership. A plan that is appropriate for this purpose (gaining senior leadership approval) is not likely to contain adequate detail to guide the actual work of developing and implementing the partnership. Once the partnership is approved, a core team with representatives from both partners should meet (probably several times) to work out a detailed project plan. An outline of the most basic steps of project management appears below.

Step 1: Create a clear statement of the *scope* of the project.
- The scope of the project is a list of all the deliverables and major tasks required.

Step 2: Identify and confirm the *requirements* (those features and characteristics of the deliverables that will determine if the deliverable is acceptable to the one who will use it).
- Identify who will use each deliverable? Who else has an interest in how it is designed and created?
- Identify requirements for each deliverable; that is what is important about this deliverable to those who will use it? (This typically involves checking with those who will use it for their input.)

Step 3: Create a *work breakdown structure*.
- The work breakdown structure looks like an org chart. It shows all of the deliverables and major tasks for the project and how they are related ... its purpose is to make sure you've thought of everything.

Step 4: Develop a *network diagram*. The network diagram is the basis for the project schedule and risk assessment.
- This is a highly technical task and should only be completed by someone with training and experience. If no one with these qualifications is available, then the schedule and budget can be built from the work breakdown structure.

Step 5: Conduct a *risk assessment* with the project team (and stakeholders as appropriate).
- The risk assessment starts with a question: What could go wrong?
- Responses are rated in terms of probability and impact (How likely is it that this will go wrong? If it does, what would be the impact?)
- Risks that are likely to happen and will have a significant impact should be addressed through preventive actions.

Step 6: Create *time estimates* and a *schedule*.
- For each task, the person responsible for that task should provide an estimate of how long it will take to complete it.

Step 7: Create a *project budget*.

Step 8: Answer other important *project management questions*.
- Who will handle external and internal communications for the project?
- How will you confirm that each deliverable meets all documented requirements before turning it over to the ones who will use it?
- Does your team have all the necessary skills and time to complete each deliverable? If not, what options are available?
- What contracts need to be written and executed?
- Who will authorize purchases for the project? How will this authorization be obtained?
- Who can approve changes to the project? Is it the same person for small changes as for large or significant changes? How will changes be communicated to those who need to know?
- How and how often will project status be reported to the project sponsor?

SUMMARY

The information and lessons about partnerships described in this document are useful in mapping out a clear path to a successful partnership; but how can districts and universities that are working toward such a partnership know they are on the right track and that their plan is likely to prove effective? SREB identified a number of conditions that should be in place if a redesigned principal preparation program is to be successful (Fry, O'Neill, & Bottoms, 2006). One of these conditions relates to partnerships and provides the content for a quick checklist districts and universities can use to self-assess the strength of the foundation for their partnership That checklist has been found to be useful by a number of universities and districts across the nation, and it is provided here as way to summarize the key ideas within this document.

REFERENCES

Browne-Ferrigno, T., & Barber, M. E. (2010, May). Successful principal-making collaborations: From the perspective of a university partner. In M. C. Mattis (Chair), *Rethinking leadership preparation by leveraging institutions and sharing the work: Lessons in district-university consumer action from multiple case studies.* Symposium at the annual meeting of the American Educational Research Association, Denver, CO.

Davis, S., Darling-Hammond, L., Meyerson, D., & LaPointe, M. (2005). *Review of research. School leadership study. Developing successful principals.* Palo Alto, CA: Stanford University, Stanford Educational Leadership Institute.

Darling-Hammond, L., LaPointe, M., Meyerson, D., Orr., M. T., & Cohen, C. (2007). *Preparing school leaders for a changing world: Lessons from exemplary leadership development programs.* Stanford, CA: Stanford University, Stanford Educational Leadership Institute. Retrieved from http://seli.stanford.edu; http://srnleads.org

Fry, B., O'Neill, K., & Bottoms, G. (2006). *Schools can't wait: Accelerating the redesign of university principal preparation programs.* Southern Regional Education Board.

Goldring, E., & Sims, P. (2005). Modeling creative and courageous school leadership through district/community-university partnerships. *Educational Policy, 19*(1), 223–249.

Hale, E. L., & Moorman, H. N. (2003). *Preparing school principals: A national perspective on policy and program innovations.* Washington, DC: Institute for Educational Leadership.

Leithwood, K., Seashore Louis, K., Anderson, S., & Wahlstrom, K. (2004). *How leadership influences student learning.* New York, NY: Wallace Foundation. Retrieved from http://www.wallacefoundation.org/. Accessed on September 14, 2005.

Milstein, M. M. (1993). *Changing the way we prepare educational leaders.* Newbury Park, CA: Corwin Press.

Orr, M. T., King, C., & LaPointe, M. (2010). *Districts developing leaders: Lessons on consumer actions and program approaches from eight urban districts.* Newton, MA: EDC.

Wheatley, M. J. (2002). *Turning to one another; Simple conversations to restore hope to the future.* San Francisco, CA: Berrett-Koehler Publishers, Inc.

Whitaker, K. (2006). *Preparing future principals.* National Association of Secondary School Principals. Retrieved from http://www.nassp.org/portals/0/content/54438.pdf

APPENDIX: RUBRIC FOR ASSESSING THE QUALITY OF UNIVERSITY/DISTRICT PARTNERSHIPS FOR PRINCIPAL PREPARATION

	Completed and In Place	Planned and In Progress	Not a Part of the Plan
Indicator 1. The partnership is formal, definitive and institutionalized.			
1.1 There is a written agreement signed by the university president and district superintendent defining how the entities will work as partners in the preparation of school principals.			
1.2 The agreement defines how the university/district partners will:			
1.2(a) Create a shared vision and program design that meets high-quality program standards and the needs of the district			
1.2(b) Develop criteria and a process for recruiting, selecting and supporting the most promising candidates			
1.2(c) Conduct substantial, high-quality field experiences			
1.3 Implementation of the partnership is a priority in both organizations, as reflected in their respective missions, program plans, staff assignments and budgets.			

	Completed and In Place	Planned and In Progress	Not a Part of the Plan
Indicator 2. Candidate screening and selection is a joint process.			
2.1. The university and district have jointly established and implemented criteria and processes for screening and selecting promising candidates for admission to the preparation program.			
2.2. The selection criteria emphasize expertise in curriculum and instruction, a record of raising student achievement and prior leadership experiences.			
2.3. Implementation of the screening and selection system is continually monitored, evaluated and improved.			
Indicator 3. The program is customized to meet district needs.			
3.1. The university and district partners work together to assess local needs for improved student learning outcomes and to incorporate district and school data, state and local standards, adopted curriculum frameworks, current change initiatives and school reform models, and assessment and accountability processes into program goals, course content and field experiences.			
Indicator 4. Resources and conditions support candidates' success.			
4.1. The university and district allocate and pool resources to provide candidates the support and conditions necessary to successfully complete the leadership preparation program, including such things as release time for course work and field experiences, tuition assistance, learning materials and expert mentoring and coaching as needed to master essential competencies.			

CHAPTER 5

A RIGOROUS RECRUITMENT AND SELECTION PROCESS OF THE UNIVERSITY OF TEXAS AT AUSTIN PRINCIPALSHIP PROGRAM

Mark A. Gooden and Richard Gonzales

ABSTRACT

There is growing national attention on the question of how the quality of leadership preparation programs can help to develop effective school leaders and thus impact student learning (Davis, Darling-Hammond, LaPointe, & Meyerson, 2005). In recent years several educational leadership preparation programs have redesigned their content and delivery to be more influential in graduates' leadership development and subsequent leadership practice focused on school improvement (Young, 2009). Davis, et al. (2005) add that exemplary programs that are effective include important components such as having a rigorous selection process in admission of candidates.

This chapter discusses the recruitment and selection mode utilized by the University of Texas at Austin Principalship Program (UTAPP), which includes several key components associated with exemplary preparation programs (Darling-Hammond, LaPointe, Meyerson, Orr & Cohen, 2007). These components include: rigorous recruitment and careful selection of participants, a cohort structure, and an emphasis on powerful authentic learning experiences (Orr, 2006). While the process has undergone some changes in reason years, it has sought to explore multiple manifestations of the candidate's leadership. As a result, the program's recruitment and selection process has evolved into the current iteration, which is outlined in this chapter.

Recently, an increasing number of questions have emerged about how to prepare leaders for schools, thus making it apparent that preparation of effective school leaders is believed by many to be important. It is also clear that leadership impacts the school improvement process, particularly in schools where students' learning needs are most acute (Leithwood, Harris, & Hopkins, 2008; Leithwood, Louis, Anderson, & Wahlstrom, 2004). Indeed almost all educational reform efforts have come to the conclusion that this nation cannot attain excellence in education without effective school leadership (Crawford, 1998; Papa, 2007). Haberman and Dill (1999) went so far as to assert that schools with students at risk and in poverty need more resources, but resources and reform efforts would be useless without a capable principal whose beliefs empower teachers and students to succeed in school regardless of their life constraints.

In light of the fact that leadership is so critical, educational reformers and those who prepare leaders will do well to focus their attention and energy on how leaders are prepared. Accordingly, Hassenpflug (2011) has argued that despite a lack of data confirming that old and new assessments actually make any difference in a future principal's leadership ability, there is an intense focus on them by faculty in preparation programs. To be fair, faculty members' decisions are often influenced by accrediting agencies such as NCATE. However, Hassenpflug argues that it is better to divert some of that focus from assessments and tests in principal-preparation programs to other important program components that may be more relevant in the preparation of leaders. She states "it is time to look at other pieces of the process to determine if the necessary questions are being asked about the preparation process, which includes the selection (or, more often, self-selection) of candidates, the pedagogy, and delivery methods used in the courses, the knowledge base and skills addressed in the educational administration courses, and the qualifications of the faculty" (p. 24).

We agree with this argument and find it to be supported by the University Council for Educational Administration (UCEA), other higher education faculty members, and even private preparation programs. The specific interest is in confirming exactly what these important components are, and exploring their effectiveness in exemplary preparation programs. This flurry of activity has resulted in growing national attention on the question of how the quality of leadership preparation programs can help to develop effective school leaders and thus impact student learning (Davis, Darling-Hammond, LaPointe, & Meyerson, 2005; Fry, O'Neill, & Bottoms, 2006). In recent years several educational leadership preparation programs have redesigned their content and delivery to be more influential in graduates' leadership development and subsequent leadership practice focused on school improvement (Young, 2009). Davis et al. (2005) add that exemplary programs that are effective include important components such as having a rigorous selection process in admission of candidates.

Adding to this research are strong reasons to really focus on developing such a process. Leithwood et al. (2008) outline what they refer to as the basics of successful leadership, which are Setting Directions, Developing People, and Redesigning the Organization. Because all of these endeavors involve working with and through people, it is reasonable to add components to the selection process that give leaders an opportunity to display interpersonal skills. Moreover, they argue that beyond these basics, a leader must understand her/his respective context of leadership including broad aspects such as the organization context (urban, suburban, rural) and level (elementary or secondary). McKenzie et al. (2008) go further and argue that a candidate must enter a principalship program with some awareness about her or his own and others' social beliefs, biases, and prejudices. They contend that with this advantage, programs can much more quickly move the candidates to learn how to become advocates and leaders of change in schools that will successfully serve students of color, poverty, linguistic differences, (dis)abilities, and various sexual orientations. This position is supported by Brown (2004) who maintains that because beliefs can change as a result of experience, it is critical for preparation programs to examine the impact of their strategies on preservice leaders' attitudes, perceptions, and practices regarding issues of social justice, equity, and diversity. However, before that impact can be measured, programs must select aspiring leaders open to exploring learning about equity and taking action.

Another important piece is understanding how to support diverse student populations, where more work clearly needs to be done. Lastly, they note a leader must understand and know how to navigate a policy context that includes many accountability constraints. In the words of Leithwood et al. (2008), "We need to be developing leaders with large repertoires of practices and the capacity to chose[sic] from that repertoire as needed, not leaders trained in the delivery of one 'ideal' set of practices" (p. 8).

We note that the recruitment and selection processes are only some of the components of exemplary preparation program as outlined by Davis et al. (2005). However, these other components and those outlined above can be supported by a well-defined, rigorous recruitment and selection preparation component that includes "performances" and assessment beyond the standard requirements of graduate record examination (GRE) scores and grade point averages (GPAs). These two traditional indicator scores, while having limited prediction of a candidate's early success in masters' coursework and appearing to correlate well with family income, have not been shown to be reliable predictors of a school leader's effectiveness. What then are the components of a rigorous recruitment and selection process that may hold such promise? Below we share some background on an exemplary program and then we outline how this program has employed a rigorous recruitment and selection process.

UNIVERSITY OF TEXAS AT AUSTIN PRINCIPALSHIP PROGRAM'S RECRUITMENT AND SELECTION PROCESS

Located in a growing urban area and part of a large research one university, UTAPP has successfully partnered with surrounding school districts to train principals for over 50 years. As noted above, the model of the UTAPP includes several key components associated with exemplary preparation programs (Darling-Hammond, LaPointe, Meyerson, Orr, & Cohen, 2007). These components include: rigorous recruitment and careful selection of participants, a cohort structure, and an emphasis on powerful authentic learning experiences (Orr, 2006). Programmatic aspects of the UTAPP model, particularly rigorous recruitment and careful selection are discussed more fully below.

Recruiting Nominees

The UTAPP selection model has been intentionally designed to recruit teacher leaders who have demonstrated abilities to apply informed practice with students and facilitate collaborative processes with peers. While the process has undergone some changes in reason years, it has sought to explore multiple manifestations of the candidate's leadership. As a result, the program's recruitment and selection process has evolved into the current iteration, which is described in more detail below.

As a first step, the recruitment process begins with contacting local district leaders and asking them to nominate individuals who have demonstrated dedication to the education all students, the ability to collaborate effectively with colleagues, and who are driven to improve the educational landscape as a school leader. At about the same time a solicitation is made to local area teachers interested in the principalship to consider applying. Additionally, we contact alumni of the program and enlist their help in identifying select individuals who might be good for the program. We also invite interested individuals to attend one of two information sessions, which are held in late fall.

The primary purpose of the information session is to introduce the nominees to our unique, coherent masters program including more about its features, current students, and award-winning faculty. In each session, nominees also hear from a practicing principal who is a graduate of the program. We ask the practicing principal to provide a sobering reality of the work of the principal but to also share the joys and triumphs of the job. For some nominees this is confirmation that they have chosen the correct program; however, for others the principal presentation is confirmation that they should reconsider. For example, nominees decide not to apply for a range of reasons including the program is too intense, a realized lack of desire to serve as a principal, or it is the wrong time in life to submit an application. During this time we also explain the process of applying in detail and answer any questions the nominees may have about the program, or how it might work for them personally.

Lastly, there is a time that the nominees participate in breakout sessions with current students to get a better understanding of specific experiences in the program. This initial process is as transparent as we can make it and it might seem counterintuitive in that it forces some nominees to reconsider. It might appear that we are sending them away from our program in a time when most programs, including ours, could use an increase in enrollment. However, if we stick to our mission of preparing leaders who seriously consider the principalship, we believe this makes sense. In fact, by following this structure in the information session, we will have given the nominees an opportunity to get a real glimpse of the principalship job and the principalship program that purports to prepare them for it.

Indeed, we facilitate their decision-making process, especially if they are unsure about whether they want to lead a school.

Converting to Applicants

The next step is for the nominees to become applicants for admission. Nominees are nominated by educational leaders, or self-nominated, but we consider them applicants once they submit applications. To apply means the nominee has been asked and has agreed to develop a program "application portfolio" containing three components: a statement of purpose, a resume, and three letters of recommendation. UTAPP provides a rubric that shares how we will assess the pieces of the information that the applicant submits. To determine their focus on personal and professional goals and to get a sense of their personal mission regarding leadership, we review their typed statement of purpose. The statement of purpose also provides a better sense of the applicant's personality and leadership philosophy and how well it aligns with the core values of the program. Specifically, referencing the criteria for a rating of excellent on the rubric, we are determining whether the essay "demonstrates excellent writing skills in terms of organization, clarity, style, and mechanics." The content should be "highly reflective of core values and vision of the program and department." We also note the applicant's purpose and future goals and whether these detail any scholarly and professional pursuits. The scores for this part range from 10 to 30 points.

We provide a resume template to the nominees, which they then use to present information about their professional accomplishments. The template is designed to quickly provide reviewers with an illustration of the applicant's current leadership accomplishments at the campus and/or district level. Our belief is that the applicant should have engaged in some leadership activities like chairing a school committee, department, or spearheading a district-wide initiative. The scores on this part range from 10 to 40 points. The thinking behind this is that the nominee has ventured beyond the classroom to explore leadership or that s/he has been noticed as someone with leadership potential.

Lastly, we review the letters of reference to see if colleagues, professors, and supervisors have recognized the candidate's leadership potential. Importantly, as we believe leaders recognize other potential leaders on some level, their principal or immediate supervisor must write one of these three letters. We also require applicants to submit traditional items like

GRE scores and undergraduate and graduate transcripts. Though we have not required a minimum score on the GRE, we have noted that our graduate school, which ultimately accepts or denies our nomination of applicants, really expects at least an 800 combined on quantitative and verbal. On the new version of the GRE, the requirement is 300 combined on quantitative and verbal, according to the Educational Testing Service (ETS). Using the transcript and focusing on upper-division course work, the graduate school calculates a GPA that should be at least a 3.0 or a rationale will eventually be required. In the initial screening, we take note of the scores mainly to see if they might cause concern later in the process. However, the majority of the weight determining whether to invite the nominees to the next step is based on the review of the statement, the resume, and the letters of reference because they start to tell the story of the applicant's leadership potential. Once all of the materials, including the statement, resume, and three letters, are collected, a team reviews them and determines which applicants will be invited to the next stage, an Assessment Center.

THE ASSESSMENT CENTER

The Assessment Center provides the applicant a chance to *demonstrate* her/his philosophy of leadership and specifically make his/her thinking clear through a set of focused educational leadership activities. These activities, which require written and/or oral responses, are described in turn below. They are Interview with Supporting Leadership Artifact; Learning Observation and Role Play; and Data Set Leadership Presentation. Such activities have relevance because today's campus leaders must be able to "focus on learning, monitor teaching and learning, build nested learning communities, acquire and allocate resources, and maintain safe learning environments" (Halverson, 2005, p. 1). As part of our rigorous selection process, each Assessment Center activity has been aligned to the Educational Leadership Policy Standards and ELCC Program Standards.

Applicants will be evaluated on the results of three activities.

The Teams

As one might imagine, the Assessment Center's review team is larger and more involved than the preliminary review team described above. For example, where the review team may have one or two professors and one or two district leaders, the Assessment Center team will have at least six members (at least two for each activity) including a team leader. To construct the teams we invite practicing leaders, current and former students, department faculty to help us select the leaders. We carefully construct the teams paying careful attention to a range of factors that vary according the team leader. For example, when building teams we look at current positions for practitioners, years in program for students, and area of expertise of faculty members. We also consider personalities of individuals and consider this factor especially when pairing members to work on one of three activity teams. Additionally, we seek to construct teams with some attention to racial, ethnic and gender diversity whenever possible.

Today's campus leaders must be able to "focus on learning, monitor teaching and learning, build nested learning communities, acquire and allocate resources, and maintain safe learning environments" (Halverson, 2005, p. 1). As part of the selection process each Assessment Center activity has been aligned to the Educational Leadership Policy Standards and ELCC Program Standards.

The Process

The Assessment Center consists of three performance-based activities – a leadership interview, a teaching/learning observation role-play, and a data analysis presentation. In the leadership interview activity, candidates meet individually with two assessors for up to thirty minutes and respond to six questions ranging topically from their interest in becoming a principal to how they would deal with the challenge of implementing change for equity and achievement in a hypothetical scenario. Additionally, candidates have the opportunity to discuss a leadership artifact representing a specific leadership contribution they have made in their school or district. There are at least two assessors for each activity, and they are provided a rubric (Appendix A) that helps them structure their review of the applicant's responses. Additionally, the questions are connected to the ELCC Program Standards.

In the teaching/learning observation role-play activity, applicants have a total of 30 minutes to complete the exercise. Each applicant is given 10 minutes to view a film clip of a classroom observation, 5 minutes to develop brief notes, and 15 minutes to respond to questions and role-play a conversation with the teacher. The questions and responses seek to identify the breadth and depth of their observations. Though applicants are called to take notes on the teacher in the video, they are asked to prepare responses to the "bad teacher" about his practice. Applicants also are then asked to role-play a conversation with the teacher in which the applicant offers feedback/constructive criticism to the teacher based on his/her observation.

Finally, in the data analysis presentation activity, applicants are given 30 minutes to complete this task. First, they make a 15-minute digital presentation of their findings from an analysis of state and federal accountability data from a hypothetical school called Anywhere School. They may designate the school as a secondary or elementary school. Specifically, the applicant receives annual yearly progress (AYP) data, abbreviated Texas state school data, and parent/teacher/student survey results for the Anywhere School. All applicants receive the data two weeks before the presentation is due. They are then instructed to show up on Assessment Center day with the presentation on a flash drive with their own laptop computer, ready to present. Additionally, the applicants should have at least three copies of the slides of the presentation. Applicants must identify data-based action steps they would take if they were principal of the Anywhere School. Below are the actual instructions that are sent to the applicants:

> You have recently been appointed as the principal of Anywhere School located in your district and have received the attached Anywhere School data set. As the incoming principal, you will have 15 minutes to make a digital presentation to district leaders outlining what you noticed in the data and your approach for the first 10, 30, and 90 days. Following your presentation, the assessment team will provide an opportunity to engage in further dialogue (approx. 15 minutes) about your ideas and/or processes.

In summary, each nominee is evaluated on performance in each activity by a team of assessors consisting of program faculty, current and former school administrators, and second-year program students. Assessors rate each candidate's performance using rubrics designed for each of the activities. After candidates have had the opportunity to participate in all three activities, the assessment team comes together to aggregate evaluation scores, discuss each candidate's performance holistically and achieve consensus on a selection recommendation.

Applicant Assessment Summary

After each candidate has completed the three activities, the assessors in three activity teams come together as a group to discuss the applicants whose performance they evaluated and complete a Candidate Assessment

Summary (Appendix B). In a collaborative process, the assessors discuss the observed strengths and areas of improvement for each applicant. The assessors then share their ratings of each candidate in the respective activities. These scores are averaged for each activity, taking into account at least two assessors' independent ratings. After an applicant's scores are averaged for the three activities, a cumulative score is calculated by summing the averages for each activity. For example, an applicant may have an average of 23 on the leadership interview, a 27 on teaching/learning observation role-play, and a 22 data analysis presentation. Final total scores for each candidate are reported in a ratio comparing their cumulative score to a possible total score of 90. So in this example our applicant's total score would be 72/90. This total score is used to provide an illustration and present an opportunity to discuss the nominee's performance and potential fit in the program more than as a rigid cutoff score. Next, a designated assessment team leader engages all six assessors in a data-driven discussion to come to consensus about a recommendation instead of a final vote on each applicant. The assessment team may submit one of four recommendations for each candidate: Yes; Yes, with reservations; Not at this time; or No. Though the first and last of these are self-explanatory, the two other recommendations are submitted with comments for consideration by the UTAPP program director who ultimately recommends candidates for admission to the university. The "Yes, with reservations" provides caveats and/or calls for ways to support the applicant who will be recommended for admission. The "not at this time" suggests a need for more development before admission will be considered. The "No" recommendation is utilized only for an applicant who we believe should not be encouraged to reapply in the future.

This recommendation process for admission to the graduate school usually happens without incident if the applicant has a combined GRE quantitative and verbal score of 800 or 300 on the GRE test and at least a 3.0 GPA. However, if either score fall below, then the program director petitions to get the student admitted. This argument in the process is made stronger based on the holistic data we have collected as part of the Assessment Center.

Preparing Assessors for the Process

Assessor training begins with their assignment to a team and an activity. Next we group assessors by the respective activities they will assess and have them evaluate a demonstration performance. Each assessor then shares her/his score and discusses what they observed and which rubric criteria they used to determine their rating of the demonstration performance. This calibration process promotes inter-rater reliability within each activity and between the assessment teams.

CONCLUSION

Despite the benefits outlined above, there are also areas of growth for the rigorous recruitment and selection process at UTAPP. For one, the option of "not at this time" can be developed into a process that gives those rejected in this way more specific instructions on how they should grow before applying next year. This practice has great potential as a developmental growth opportunity but is not yet well developed. Another challenge is that this is a human process, and therefore there is some room for error. Though there are many eyes watching and several hands on board, the possibility remains that the process can recommend individuals that present well in the Assessment Center but may have personality types or areas of needed improvement that adversely impact their participation in the program. On the other hand, the process may exclude those who can really benefit from the program though they do poorly in the Assessment Center for one reason or another.

A general strength of UTAPP recruitment and selection model is that it evaluates candidates' potential in relevant areas including academic prowess, current performance on hands-on leadership activities, their beliefs about social justice and equity in schools. As noted above, this selection decision is part of a holistic process. It also has greater relevance to the work of the school building leader. Another strength is the collaborative nature of the Assessment Center, evaluation and recommendation process. It is good to get as many different impressions as possible of every candidate's leadership potential. Another positive aspect about the recruitment and selection process is it involves external school leaders in addition to university officials, thereby broadening the scope and type of expertise that goes into this important process of choosing the next generation of leaders in central Texas. The process of completing the Assessment Center also creates allies and potential partnerships. Current students in our program get to be a part of the process of interviewing.

REFERENCES

Brown, K. M. (2004). Leadership for social justice and equity: Weaving a transformative framework and pedagogy. *Educational Administrative Quarterly, 40*(1), 79–110.

Crawford, J. (1998). Changes in administrative licensure: 1991–1996. *UCEA Review, 39*(3), 8–10.

Darling-Hammond, L., LaPointe, M., Meyerson, D., Orr, M. T., & Cohen, C. (2007). *Preparing school leaders for a changing world: Lessons from exemplary leadership development programs.* Stanford, CA: Stanford Educational Leadership Institute.

Davis, S., Darling-Hammond, L., LaPointe, M., & Meyerson, D. (2005). *Developing successful principals.* Stanford, CA: Stanford Educational Leadership Institute.

Fry, B., O'Neill, K., & Bottoms, G. (2006). *Schools can't wait: Accelerating the redesign of university preparation programs.* Atlanta, GA: Southern Regional Education Board.

Haberman, M., & Dill, V. (1999). Selecting star principals for schools serving children in poverty. *Instructional Leader, 7*(1), 1–5, 11–12.

Halverson, R. (2005). *IFL principal workshop: School leadership rubrics.* Madison, WI: University of Wisconsin.

Hassenpflug, A. (2011, May 18). Principal preparation: Moving beyond assessment. *Education Week,* 24–25.

Leithwood, K., Harris, A., & Hopkins, D. (2008). Seven strong claims about successful school leadership. *School Leadership and Management, 28*(1), 27–42.

Leithwood, K., Louis, K. S., Anderson, S., & Wahlstrom, K. (2004). *How leadership influences student learning.* New York, NY: Wallace Foundation.

McKenzie, K., Christman, D. E., Hernandez, F., Fierro, E., Capper, C. A., Dantley, M., et al. (2008). From the field: A proposal for educating leaders for social justice. *Educational Administration Quarterly, 44*(1), 111–138.

Orr, M. T. (2006). Mapping innovation in leadership preparation in our nation's schools of education. *Phi Delta Kappan, 87*(7), 492–499.

Papa, F., Jr. (2007). Why do principals change schools? A multivariate analysis of principal retention. *Leadership & Policy in Schools, 6*(3), 267–290.

Young, M. D. (2009). The politics and ethics of professional responsibility in the educational leadership professoriate. *UCEA Review, 51*(2), 1–4.

APPENDIX A: SAMPLE ACTIVITY AND RUBRIC: CLASSROOM OBSERVATION

Activity Description

Candidates will have 30 minutes to complete this activity. Each candidate will have 10 minutes to view a film clip of a classroom observation, 5 minutes to develop brief notes, and 15 minutes to respond to questions and role-play a conversation with the teacher.

Assessor Roles

- Prior to beginning, determine who will ask questions and serve as timekeeper.
- Both assessors may take notes on responses.
- Timekeeper will stop the candidate at the end of the session – even if he/she has not yet answered all of the questions.
- Collect the candidate's written notes at the end of the session.
- Individually complete scoring rubric.

ELCC Standards

While other areas may be addressed by this activity, the ELCC Standards specifically targeted include: 2.1, 2.4, 2.6, 2.7, 2.8, 2.9, 3.5

Process: Candidate views film for 10 minutes
Candidate has 5 minutes to make notes
Candidate has 15 minutes to respond to follow-up questions

Post-Observation Questions

1. What did you notice about the lesson?
2. What else would you like to know about what you have observed?
3. Assume that I am the teacher. Role-play the conversation you would have with me following this observation.
4. What might be your next steps?
5. Reflect on your role-play performance as the observer giving feedback to the teacher. What did you notice about your performance during this activity?

Learning Teacher Observation Rubric

5
- Candidate inappropriately labels weaknesses/strengths
- Does not communicate effectively with teacher
- Responses demonstrate lack of understanding of learning objectives, instructional methods, and/or assessment knowledge.
- Candidate is unable to reflect on their performance in this role.

10
- Candidate identifies key strengths and/or weaknesses of the lesson focused on student behavior
- Candidate tells teacher how to improve.
- Responses support limited understanding of instructional methods and/or assessment knowledge.

20
- Candidate identifies strengths and/or weaknesses of the lesson focused on teacher behavior
- Candidate tells teacher how to improve, but also engages teacher in reflective thinking or inquiry.
- Responses support understanding of instructional methods and/or assessment knowledge.

30
- Candidate identifies strengths and weaknesses of the lesson focused on student learning
- Candidate engages teacher in reflection and inquiry and leads teacher to diagnose lesson
- Response supports deep understanding of instructional methods, and/or assessment knowledge
- Candidate reflects honestly and accurately about their approach.

APPENDIX B: CANDIDATE ASSESSMENT SUMMARY

Candidate Name: _____

School/Position: _____

Candidate Nominated by: _____

Team Facilitator

Lead discussion of each candidate. Complete the following information on each candidate assigned to your Assessment Center Team. Record 3–5 strengths and targets for growth identified by team members. Complete the score sheet by entering each assessor's initials and scores for each activity, and averaging the activity scores.

Candidate's Strengths	**Candidate's Areas to Target or Improve**	**Candidate Score Sheet**
Assessor 1 – Initials: Interview & Artifact 30 Points	Assessor 2 – Initials:	Average:
Assessor 3 – Initials: Learning Observation 30 Points	Assessor 4 – Initials:	Average:
Assessor 5 – Initials: Leadership Presentation 30 Points	Assessor 6 – Initials:	Average:
Team Comments:		TOTAL SCORE: /90

Team Consensus

As a team, discuss the candidate as a potential member of the UTAPP program. Come to a consensus as to whether or not the team recommends this candidate for consideration for UTAPP program.

- Yes, definitely.
- Yes, with reservations. Include specific reservations in team comments section.
- Not at this time. Candidate will be encouraged to apply again in the future.
- No. Candidate will not be encouraged to apply again in the future.

CHAPTER 6

LEARNING-CENTERED LEADERSHIP DEVELOPMENT PROGRAM FOR PRACTICING AND ASPIRING PRINCIPALS

Jianping Shen and Van E. Cooley[†]

ABSTRACT

In this chapter we discuss the content and process of the Learning-Centered Leadership Development Program for Practicing and Aspiring Principals. In terms of the content, based on extensive literature review the program focuses on seven dimensions of principal leadership associated with student achievement. In terms of process, one pair of practicing and aspiring principals from each school engage in five levels of learning – moving from (a) experiential, to (b) declarative, to (c) procedural, to (d) contextual, and to (e) evidential. The pair of practicing and aspiring principals works with two additional teacher leaders to develop sufficient leadership density in the school to plan and implement renewal activities along the seven dimensions to improve student achievement. We also reflect upon the lessons learned from implementing the program.

[†]Deceased

INTRODUCTION

Western Michigan University (WMU) and 12 eligible, high-needs public school districts in Michigan collaborate to conduct the *Learning-Centered Leadership Development Program for Practicing and Aspiring Principals*. The project involves working with 50 pairs of practicing and aspiring principals (with each pair from the same school and a total of 100 participants) over a five-year period. Participating high-needs schools are from urban and rural settings. The *Learning-Centered Leadership Development Program* engages practicing and aspiring principals in the learning and practice of seven dimensions of principal leadership empirically related to higher student achievement. The seven dimensions, based on a synthesis of empirical research displayed in Table 1 later, include (a) commitment and passion for school renewal, (b) safe and orderly school operation, (c) high, cohesive, and culturally relevant expectations for students, (d) coherent curricular programs, (e) distributive and empowering leadership, (f) real-time and embedded instructional assessment, and (g) data-informed decision-making. The learning and practice of school leadership is based on a professional development model that includes knowing what is important and why, how to do it, what results to look for, and how to make adjustments (adapted from Waters, Marzano, & McNulty, 2003). In this chapter, we will discuss the features of the project and the underlying ideas.

TWO KEY ELEMENTS OF THE PROJECT: CONTENT AND PROCESS[1]

The proposed project has a solid conceptual framework which consists of two key elements. The first key element is the content — the seven dimensions of school principalship that are empirically associated with improving student achievement. The second element is the process — the theory of learning and practice for adults in a complex organization. Learning activities range from knowing what is important and why (experiential), to what to do (declarative), to how to do it (procedural), to when to do it (contextual), and to what to look for as to results and how to make adjustments (evidential) (adapted from Waters et al., 2003). From the process standpoint, principals, aspiring principals and school improvement team members are engaged in "renewal activities" aligned with the seven dimensions

Table 1. Principal Leadership Dimensions and Elements Empirically Associated with School Improvement and Student Achievement.

Dimensions	Elements in Marzano's Balanced Leadership	Elements in Other Research
(A) Commitment and passion for school renewal	• Affirmation • Change agent • Optimizer • Flexibility • Intellectual stimulation	• Self-efficacy (Smith, Guarino, Strom, & Adams, 2006), self-confidence, responsibility, and perseverance; rituals, ceremonies, and other symbolic actions (Cotton, 2003) • Influence of principal leadership on school process such as school policies and norms, the practices of teachers, and school goals (Hallinger & Heck, 1996) • The integration of transformational and shared instructional leadership (Marks & Printy, 2003) • Visibility (Witziers, Bosker, & Kruger, 2003) • Purposes and goals (Leithwood & Jantzi, 1999) • Encouraging teachers to take risks and try new teaching methods (Sebring & Bryk, 2000)
(B) Safe and orderly school operation	• Order • Communication • Discipline	• Safe and orderly school environment; positive and supportive school climate; communication and interaction; interpersonal support (Cotton, 2003) • Governance (Heck, 1992; Heck & Marcoulides, 1993) • Planning; structure and organization (Leithwood & Jantzi, 1999) • Minimizing classroom disruptions (Sebring & Bryk, 2000)
(C) High, cohesive, and culturally relevant expectations for students	• Culture • Focus • Outreach • Ideals/beliefs	• Goals focused on high levels of student learning; high expectations of students; community outreach (Cotton, 2003)

Table 1. (*Continued*)

Dimensions	Elements in Marzano's Balanced Leadership	Elements in Other Research
		• Climate (Heck, 1992; O'Donnell & White, 2005) • Leadership of parents positively associated with student achievement (Pounder, 1995) • School mission, teacher expectation, school culture (Hallinger & Heck, 1996) • Defining and communicating mission; achievement orientation (O'Donnell & White, 2005; Witziers et al., 2003) • Culture (Leithwood & Jantzi, 1999) • Collective efficacy (Goddard, 2001; Goddard, Hoy, & Hoy, 2004; Goddard & Salloum, 2011; Manthey, 2006; Moolenaar et al., 2012; Ware & Kitsantas, 2007) • Collective responsibility (Lee & Smith, 1996; Wahlstrom & Louis, 2008) • Culturally relevant pedagogy (Boykin & Cunningham, 2001; Dill & Boykin, 2000; Hurley et al., 2009; Ladson-Billings, 1994, 1995a, 1995b, 1998)
(D) Coherent curricular programs	• Curriculum, instruction, assessment • Knowledge of curriculum, instruction, and assessment	• Instructional organization (Hallinger & Heck, 1996; Heck,1992; Heck & Marcoulides, 1993) • The integration of transformational and shared instructional leadership (Marks & Printy, 2003) • Supervising and evaluating the curriculum; coordinating and managing curriculum (Witziers et al., 2003)

Table 1. (*Continued*)

Dimensions	Elements in Marzano's Balanced Leadership	Elements in Other Research
		• Instructional program coherence (Newmann et al., 2001; Youngs et al., 2011)
(E) Distributive and empowering leadership	• Input • Resources • Visibility • Contingent reward • Relationship	• Shared leadership and staff empowerment; visibility and accessibility; teacher autonomy; support for risk taking; professional opportunities and resources (Cotton, 2003; Hallinger & Heck, 2010) • Cultivating teacher leadership for school improvement; shared instructional leadership (Marks & Printy, 2003) • Promoting school improvement and professional development (Witziers et al., 2003) • Teacher empowerment (Marks & Louis, 1997) • Professional community (Louis, 2006; Louis et al., 1996; Marks & Louis, 1997; Spillane, Halverson, & Diamond, 2001; Wahlstrom & Louis, 2008) • Social trust (Cosner, 2009; Sebring & Bryk, 2000)
(F) Real-time and embedded instructional assessment	• Curriculum, instruction, assessment • Knowledge of curriculum, instruction, and assessment	• Instructional leadership; classroom observation and feedback to teachers (Cotton, 2003) • Instructional organization (Hallinger & Heck, 1996; Heck, 1992; Heck & Marcoulides, 1993) • The integration of transformational and shared instructional leadership (Marks & Printy, 2003) • Monitoring student progress (Witziers et al., 2003) • Instructional program coherence (Newmann et al., 2001)

Table 1. (Continued)

Dimensions	Elements in Marzano's Balanced Leadership	Elements in Other Research
(G) Data-informed decision-Making	• Monitors/ evaluates • Situational awareness	• The practice of teachers; student opportunity to learn; academic learning time (Hallinger & Heck 1996; Shen & Cooley, 2008; Shen et al., 2010, 2012a) • Supervising and evaluating the curriculum (Witziers et al., 2003) • Information collection (Celio & Harvey, 2005; Leithwood & Jantzi, 1999; Shen et al., 2010; 2012a; Shen, Cooley, Marx, Kirby, & Whale, 2012b) • Organizational learning (Marks, Louis, & Printy, 2000; Schechter, 2008; Schechter & Feldman, 2010).

that will ultimately improve student achievement. Renewal activities are school-based improvement initiatives developed by principals and aspiring principals to address an identified weakness or shortcoming related to the seven dimensions.

The First Element of the Conceptual Framework for Learning-Centered Leadership Development Program: The Seven Dimensions as the Content

The program is based on current knowledge from research and effective practice. Principals, particularly those in high-need schools, face intensive pressure to raise student achievement. It has been increasingly argued that the main responsibility of school leadership is the improvement of teaching and student learning (Spillane, 2003).

Principals make a difference in student learning (e.g., Bossert, Dwyer, Rowan, & Lee, 1982; Goldring & Pasternak, 1994; Hallinger & Heck, 1996; Heck, Larson, & Marcoulides, 1990; Heck & Marcoulides, 1992; Knuth & Banks, 2006; Leithwood, Louis, Anderson, & Wahlstrom, 2004; Marcoulides & Heck, 1993; Marzano, Waters, & McNulty, 2005; Owings, Kaplan, & Nunnery, 2005; Waters & Kingston, 2005). However, the validity of the existing mechanisms for developing, certifying, and credentialing principals needs improvement. One shortcoming of the current paradigm of principal preparation is that the focus is more on general leadership characteristics and management functions than on leadership behaviors related to student achievement (Shen et al., 2005). Based on the Balanced Leadership study (Marzano et al., 2005) and 25 additional high-quality studies (see Table 1), as well as our projects funded by the US Department of Education and The Wallace Foundation, we developed the Learning-Centered Leadership Development Program for Practicing and Aspiring Principals. We are using this intervention program to work with participants on seven dimensions of principal leadership in Table 1.

Table 1 illustrates that the seven dimensions of the *Learning-Centered Leadership Development Program* represent current knowledge from research and best practices. The seven dimensions of principal leadership are based on two streams of literature. The first stream includes large-scale meta-analyses, such as those by Marzano et al. (2005) and Cotton (2003). These meta-analyses consist of syntheses of the literature on the relationship between principal leadership and student achievement. However, the meta-analyses used original studies as data sources and accordingly, there are additional requirements for studies to be included in the meta-analyses. In other words, meta-analyses have limitations in terms of what studies are included. For example, the meta-analysis by Marzano et al. (2005) set criteria such as "The study involved K-12 students," "effect sizes in correlation form were reported or could be computed" (p. 28). Thus, the second stream of our literature includes those recent, influential studies that were not included in the meta-analyses. We included research ideas such as the integration of transformational and shared instructional leadership (Marks & Printy, 2003; Hallinger & Heck, 2010), collective efficacy (Goddard, 2001; Goddard, Hoy, & Hoy, 2004; Manthey, 2006; Ware & Kitsantas, 2007; Moolenaar, Sleegers, & Daly, 2012; Goddard & Salloum, 2011), collective responsibility (Lee & Smith, 1996; Wahlstrom & Louis, 2008), culturally relevant pedagogy (Boykin & Cunningham, 2001; Dill & Boykin, 2000; Ladson-Billings, 1994, 1995a, 1995b, 1998; Hurley, Alle, & Boykin, 2009), instructional program coherence (Newmann, Smith, Allensworth, & Bryk, 2001; Youngs, Holdgreve-Resendez, & Qian, 2011), professional community (Louis, Marks, & Kruse, 1996; Marks & Louis, 1997; Louis, 2006; Wahlstrom & Louis, 2008), social trust (Sebring & Bryk, 2000; Cosner, 2009), organizational learning (Marks et al., 2000; Schechter, 2008; Schechter & Feldman, 2010), and using data for decision-making (Celio & Harvey, 2005; Leithwood & Jantzi, 1999; Shen et al., 2010, 2012a,

2012b). By utilizing the research findings from the empirical studies, the Learning-Centered Leadership Development Program reflects comprehensive, up-to-date knowledge from research and effective practice.

The Second Key Element of the Learning-Centered Leadership Development Program: The Five-Level-of-Learning Process to Engage Practicing and Aspiring Principals in School Renewal in a Complex System

In the foregoing, we presented the seven dimensions as the content for the Learning-Centered Leadership Development Program. In this section, we discuss the five-level-of-learning process to conduct the learning activities, which is the second key element of the project. The following table illustrates how we conduct the program.

There are four major groups of learning activities for participants. First, each participant participates in a workshop for each of the seven dimensions of principal leadership (each workshop is a distinct module focusing on one leadership dimension). The workshops utilize the theories of adult learning to emphasize job-embededness and reflection on participants' practices (Darling-Hammond, 1998). Second, as an extension of each workshop, each pair of practicing and aspiring principals (from the same school), together with a mentor and the school's stakeholders, examine and reflect upon current and desired practice of leadership dimensions in the school. Practicing and aspiring principals, together with teacher leaders in their school then develop a minimum of one renewal activity related to each dimension. For example, in relation to the dimension of *data-informed decision-making*, a pair of practicing and aspiring principals might begin or modify the use of data while observing teachers as part of the instructional supervision and evaluation process. Third, based on the development work in the previous point, the pair of practicing and aspiring principals implements, in partnership with the school's stakeholders and the mentor, designs and implements at least one renewal activity for each of the seven dimensions. Finally, the participants and the project staff form a learning community to facilitate the sharing and reflecting upon their collaborative thinking and actions.

As illustrated in Table 2 and the four learning activities discussed in the previous paragraph, the continuum of four major learning activities differs from the usual professional development practices. First, project activities focus on knowledge and skills at different levels, ranging from

Table 2. Levels of Learning: A Seamless, Actions-oriented Approach (The Second Key Element of the Proposed Project).

Five Levels of Learning	Training for Each Dimension	Mentoring and Developing the Renewal Activities with Stakeholders	Mentoring and Implementing the Renewal Activities with Stakeholders	Learning and Sharing
Experiential (knowing what is important and why)	X			
Declarative (knowing what to do)	X			
Procedural (knowing how to do it)		X	X	
Contextual (knowing when to do it)			X	
Evidential (knowing what to look for as to results and how to make adjustments)				X

(a) *experiential*, to (b) *declarative*, to (c) *procedural*, to (d) *contextual*, and to (e) *evidential*. Second, proposed activities are action-oriented and job embedded. With the support of a mentor, the school's stakeholders and the project staff, each pair of practicing and aspiring principals plans and actually implements renewal activities in their school. Finally, project activities are results oriented. Working with participants, the evaluation component of the project investigates the outcome of renewal activities participants choose to implement.

In summary, the two elements for the proposed project are intended to connect the content ("what") with the process ("how") so that the proposed project impact practicing and aspiring principals, teachers and schools, and ultimately students. The following conceptual framework summarizes the project (Fig. 1).

The conceptual framework represents a systematic approach to school improvement with each of the inter-related steps closely aligned. Successful implementation is dependent on content knowledge as well as the breadth and depth in the implementation of the seven dimensions related to increasing student achievement.

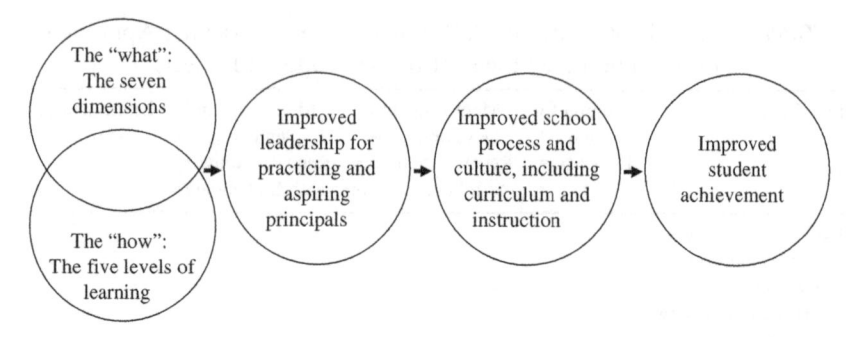

Fig. 1. A Schematic Presentation of the Conceptual Framework of the Project.

GOALS OF THE PROPOSED PROJECT

Goals provide direction to principals, aspiring principals and teachers as they implement the renewal activities associated with the seven dimensions. Each of the seven dimensions along with project goals for each dimension is presented in Table 3.

Outcomes of the Project. As part of the project evaluation, we are conducting rigorous analysis of the outcomes related to (a) principals, (b) school process and culture, and (c) student achievement. The evaluation focuses on those dimensions associated with the intervention (Table 4).

The three distinct measures will provide a comprehensive database to determine the impact of the seven dimensions on student learning. Multiple measures should provide clear evidence on the effectiveness of the Learning-Centered Leadership Development Program.

RENEWAL ACTIVITIES

The Notion of "Renewal"

As mentioned in the foregoing, the content and process of the project lead to renewal activities in each school. John Goodlad is the leading author who advocates the notion of *renewal* (Goodlad, 1987, 1994; Shen, 1999). The traditional model of Research, Development, Dissemination, and Evaluation (RDDE) takes a top-down approach, and the term *reform* is associated with the RDDE Model. Goodlad advocates for a Dialogue,

Table 3. Specified and Measurable Goals of the Project.

Dimensions	Goals
(A) Commitment and passion for school renewal	• Adjust leadership approaches to fit the current reality • Engage in school renewal activities • Recognize success and failure • Ensure teachers are aware of most recent best practice
(B) Safe and orderly school operation	• Adhere to standard operating procedures • Communicate well with teachers and students • Reduce factors that detracts teachers from their teaching • Develop a positive and supportive school climate
(C) High, cohesive and culturally relevant expectations for students	• Foster a collective efficacy for students • Establish clear goals for students • Be an advocate to communicate the expectation with stakeholders • Demonstrate a strong belief in high expectations for students
(D) Coherent curricular programs	• Be actively involved in curriculum-related activities • Work with teachers to align the standards and curriculum • Visit classrooms to supervise the implementation of the alignment • Ensure the coherence among various renewal initiatives in school
(E) Distributive and empowering leadership	• Engage teachers in decision-making • Promote quality interactions with teachers • Celebrate teachers' accomplishments • Have good relationships with teachers • Secure sufficient resources for teachers' work
(F) Real-time and embedded instructional assessment	• Establish a formative assessment system consistent with the curriculum and the state's accountability measures • Facilitate teachers' use of formative assessment data in key subjects for diagnostic purpose • Promote the notion that assessment is part of instruction • Facilitate teacher growth via classroom observation and objective feedback

Table 3. (*Continued*)

Dimensions	Goals
(G) Data-informed decision-making	• Develop a system to collect major streams of data on topics such as student achievement, instructional practice, and parent engagement • Know the status of the school based on data • Is able to analyze data and initiate first-order and second-order renewal activities • Is able to evaluate the impact of the renewal activities

Table 4. How will the Outcomes of the Program be Measured?

Outcomes	Instrument or Data Source
Improved principal's leadership	Measured by Vanderbilt Assessment of Leadership in Education (VAL-ED)
Statistically improved school culture and process	Measured by an instrument on school process
Statistically improved student achievement	Measured by student achievement in math and reading as reflected in MEAP (Michigan Educational Assessment Program)

Decision, Action and Evaluation (DDAE) model, which is associated with the term *renewal*. *Reform* has the connotation of imposing an alternative, while *renewal* has the connotation that change is a nonlinear and only vaguely goal-oriented approach to explore the possibilities of alternatives. Goodlad argues that for renewal to occur, there must be some combination of internal responsiveness and external stimulation; for renewal to continue, there must be some continual, productive, and creative tension between the internal and external. The project is designed around Goodlad's notion of *renewal* rather than the typical notion of *reform*. Renewal activities are the centerpiece of the project and represent actionable behaviors based on research and best practices that when systematically implemented, have a strong probability to increase student achievement.

Theory into Best Practice: The Renewal Matrix

Renewal activities are theory-to-best-practice, job-embedded actions. The project team, consisting of both university and school personnels, stresses that renewal activities should address one or more of the identified barriers to learning in each building. Principals, aspiring principals, and school improvement members (teams) are instructed to develop one renewal activity for each of the seven dimensions; however, where there are appropriate connections from one dimension to another, teams may combine renewal activities with the understanding that each of the seven dimensions of leadership must be addressed. The seven dimensions of leadership represent a system and each dimension must be adopted to maximize student learning.

The process of identifying renewal activities to address areas in need of improvement resulted in creative tension for principals, aspiring principals, school improvement team members, and mentors. To facilitate implementation, a planning activity matrix was developed (Table 5). The matrix is aligned with Goodlad's DDAE model. The matrix provides a roadmap for development and implementation of renewal activities. The matrix is a professional development model that includes 10 interconnected steps designed to guide teams through the renewal activity development and implementation process. Teams initially identified issues or barriers related to each dimension that inhibited or compromised student learning. Once areas of need were identified, team members differentiated proposed renewal activities from current practices to determine what was currently being done at the school and district levels for the respective dimension. This involved a gap analysis between existing and desired practices. Team members were also asked to connect renewal activities to the building's school improvement plan to effectively use their time and to avoid duplicating activities.

Prior to moving to the implementation phase, teams must identify how the renewal activities will increase student achievement. Our observations revealed "spirited dialogue" and "debate." If team members could not identify at the onset how the activities would increase student learning, teams deemed the renewal activities as inappropriate. These discussions resulted in team building and a targeted focus on results by the entire team. Determining how the activity would increase student learning was a significant challenge for many teams.

The implementation phase involves identification of other stakeholders, including both "significant" and "resistant others." Over the years, teachers have been involved in numerous reform initiatives which resulted in a mindset that No Child Left Behind (NCLB) reform will also in time go away. However, NCLB is different because teachers and administrators are now being held accountable for student performance and the accountability is here to stay. The result is a situation in which teachers and administrators are cognizant that changes need to be in a number of areas to

Table 5. Renewal Activity Matrix.

Implementation Steps	Passion and Commitment for School Renewal Data-Informed Decision-Making	Safe and Orderly School Operation	High, Cohesive, and Culturally Relevant Expectations for Students	Distributive and Empowering Leadership	Coherent Curricular Programs	Real-Time Embedded Assessments	Data-Informed Decision-Making
Proposed renewal activity(s) (list new activity(s) beyond the current practice							
Current practices in this area. What is being done now at the school or district level?							
Gaps in current practice – what can be done to improve?							
Connection to school improvement plan							
How will renewal activities increase student achievement?							
Identify stakeholders or significant others that need to be involved.							
Forces for and against change							
Requires technical assistance							
Timeline for implementation							
What measures will be used to determine if renewal activities are successful?							

avoid potential actions taken by the state. In order to address the sanctions associated with NCLB, for our project expanding and developing a team with multiple voices is deemed an important step in the change process and a step welcomed by principals and other team members. To successfully address program deficiencies and implement new programs that impact student learning, teams must identify forces for and against the change. They include conditions, policies, past practices, and political elements that need to be reconciled for change to occur. Renewal activities often deviate from current practice. In other instances, central official personnel may resist activities developed by the team. The process involves considerable thought and discussion and all stakeholders must have a clear understanding of why the renewal activities are important. When content is aligned with best practice, the opportunity for change is increased.

Another component of the planning process is for teams to identify technical assistance required to implement concepts. The seven dimensions have been in the literature for years, although implementation has been piecemeal or nonexistent. Teachers and administrators often do not have the knowledge and skill to implement renewal activities. Teachers and administrators must be provided targeted professional development to develop, implement, and nurture renewal activities. Closely related to professional development is establishing a timeline for renewal activity implementation. Timelines should also include roles and responsibilities for team members so that each stakeholder is held accountable for their role in the implementation process.

The final and one of the most important steps is for team members to establish acceptable criteria used to determine if renewal activities are successfully implemented. We emphasize that evidence must be closely related to data rather than intuition. Student achievement is most often measured by standardized test results. However, leadership inventories, climate surveys, formative and summative classroom assessments, observations, interviews, and other data can be used as criteria to determine renewal activity success (Shen et al., 2010). Team members are encouraged to embrace the assessment process with the realization that change requires time, patience, and, thoughtful modifications throughout the implementation process.

The renewal activity matrix is not without limitations. Our observations revealed serious discussions among teachers, principals, and aspiring principals. In some instances, mentors were asked to intervene when building teams could not agree on a particular issue. Seasoned mentors ask clarifying questions and allowed teams to develop their own remedies. This approach resulted in additional time for discussion as well as some frustration and tension. However, in the final analysis, teams must develop and support their respective renewal activities. There are no quick fixes to the process. We noticed a few teams moving through the process without serious discussion. These teams were challenged to go back to the drawing board.

An Example of Renewal Activities from a School

Team completion of their renewal activity matrix represents a planning framework for engaging in renewal activities along the seven dimensions. The process to complete the matrix was designed for the team to begin to discuss and formulate ideas, strengths, and to move toward implementation of renewal activities. The project staff surmised that seeing the seven dimensions of leadership in a matrix would enable the team to make connections between dimensions. Team members stated that they were grateful for the opportunity for teachers and the principal to work together in a comfortable, nonthreatening setting. They valued the opportunity to share, exchange ideas, and to participate in spirited discussions. It was obvious that leadership did not always rest solely with the principal as teachers and the aspiring principals often led the discussions taking the lead on issues facing their school.

Renewal Activity in a School: An Exampe

The renewal activity planning matrix helped to identify areas of need providing concrete steps for implementations. Following is one example of proposed renewal activities focusing on coherent curriculum programs.

The team, comprised of the principal, one aspiring principal, and two additional elementary teachers, concluded they needed to create and implement a consistent curriculum in all subject areas. In terms of current practices and what was being done in their building, team members noted the building and district curriculum was inconsistent and resources were described as inadequate. Consensus was the curriculum must be consistent with vertical and horizon articulation in the school and district. The team also noted that teachers should have access to a wide range of resources that support the curriculum.

In terms of connecting renewal activities to the school improvement plan, the team noted the need to connect pacing guides, grade-level expectations, and common core standards with a comprehensive curriculum. The team concluded that a consistently implemented curriculum would increase student achievement providing scope and sequencing at all grade levels. The team stressed teachers, parents, administrators (buildings and central office) and students needed to be involved in the curriculum development process.

Team members also identified forces for and against change. The team proclaimed that "reform could not stop at the classroom door." All teachers and administrators needed to be on board and teachers, students, parents, and administrators must be held accountable for curriculum creation, implementation, curriculum delivery, and remediation efforts. The issue of transient students or students moving from building to building throughout the school year was identified as a problem. Team members felt that remediation or catch-up measures needed to be in place and that curriculum articulation with limited pacing could help to alleviate the problem of students moving from school to school.

Team members strongly recommended comprehensive professional development for all stakeholders. Participants need to understand why change was necessary and be given the knowledge and support to develop an articulated curriculum. As to the timeline, the agreement was that the renewal activity must be implemented immediately.

In terms of assessment, team members recommended a broad-brush approach focusing on both summative and formative assessments. The principal, aspiring principal, and teachers clearly understood the state test would be the most important measure, but that other assessments would provide teachers information to make instructional changes during the school year.

Completion of the matrix provided the team with the information needed to develop the renewal activities. The ability to see all seven dimensions on one chart allowed team members to connect dimensions and to begin to understand the systemic process. There were areas on the matrix that required additional discussion and development. The process included a gap analysis, identification of stakeholders, barriers, and opportunities, an understanding of desire outcomes or how the program would impact achievement, required professional development along with timelines, and assessment procedures.

LESSONS LEARNED

In the foregoing, we discuss the rationale, design, and implementation of our Learning-Centered Leadership Development Program. We highlight the seven dimensions of principal leadership that are associated with student achievement. We also emphasize the employment of adult learning theories to make the project (a) job embedded and (b) reflective upon their experiences through five levels of learning – moving from (a) *experiential*, to (b) *declarative*, to (c) *procedural*, to (d) *contextual*, and to (e) *evidential*. In the following, we discuss the lessons that we have learned.

The Leadership Density in Each School

The project requires a pair of practicing and aspiring principals from each school. We observe that the practice of pairing practicing and aspiring principals from each school (a) creates efficiency, (b) promotes the interaction of perspectives from the principal (the practicing principal), the teacher leader (the aspiring principal) and the mentor, and (c) facilitates the development and implementation of renewal activities in the school. One year into the project, we realize that to include two more teachers from each school is even more beneficial. Observing how a team of four from each school engages in developing and implementing renewal activities lead to the lesson that we must have sufficient leadership density from each school in order to make renewal activities feasible, both from the human resource perspective and political perspective.

Just Like How a Good Teacher Teaches, There Must Be Scaffolding for the Participants

As discussed in the foregoing, there are four major groups of learning activities for the participants: (a) each practicing and aspiring principal participates in a workshop for each of the seven dimensions of principal leadership; (b) as an extension of each workshop, each pair of practicing and aspiring principals, together with a mentor and the school's stakeholders, examines the practice of that leadership dimension in the school, and develop at least one renewal activity related to each dimension; (c) working with the school's stakeholders and the mentor, each pair of practicing and aspiring principals implements at least one renewal activity for each of the seven dimensions; (d) the participants, the project staff, and mentors form a learning community (both on-line and face-to-face), sharing and reflecting upon their thinking and actions. The continuum of four major activities rang from (a) *experiential*, to (b) *declarative*, to (c) *procedural*, to (d) *contextual*, and to (e) *evidential* (adapted from Waters et al., 2003). The scaffolding of the learning experience makes it feasible for participants to engage in renewal activities.

No Busy Work: A Coherent, Sustained Program Connected with Participants' Ongoing Professional Lives

The activities constitute a *coherent p*rogram for the following two reasons. First, there is a strong conceptual framework underling the proposed activities. The content of the program (i.e., the seven dimensions) and the conduct of the program (i.e., the learning activities that ranged from *experiential*, to *declarative*, to *procedural*, to *contextual*, and to *evidential*) connects the "what" and the "how". The connection of the "what" and "how" points to the coherence of the program − a job-embedded, action-focused, and results oriented project with an emphasis on student learning. Second, the project also takes into account the conditions under which practicing and aspiring principals work (Wallace Foundation, 2006). Too often a project focuses on improving the knowledge, skills, and behaviors of practicing and aspiring principals, with no attention to the context and condition under which they work. The project investigates the condition and context along the seven dimensions for participants, and develops the most appropriate training activities for the dimensions. Incorporating into the training program the context and condition under which practicing and aspiring principals work so that participants could effectively apply what they have learned is also an indicator of the coherence of the proposed project. The project lasts 2.5 years for each cohort. The *sustained* program makes it possible for participants to develop and implement renewal activities.

Tools are Needed to Facilitate Participants' Work

Participants felt that the renewal activity matrix is a useful tool. Completion of the matrix provided teams with the information to develop their renewal activities. The ability to see all seven dimensions on one chart allowed teams to connect dimensions and to begin to understand the systemic process. There is a need of similar tools to facilitate participants' work.

CONCLUDING THOUGHTS

The focus of the Learning-Centered Leadership Development Program is on renewal activities that principals and teachers can implement to improve student achievement. The seven dimensions of leadership provide a cohesive, systemic approach to renewal activities with emphasis on addressing researched-based areas found to impact student achievement. We believe the key to success is to systematically address all dimensions through the development and implementation of renewal activities. The renewal activity concept is closely aligned with the work of Goodlad, whose DDAE model serves as the foundation for the renewal activity process. The matrix is a tool for principals, aspiring leaders, and teachers to plan and organize their school improvement work. The matrix provides a framework for teachers and administrators to begin to address issues that diminish student learning. The Learning-centered Leadership Development Program holds considerable promise as this is an attempt to systematically address the factors that positively impact student learning.

NOTE

1. The section was based on Shen, J., Cooley, V., Ma, X., Reeves, P., Burt, W., Rainey, J.M., & Yuan, W. (2012). Data-informed decision-making on high-impact strategies: Developing and validating an instrument for Principals. *Journal of Experimental Education, 80*(1), 1–25. The source and the publisher Taylor and Francis are acknowledged. The materials were used with permission from the publisher.

REFERENCES

Bossert, S., Dwyer, D., Rowan, B., & Lee, G. (1982). The instructional management role of the principal. *Educational Administration Quarterly, 18*(3), 34–64.
Boykin, A. W., & Cunningham, R. T. (2001). The effects of movement expressiveness in story content and learning context on the analogical reasoning performance of African American children. *Journal of Negro Education, 70*(1-2), 72–83.
Celio, M. B., & Harvey, J. (2005). *Buried treasure: Developing a management guide from mountains of school data.* New York, NY: Wallace Foundation.
Cosner, S. (2009). Building organizational capacity through trust. *Educational Administration Quarterly, 45*(2), 248–291.
Cotton, K., & Association for Supervision and Curriculum Development. (2003). *Principals and student achievement: What the research says.* Alexandria, VA: ASCD.

Darling-Hammond, L. (1998). Teacher learning that supports student learning. *Educational Leadership, 55*, 6–11.

Dill, E. M., & Boykin, A. W. (2000). The comparative influence of individual, peer tutoring, and communal learning contexts on the text recall of African American children. *Journal of Black Psychology, 26*(1), 65–78.

Goddard, R. D. (2001). Collective efficacy: a neglected construct in the study of schools and student achievement. *Journal of Educational Psychology, 93*, 467–476.

Goddard, R. D., Hoy, W. K., & Hoy, A. W. (2004). Collective efficacy beliefs: Theoretical developments, empirical evidence, and future directions. *Educational Researcher, 33*(3), 1–13.

Goddard, R. D., & Salloum, S. (2011). Collective efficacy beliefs, organizational excellence, and leadership. In K. Cameron & G. Spreitzer (Eds.), *Positive organizational scholarship handbook* (pp. 642–650). Oxford, UK: Oxford University Press.

Goldring, E., & Pasternak, R. (1994). Principals' coordinating strategies and school effectiveness. *School Effectiveness and School Improvement, 5*(3), 239–253.

Goodlad, J. I. (Ed.). (1987). *The ecology of school renewal. The 86th yearbook of the national society for the study for education, part I.* Chicago, IL: University of Chicago Press.

Goodlad, J. I. (1994). *Educational renewal: Better teachers, better schools.* San Francisco, CA: Jossey-bass.

Hallinger, P., & Heck, R. H. (1996). Reassessing the principal's role in school effectiveness: A review of empirical research, 1980–1995. *Educational Administration Quarterly, 32*(1), 5–44.

Hallinger, P., & Heck, R. H. (2010). Collaborative leadership and school improvement: Understanding the impact on school capacity and student learning. *School Leadership & Management, 30*(2), 95–110.

Heck, R. H. (1992). Principals' instructional leadership and school performance: Implications for policy development. *Educational Evaluation and Policy Analysis, 14*(1), 21–34.

Heck, R., Larson, T., & Marcoulides, G. (1990). Principal instructional leadership and school achievement: Validation of a causal model. *Educational Administration Quarterly, 26*, 94–125.

Heck, R., & Marcoulides, G. (1992). Principal assessment: Conceptual problem, methodological problem, or both? *Peabody Journal of Education, 68*(1), 124–144.

Heck, R. H., & Marcoulides, G. A. (1993). Principal leadership behaviors and school achievement. *NASSP Bulletin, 77*(553), 20–28.

Hurley, E. A., Alle, B. A., & Boykin, A. W. (2009). Culture and the interaction of student ethnicity with reward structure in group learning. *Cognition and Instruction, 27*(2), 121–146.

Knuth, R., & Banks, P. (2006, March). The essential leadership model. *NASSP Bulletin, 90*(1), 4–18.

Ladson-Billings, G. (1994). *The dreamkeepers: Successful teachers of African American children.* San Francisco, CA: Jossey-Bass.

Ladson-Billings, G. (1995a). Toward a theory of culturally relevant pedagogy. *American Educational Research Journal, 32*, 465–491.

Ladson-Billings, G. (1995b). But that's just god teaching? The case for culturally relevant pedagogy. *Theory into Practice, 34*, 159–165.

Ladson-Billings, G. (1998). Teaching in dangerous times: Culturally relevant approaches to teacher assessment. *The Journal of Negro Education, 67*, 255–267.

Lee, V., & Smith, J. B. (1996). Collective responsibility for learning and its effects on gains in achievement and engagement for early secondary school students. *American Journal of Education, 104*(2), 103–147.

Leithwood, K. A., & Jantzi, D. (1999). The relative effects of principal and teacher sources of leadership on student engagement with school. *Educational Administration Quarterly, 35*(Suppl), 679–706.

Leithwood, K., Louis, K. S., Anderson, S., & Wahlstrom, K. (2004). *How leadership influences student learning*. Center for Applied Research and Educational Improvement, University of Minnesota, Minneapolis, MN. Retrieved from http://www.wallacefoundation.org/NR/rdonlyres/E3BCCFA5-A88B-45D3-8E27-B973732283C9/0/ReviewofResearchLearningFromLeadership.pdf. Accessed on January 31, 2008.

Louis, K. S. (2006). Changing the culture of schools: professional community, organizational learning, and trust. *Journal of School Leadership, 16*(5), 477–489.

Louis, K. S., Marks, H. M., & Kruse, S. D. (1996). Teachers' professional community in restructuring schools. *American Journal of Education, 33*(4), 757–798.

Manthey, G. (2006). Collective efficacy: Explaining school achievement. *Leadership, 35*(3), 23–36.

Marcoulides, G., & Heck, R. (1993). Organizational culture and performance: Proposing and testing a model. *Organization Science, 4*(2), 209–225.

Marks, H. M., & Louis, K. S. (1997). Does teacher empowerment affect the classroom? The implications of teacher empowerment for instructional practice and student academic performance. *Educational Evaluation and Policy Analysis, 19*, 245–275.

Marks, H. M., Louis, K. S., & Printy, S. M. (2000). The capacity for organizational learning: Implications for pedagogy and student achievement. In K. Leithwood (Ed.), *Organizational learning and school improvement* (pp. 239–266). Greenwich, CT: JAI.

Marks, H. M., & Printy, S. M. (2003). Principal leadership and school performance: An integration of transformational and instructional leadership. *Educational Administration Quarterly, 39*(3), 370–397.

Marzano, R. J., Waters, T., & McNulty, B. A. (2005). *School leadership that works*. Alexandria, VA: Association for Supervision and Curriculum Development.

Moolenaar, N. M., Sleegers, P. C., & Daly, A. J. (2012). Teaming up: Linking collaboration networks, collective efficacy, and student achievement. *Teaching and Teacher Education: An International Journal of Research and Studies, 28*(2), 251–262.

Newmann, F. E., Smith, B., Allensworth, E., & Bryk, A. S. (2001). Instructional program coherence: What it is and why it should guide school improvement policy. *Educational Evaluation and Policy Analysis, 23*, 297–321.

O'Donnell, R. J, & White, G. P. (2005). Within the accountability era: Principal instructional leadership behaviors and student achievement. *NASSP Bulletin, 89*(645), 56–72.

Owings, W. A., Kaplan, L. S., & Nunnery, J. (2005). Principal quality, ISLLC standards, and student achievement. *Journal of School Leadership, 15*(1), 99–119.

Pounder, D. G. (1995). Leadership as an organization-wide phenomenon: Its impact on school performance. *Educational Administration Quarterly, 31*(4), 564–588.

Schechter, C. (2008). Organizational learning mechanisms: Its meaning, measure, and implications for school improvement. *Educational Administration Quarterly, 44*(2), 155–186.

Schechter, C., & Feldman, N. (2010). Exploring organizational learning mechanisms in special education. *Journal of Educational Administration, 48*(4), 490–516.

Sebring, B., & Bryk, A. (2000). School leadership and the bottom line in Chicago. *Phi Delta Kappan, 81*, 440–443.

Shen, J. (1999). Connecting educational theory, research, and practice: John I. Goodlad's research. *Journal of Thought, 34*(4), 25–96.
Shen, J., & Associates. (2005). *School principals.* New York, NY: Peter Lang.
Shen, J., & Cooley, V. (2008). Critical issues in using data for decision-making. *International Journal of Leadership in Education, 11*(3), 319–329.
Shen, J., Cooley, V., Ma, X., Reeves, P., Burt, W., Rainey, J. M., & Yuan, W. (2012a). Data-informed decision-making on high-impact strategies: Developing and validating an instrument for principals. *Journal of Experimental Education, 80*(1), 1–25.
Shen, J., Cooley, V. E., Marx, G., Kirby, E., Whale, D. E. (2012b). Data-informed decision-making: A guidebook for data points and analyses for the school improvement team. In J. Shen (Ed.), *Tools for improving school principalship* (pp. 137–168). New York, NY: Peter Lang.
Shen, J., Cooley, V., Reeves, P., Burt, W., Ryan, L., Rainey, J. M., & Yuan, W. (2010). Using data for decision-making: Perspectives from 16 principals in Michigan, USA. *International Review of Education, 56,* 435–456.
Smith, W., Guarino, A., Strom, P., & Adams, O. (2006). Effective teaching and learning environments and principal self-efficacy. *Journal of Research for Educational Leaders, 3*(2), 4–23.
Spillane, J. P. (2003). Educational leadership. *Educational Evaluation and Policy Analysis, 25,* 343–346.
Spillane, J. P., Halverson, R., & Diamond, J. B. (2001). Investigating school leadership practice: A distributed perspective. *Educational Researcher, 30*(3), 23–28.
Wahlstrom, K. L., & Louis, K. S. (2008). How teachers experience principal leadership: The roles of professional community, trust, efficacy, and shared responsibility. *Educational Administration Quarterly, 44*(4), 458–495.
Wallace Foundation. (2006). *Leadership for learning: Making the connection among state, district, and school policies and practices.* New York, NY: Wallace Foundation.
Ware, H., & Kitsantas, A. (2007). Teacher and collective efficacy beliefs as predictors of professional commitment. *Journal of Educational Research, 100*(5), 303–310.
Waters, T., & Kingston, S. (2005). The standards we need. *Leadership, 62*(16), 14–39.
Waters, T., Marzano, R. J., & McNulty, B. (2003). *Balanced leadership: What 30 years of research tells us about the effect of leadership on student achievement.* Aurora, CO: Mid-continent Research for Education and Learning. Retrieved from http://www.mcrel.org
Witziers, B., Bosker, R. J., & Kruger, M. L. (2003). Educational leadership and student achievement: The elusive search for an association. *Educational Administration Quarterly, 39*(3), 398–425.
Youngs, P., Holdgreve-Resendez, R. T., & Qian, H. (2011). The role of instructional program coherence in beginning elementary teachers' induction experiences. *The Elementary School Journal, 111*(3), 455–476.

CHAPTER 7

PREPARING AND SUPPORTING PRINCIPALS IN RURAL SOUTH DAKOTA SCHOOLS

Jeanne Cowan and Janet Hensley

ABSTRACT

The Partnership for Improvement in Rural Leadership and Learning (PIRLL) grant had a goal of improving school leadership in rural and remote locations across South Dakota. The work included recruitment and training of aspiring principals as well as capacity building for practicing principals. The two key elements used to meet this goal were development of a customized principal preparation program and providing On-site mentoring and professional development for practicing principals. A desired outcome was to increase the capacity and availability of school leaders who would be culturally responsive to the needs of students and remain in high-needs schools in South Dakota.

The goal of the Partnership for Improvement in Rural Leadership and Learning (PIRLL) grant was to inspire improvements in educational outcomes for students in rural South Dakota by building the capacity and availability of educational leaders who would serve in high-needs schools. The project had two objectives: to recruit, instruct, and support 50 aspiring school leaders to become prepared and credentialed to serve high-needs schools; and to build the capacity of sixty practicing principals and assistant principals through professional development that was embedded in their local practice and was responsive to the needs of students served, as well as to the culture of their local communities. The purpose of this chapter was to describe how the project implemented two key elements and their implications.

Participants in this project were from schools and districts located on or near one of the state's nine Native American reservations and in the most rural areas of South Dakota. These schools were identified for improvement or were on alert for improvement in reading, math or both. The majority of the schools served are in the three poorest counties in the United States. To further understand the intense socioeconomic needs of the students in these schools, information from Benson, Lies, Okunade, and Wunnava (2009) stated that:

> According to Indian Services Medical Records and the US Census Bureau, the Pine Ridge NAIR population is about 50,000, annual median income is about $2,600, infant mortality is roughly three times the US average, half of the population is under 18 years old, 70% of the children are poor, some 40% of the population is diabetic, the suicide rate is more than 72% higher than the US average, and the life expectancy is 55 years for male and 60 years for females. (p. 3)

According to the US Census Bureau, 22% of the residents of Todd County speak a language other than English in the home. US Department of Education (2011) Secretary Arne Duncan highlighted the importance of focusing on the education of Native American students by stating, "We have to dramatically improve the quality of education in Indian Country and for Native American students, whether they live on reservations or not" (p. 1). A recent 20/20 program called *Children of the Plains* further illustrates the contextual factors of those served by this grant and portrays the lives of children living there (Sawyer, 2011).

Two key elements of the PIRLL program were designed and implemented in response to the rural setting and the context described above: (1) a customized program for principal preparation and (2) an on-site mentoring and professional development program for practicing principals.

KEY ELEMENT ONE: CUSTOMIZED PRINCIPAL PREPARATION PROGRAM

The first key element that was critical to the success of the PIRLL program focused on recruitment; collaboration with the South Dakota Board of Regents and Sinte Gleska University; relevant instructors; updated curricular content; a yearlong internship; and course evaluation and adjustments.

Recruitment

The PIRLL project's first step was to address the recruitment of aspiring leaders who would be well prepared and available to accept positions in high-needs rural schools. PIRLL focused on existing teacher-leaders within the partner schools and districts as a primary source for recruitment. Already connected to their community, these teacher-leaders presented the greatest potential for retention as building principals. As South Dakota Secretary of Education Dr. Melody Schopp (personal communication, 2009) indicated to the current PIRLL master's cohort, "PIRLL provides the potential to build a leadership cohort from within, with those of you who understand the culture and the schools in which you are serving." This is sometimes referred to as "growing your own leaders."

According to Browne-Ferrigno and Allen (2006), "Transient student populations, ethnic and cultural diversity, and achievement gaps also contribute to creating hard-to-staff schools in both urban and rural settings" (p. 1). Students in the two cohorts signed a contract stating that upon completion of their PK-12 administrative degrees and licensure, they would continue to serve in rural high-needs South Dakota schools for three years and apply for at least three principal positions in those schools determined as high-needs by the Census Poverty Data by Local Educational Agency reports.

Collaboration of Partners

One of the main successes of this project was the groundwork in coordinating all of the major partners. Project staff worked with leaders of the various partner organizations to gain statewide and joint university commitment to a hybrid master's degree program in PK-12 Administration. Coursework from both the University of South Dakota and Sinte Gleska University (located on the Rosebud Sioux Indian Reservation) was used. A thorough Memorandum of Understanding (MOU) was signed by leaders in the following agencies: South Dakota Department of Education, South Dakota Board of Regents, Sinte Gleska University, University of South Dakota, and Technology and Innovation in Education. The MOU allowed for a contextually rich and relevant instructional design leading to hybrid graduate degrees in educational administration and completion of all requirements for certification as a school administrator. The importance of this preliminary work for the MOU, which included state, local, and tribal agencies, is noted in the summary statements from *Tribal Leaders Speak: The State of Indian Education* (2011). According to summary statements from this report, "In the consultations, federally recognized tribes and American Indian educators indicated that 'disconnects' between these different education systems and funding streams cause a significant disruption in accountability, efficient resource allocation, and quality education delivery" (p. 14).

Throughout the four-year period, as courses were designed to accommodate the rural and geographically isolated nature of these high-needs districts and the desire to have relevant and current content in their instructional courses, the MOU was of great value in ensuring continuing endorsement by all partners. This collaboration served as the basis for the coursework which emphasized the day-to-day issues pertinent to these rural high-needs districts and established the partnership for this hybrid program.

Instructors

The PIRLL project engaged instructors who were currently active in educational initiatives and roles across the state. These instructors included the South Dakota State Secretary of Education, the Leadership Development Director from South Dakota Associated School Boards, practicing principals and assistant superintendents — all of whom were educational leaders who placed a strong emphasis on student achievement. These instructors had a high commitment to the success of the goals of the PIRLL grant and took extra effort in ensuring that the coursework was relevant and addressed current issues such as the implementation of the Common Core Standards and the newly adopted South Dakota Framework for Teaching.

Instructors went beyond expectations in giving relevant, specific and frequent feedback to each individual participant. Because the success and growth of each participant was a priority, project directors had frequent interaction with the individual students providing encouragement and support. Use of a wiki space (http://pirll.tie.wikispaces.net) (see appendix) aided in the communication and accessibility of relevant materials and information. The frequent interactions among instructors, students and project directors were a valuable component.

Curriculum

Project coordinators were able to design the content for each course, ensuring updated curricula. Central to the curriculum was the use of The Interstate School Leaders Licensure Consortium (ISLLC) Standards which were developed by the Council of Chief State School Officers (2008); current national trends; current university syllabi; and leadership components. Preservice administrative programs emphasized leading individual and organizational change processes; fostering school improvement; using data for instructional improvement; and leading effective professional development (Darling-Hammond, LaPointe, Meyerson, Orr, & Cohen, 2007). Each class incorporated and emphasized these concepts. Also included in the curriculum were activities showing the relationship between the ISLLC Standards and the 21 Leadership Responsibilities identified by Marzano, Waters, and McNulty (2005). As one program participant stated, "... I thought the focus on being an instructional leader as an administrator was very important. This was the focus in many of the classes within the program."

The ISLLC Standards were infused into all coursework, starting with Introduction to Administration which included activities from *Practicing the Art of Leadership: A Problem-Based Approach to Implementing the ISLLC Standards* (Green, 2008). Various scenarios from this book were used during classes throughout the program. The PIRLL project also used the Educational Leadership Constituent Council (ELCC) Program Standards to guide the planning and implementation of coursework and internship, as required by the National Council for Accreditation of Teacher Education (NCATE) and adopted by the South Dakota Board of Regents. There was continuity between the ISLLC Standards and the ELCC Standards; however, South Dakota has not yet established state standards for principals.

University comprehensive exams were modified to match the change to current curricular content. An exit presentation and interview were conducted by the university supervisors to assess each individual's growth during the course of the 32 administrative credits. Rubrics were developed for both the portfolio and the interview. This culminating activity assisted students in summarizing their learning from their studies and helped prepare them for the administrative position interviewing process.

Internship

The student requirements for the master's program included an internship, for which *A Handbook for Educational Leadership Interns: A Rite of Passage* (Cunningham, 2006) was an integral part. Many components of this book, based on the ISLLC framework, were shared with principals and superintendents in advance of the student's internship. This handbook provided specific examples of possible activities under each ISLLC standard which helped districts utilize the intern's skills to work on important projects for the school and district. The length of the internship was a full year, giving students the opportunity to participate in an annual sequence of activities.

During the internship, students were required to complete a diversity experience, shadowing a principal from a district which was different from the district in which they were currently employed. In the program exit survey, one student noted,

> I felt that the diverse experience – shadowing a principal out of our district was very informative for me and I loved seeing the way their school functioned and the advice I received. Being a member of the Building Leadership Team (BLT), this experience gave me many personal experiences that will benefit my career as I pursue it. I learned many aspects of being a leader during this and it gave me many hands-on experiences that applied to what we were learning in the cohort. (personal communication, 2010)

The internship provided a prime example of the collaboration by instructors and project directors through the integration of student coursework and project expectations. In the course called *Administration and Supervision*, each student designed a teacher evaluation instrument using Danielson's *Enhancing Professional Practice: A Framework for Teaching* (2007), on which the South Dakota Teacher Framework is based. Students then continued their learning by implementing these evaluation instruments during their internship. In addition to benefiting the interns this also provided the districts with a model. During Introduction *to Educational Administration*, students orally presented their personal vision about learning and leading. In their portfolio presentation at the conclusion of their master's courses, students reflected on their initial vision and described any evolution that had taken place over the course of the two-year program.

Evaluation

Surveys were administered for each course in addition to an exit survey for the entire administrative program (see appendix). Project leadership looked thoroughly at all comments and ratings and made adjustments as needed. Through the exit survey rating the entire program, 100% of students agreed or strongly agreed that *the content of the courses included a balance of theory and practical information* and *the content of the courses was relevant to my developing career*. For the Internship course, a self-assessment and an assessment by the field supervisor were required by the university.

The design of the second master's cohort incorporated input from the first cohort. Face-to-face meetings were deemed important by participants, so at least one was held for each course, generally at a central location in the state. One need identified by the first cohort was for increased conversation with the field supervisor (principal) regarding each intern. Again, the wide geographical nature of the state and the involved districts presented a challenge in these interactions. In an effort to further communications with principals, superintendents, and school boards, project leaders shared newsletter updates in both paper and digital formats.

End-of-class and exit surveys indicated a need for additional community and cultural aspects, thus a community/culture course was added. Surveys also indicated differences in instructor requirements for American Psychological Association (APA); therefore course instructors in the second cohort collaborated and developed a graduated APA requirement for each course. Having instructors collaborate and agree on common requirements was a benefit. Instructors also agreed on requirements for student online discussion posts.

Experience from the first cohort indicated that the PIRLL grant needed to further emphasize the desire and intent of the participant to enter the administrative field during the application process. This process was intensified by including responses to a statement of purpose about their core beliefs regarding school leaders in high-needs schools; their purpose for attaining an administrative degree; leadership experiences; mentoring experiences; collaboration; additional professional experiences; and service to their school or district. These components are emphasized by Norton (2002). Applicants also submitted three references, including one from their direct supervisor. This emphasized the endorsement of the applicant by the district in identifying and preparing the next generation of school leaders and served as a reference when initiating the administrative internship.

To summarize the first key element, it was important to have a MOU from all state and university partners indicating their support for a hybrid program and directed at the project's goals. It was critical to have instructors who were embedded in the project goals and able to work collaboratively with other instructors to create a continuum of educational content that was relevant to rural high-needs districts with an emphasis on leadership skills which ultimately improve student achievement. It was imperative that both instructors and project leaders had frequent contact with students to ensure their success. Teachers in the graduate program were selected from high-needs rural schools to ensure their understanding and continued commitment to serving as school leaders in those settings. A contract with each student to ensure their continued work in high-needs schools and a desire to serve as principals in those schools was essential.

By the end of the five-year grant, 68 students completed their PK-12 Educational Administration degree and became credentialed to serve as PK-12 administrators. The PK-12 certification was a benefit to the many small districts that have combined principal duties to cover both elementary and secondary assignments. The need for principals to wear many hats and address many roles was noted by Darling-Hammond et al. (2007) who stated, "Contemporary school administrators play a daunting array of curriculum and assessment experts, budget analysis, facility managers, special program administrators, and community builders" (p. 2). This was even more relevant in small rural districts since there was frequently only one principal in the school and sometimes for the entire district.

KEY ELEMENT TWO: MENTORING AND PROFESSIONAL DEVELOPMENT FOR PRACTICING PRINCIPALS

The PIRLL grant provided for the design and implementation of an annual yearlong Leadership Academy for practicing principals and assistant principals. A key element of this program was the use of mentors to provide personal and professional support which was on-site and job embedded. Given the context of remote locations and the demands on principals in these high-needs schools, it was imperative to deliver professional development to participants in the most time efficient and convenient manner possible. Thus, each principal and assistant principal was matched with a mentor who met with them regularly throughout each academic year. By building relationships and providing targeted professional development that was also connected to school improvement goals, mentors provided principals and assistant principals with opportunities formerly unavailable in rural South Dakota.

The structure for the mentoring support and for building principals' leadership capacity was provided by the yearlong Leadership Academy which included two whole-group face-to-face events each year, monthly mentor visits, and in the fourth year, a more deliberate use of technology. Using a blended coaching model, principals and assistant principals were encouraged to take advantage of their mentors' experience and knowledge for concerns or issues related to their daily professional responsibilities as well as their personal skills.

The mentors recruited for this program were recently retired principals who had demonstrated leadership skills, had experience in rural South Dakota settings, and who possessed the ability to support practicing principals and assistant principals. According to a policy brief published by the Institute for Educational Leadership (IEL, 2004), "Ongoing relationships with skilled and carefully matched mentors offer a powerful source of leadership preparation and support" (p. 4). In an effort to build their skills and capacity, the PIRLL project provided mentors with ongoing professional development in several areas, including eight days of training in cognitive coaching. Other topics included Marzano and Water's 21 Leadership Responsibilities, especially those associated with second level change or leading an effective Professional Learning Community (PLC); sensitivity to issues related to poverty; and understanding of Native American culture and education. Mentors often functioned as their own support group or network, sharing agendas and mentoring strategies.

Mentor roles and responsibilities included monthly face-to-face meetings with their mentees with telephone and e-mail correspondence between visits. During the on-site meetings, the mentors provided targeted professional development and guided the principals' development of individual Leadership Action Plans (LAP) with an emphasis on reflection and the use of evidence to measure the effectiveness of their goals. Each mentor submitted a monthly log for each principal with whom they worked. These logs included the number of face-to-face meetings, phone and e-mail contacts, and hours of professional development at each visit. Mentors also included comments, observations, and evidence of progress on each principal's leadership action plan.

The PIRLL mentors embraced their mentoring role and showed a sincere desire to be as helpful and effective for their principal mentees as possible. The relationships between mentor and principal developed over the course of the project as well, making the support offered more personal and relevant to each principal's specific situation and needs. Increased time spent training and communicating with mentors has also been a successful strategy for the project. Dr. Richard Bordeaux, a member of the Rosebud Sioux Tribe, a PIRLL mentor and chair of the EDAD department at Sinte Gleska University, described the mentors' role as "promoting in our mentees a position of identifying, protecting and fostering the resiliency factors of their students which will minimize the effects of the risk factors [present in the project schools]" (personal communication, 2011). In one end-of-year survey, 100% of the principals (mentees) responded *Very True* or *Mostly True*, "Working with my mentor has given me ideas for reflection on my administrative activities and professional growth."

Professional development for principals focused on leadership for improved student achievement. Bizzell (2011) stated, "If professional development is to make an impact on practice, it must be delivered over time, job embedded and allow for reflection" (p. 5). He added that it must also be connected to school improvement goals and student achievement.

A template for the LAP was provided each year by project leaders and each principal wrote a minimum of three goals each year. One project-level goal was the same for all participants and required that they lead an effective PLC. Suggested action steps under this goal included application of at least one of the Leadership Responsibilities associated with leading an effective PLC (from their self-assessment). A second goal was written which connected to school-wide improvement planning or initiatives required by their own districts or at their schools. A final goal was developed for personal growth, based on the principal's self-assessment or on the National Association of Secondary School Principals (NASSP) 360 Survey. Most of the LAPs were developed collaboratively with mentors and then submitted to project staff.

In an end-of-year survey, 100% of participants responded *Very True* or *Mostly True* that, "Creating and following the Leadership Action Plan helped me improve in specific ways and/or accomplish specific goals." Improvements included improved student achievement, leadership skills, and personal growth. Additional professional development topics for principals included leadership of effective professional learning communities, addressing team dysfunctions, and the 21 Leadership Responsibilities. According to Bizzell (2011), "There is considerable agreement regarding the specific leadership skills necessary to foster enhanced student achievement and these skills align with accepted standards for school leaders"

(p. 10-11). There was also a high degree of similarity between the ISLLC Standards introduced to the aspiring leaders (PIRLL Objective 1) and the 21 Leadership Responsibilities which were implemented by the practicing principals (PIRLL Objective 2).

The PIRLL grant embraced several partnerships and connections with other initiatives. The PIRLL goal and objectives aligned with those of the South Dakota Incentives Plus (SDI+), a federal Teacher Incentive Fund (TIF) grant; both sought to build the capacity of school administrators who serve in high-needs schools. In partnering with SDI+, PIRLL maximized its resources and integrated efforts aimed at supporting the development of principals in high-needs schools. A concerted effort was also made to align professional development provided to the PIRLL principals with statewide initiatives such as the adoption of the South Dakota Framework for Teaching and the Common Core Standards. Book studies and graduate classes which supported project goals were also offered at no cost. The PIRLL grant provided strong links between retired principals and practicing principals, and also between practicing principals and aspiring leaders for whom they now serve as internship supervisors. In the latter years of the project, there was an increased use of technology with the addition of webinars and a virtual PLC aimed at maximizing networking and collaboration among colleagues across the project. It is hoped that this virtual networking is a connection that can be scaled up, supported and sustained at a statewide level.

Retention of principals (and superintendents) in these high-needs schools was challenging. Only one district had the same administrative team for the entire grant period and extra time and effort were required annually to assist new principals in acquiring necessary knowledge and skills previously introduced to returning principals. Every participant who began participating in the mentoring program chose to continue with the activity. By the second year, 100% of the eligible principals and assistant principals elected to be a part of the on-site mentoring and professional development program offered through the grant. The other important fact in the area of retention is that the same cadre of mentors was retained during the grant. This benefited the project, the participants, and the mentors.

According to South Dakota Secretary of Education Dr. Melody Schopp (personal communication, 2010), "We have seen that having mentors who can come to the principals to provide support where they are and work has been a unique method. While we have always struggled to provide ongoing support and funds for mentoring, it is something we need to consider continuing to find ways to help keep this work going."

To summarize the second key element, the support provided by on-site mentors was practical and focused, specific to each administrator's unique contexts and responsive to his or her needs. It enhanced school leadership skills and effective leadership of professional learning communities which emphasized increased student success. In addition, the retention rate for principals and assistant principals has increased.

CONCLUSIONS AND IMPLICATIONS

The two project objectives supported by this grant have had a significant leadership impact on the participants, their schools and districts, and across South Dakota. The first key element allowed 68 aspiring school leaders to earn degrees and become certified to lead high-needs rural South Dakota schools. Some newly credentialed participants were hired immediately upon receiving their degrees and began serving as principals, superintendents, and special-area directors. Others have utilized their skills, strategies, and knowledge to address current educational trends as teacher-leaders and members of their BLT.

The second key element addressed capacity building for over 60 current principals practicing in rural and remote sites across the state. It included a Leadership Academy and an on-site mentoring program which provided solid, consistent support from experienced mentors. Principals and assistant principals set specific goals and made plans to achieve them. They also increased their knowledge and skills with regard to leadership in their school contexts. Due to the PIRLL grant's training, support, and emphasis on building relationships, participants were better prepared to influence and effectively guide their schools, districts and learning communities. This was reflected by principals and their mentors in year-end reflections. In one survey, 80% of the principals responded *Very True* or *Mostly True*, "Student learning has been impacted by my participation in the Leadership Academy, Summer Institute and working with my mentor." In their year-end reflections, principals identified several recurring themes:

- Use of new leadership strategies, such as World Café to develop vision and mission statements
- Improved culture, communication and staff-student relationships
- Use of data to narrow instructional focus and improve student learning
- Effective leadership of a PLC.

Implications for preparing aspiring principals to serve in rural high-needs schools include the necessity of designing of a customized graduate program. Such a program needs to include a close working relationship with institutions of higher education and their governing board; an emphasis on relevant course design and content taught by instructors who are current in their fields and knowledgeable about rural and cultural issues; a yearlong internship; and extensive and regular use of formative assessments to provide responsiveness to program and student needs. Before enrolling in the program, students must commit to working three years in a high-needs school after they receive their degrees.

Implications for the support of principals in rural high-needs schools include the necessity for job-embedded on-site professional development and mentoring, based on the needs of each principal. Development and implementation of a personalized Leadership Action Plan can provide evidence of goal completion if it is regularly monitored by experienced mentors. An on-site program has financial implications in rural areas due to the distance between sites; however, the benefits of having the principal remain at his or her school for professional development and mentoring outweigh the expenses incurred by mentor travel.

Due to the PIRLL grant, over 130 aspiring and practicing principals have built their leadership capacity, and formed a cohort with whom to network, as they tackle the challenges of serving as school leaders in rural high-needs schools.

REFERENCES

Benson, D. A., Lies, A., Okunade, A. A., & Wunnava, P. V. (2009). *Small business economics of the Lakota fund on the Native American Indian reservation*. IZA Discussion Paper No. 3933. Bonn, Germany.

Bizzell, B. E. (2011). *Professional development of school principals in the rural Appalachian region of Virginia*. Doctoral dissertation. Retrieved from Virginia Tech digital library and archives.

Browne-Ferrigno, T., & Allen, L. W. (2006). Preparing principals for high-needs rural schools: A central office perspective about collaborative efforts to transform school leadership. *Journal of Research in Rural Education, 21*(1), 1.

Council of Chief State School Officers. (2008). *Educational leadership policy standards: ISLLC 2008*. National Policy Board for Educational Administration.

Cunningham, W. G. (2006). *A handbook for educational leadership interns: A rite of passage*. Boston, MA: Pearson.

Danielson, C. (2007). *Enhancing professional practice: A framework for teaching* (2nd ed.). Alexandria, VA: Association for Supervision and Curriculum Development.

Darling-Hammond, L., LaPointe, M., Meyerson, D., Orr, M., & Cohen, C. (2007). *Preparing school leaders for a changing world: Lessons from exemplary leadership development programs.* Stanford, CA: Stanford University.

Green, R. L. (2008). *Practicing the art of leadership: A problem-based approach to implementing the ISLLC standards* (3rd ed.). Boston, MA: Pearson.

Institute for Educational Leadership (IEL). (2004). *Preparing leaders for rural schools: Practice and policy considerations.* Retrieved from http://www.iel.org/pubs/ruralleaders.pdf

Marzano, R., Waters, T., & McNulty, B. (2005). *School leadership that works: From research to results.* Alexandria, VA: Association for Supervision and Curriculum Development.

Norton, J. (2002). *Preparing school leaders: It's time to face the facts.* Atlanta, GA: Southern Regional Education Board. Retrieved from http://www.wallacefoundation.org/knowledge-center/school-leadership/principal-training/Documents/Redesigning-Leadership-Preparation-for-Student-Achievement.pdf.

Sawyer, D. (Reporter). (2011). *Hidden America: Children of the plains* [Television series episode]. In D. Sloan (Executive Producer), 20/20. New York, NY: ABC News.

US Department of Education. (2011). *Tribal leaders speak: The state of Indian Education, 2010.* Retrieved from http://www2.ed.gov/about/inits/ed/indianed/consultations-report.pdf

APPENDIX

http://pirll.tie.wikispaces.net/PIRLL+General+Information

ELCC Standards
End-of-class Survey
Internship Portfolio Presentation Rubric
Internship Portfolio Rubric
ISLLC Standards
Leadership Action Plan Template
Master's Contract Template
Master's Program Exit Survey
Mentor Survey
Principal Survey
Statement of Purpose Rubric
21 Leadership Responsibilities

CHAPTER 8

RE-DESIGNING LESSONS, RE-ENVISIONING PRINCIPALS: DEVELOPING ENTREPRENEURIAL SCHOOL LEADERSHIP

Kristy Hebert, Josh Bendickson, Eric W. Liguori, K. Mark Weaver and Charles Teddlie

ABSTRACT

Social entrepreneurs and market-driven organizations are those that hold themselves accountable to both social and financial outcomes; they advance their mission by building focused strategies and sustainable business models that address customer needs and yield competitive advantage. In order to apply these market-based approaches toward social solutions, leaders must first be equipped with skills and resources to build organizational capacity that can deliver results. Wendy Kopp, Founder and Executive Director of Teach for America, recently summarized this point during a convening at the Annie E. Casey Foundation of leaders across sectors: "There's nothing more important than talent and team in organization building as we think about how to get where we want to go". Teach for America address. Annie E. Casey Foundation Baltimore, MD).

This chapter showcases this principle in action through the work of a nonprofit in Louisiana, Advance Innovative Education (AIE), which is gaining national attention for its innovative approach to education reform. AIE is improving student outcomes one school at a time by transforming school principals into social entrepreneurs. Its program draws on best practices across sectors and teaches school leaders how to harness market forces to deliver better educational opportunities to children.

INTRODUCTION

The majority of public school children (K-12) are educationally under served (Weber, 2010). They are not reaching their academic potential, as evidenced by high drop-out rates, low college graduation numbers, and abysmal academic achievement. Historic efforts to improve schools have rarely achieved their intent. Current methods of addressing the needs for improved school and student performance are unfortunately not functioning as intended (Weber, 2010).

The social impact of an unhealthy public education system is vast and far-reaching, and previous attempts to fill the gaps have failed for the most part. While some legislation has been approved to provide policy to support reform in public education, this policy is meaningless unless carried out by appropriately trained educational leaders. School leaders who embrace the tenets of social entrepreneurship are able to envision successful strategies and programs that have a high probability of improving the education sector (Weaver et al., 2012). Few current leaders understand that schools are a revenue-generating business with a social-value-generating structure (Cornwall, 2003).

Although a decrease in state and local revenues has had implications on education in many regions, federal funds to support public education have helped make up for this deficiency including an approximately $100 billion stimulus package (Hanushek, 2010). As a result, schools are able to invest in innovative programs to enhance learning environments; however, few leaders in public schools have awareness, much less an understanding, of how to leverage these funds. These issues as well as other fundamental concerns are addressed in the subsequent sections of this chapter. We address the creation of principals as social entrepreneurs and some of the implications. Lastly, through the use of data analysis, we address some of the lessons learned in the project.

CREATING SOCIAL ENTREPRENEURS: AIE, LSU, AND RLRP

AIE (a 501(c)(3) nonprofit founded in Louisiana), along with the E.J. Ourso College of Business at Louisiana State University, has created Re-designing Lessons, Re-envisioning Principals (RLRP), a nontraditional pathway to prepare educational leaders. RLRP is a principal development program based on developing individuals who will operate schools as successful nonprofits. Business and education principles intersect to develop educational leaders who focus on the "double bottom line," ensuring that schools are always focused on their mission and producing results for their clients, while at the same time generating the revenue required to operate the core business and reinvest profits into new or expanded services.

The dominant (traditional) models of education are failing and the silos and bureaucracy present do not enable the changes necessary to move forward (Wolk, 2011). Thus, there is an urgent need to produce school leaders with the capacity to tackle these unique challenges. These challenges may include either repairing broken systems or creating ones that provide a platform for success. Education needs leaders who are social entrepreneurs, possess turnaround skills, and have the ability to organize and serve their clients. Essentially, principals must be CEOs of their schools (Cornwall, 2003).

Business and economic development principles are strongly tied to the reform of public education (cf., Peterson, 2010; Weaver et al., 2012). In fact, economic growth is dependent upon schools that can produce students who have 21st-century skills and knowledge — for current needs as well as those not yet identified (e.g., Isenberg, 2011). Creating a proficient labor pool is of utmost importance in building stronger local economies. While students are usually the component that most readily comes to mind in thinking of the expansion of quality work force development, teachers play an incredibly important role. RLRP principals recognize that a quality teaching force impacts real dollars in communities, and what it means to transform potential into exponential as depicted and described in Fig. 1 (Louisiana Governor's Legislative Package, January, 2012).

The applicants to RLRP are looking to be catalysts of change — to develop *their* potential. RLRP customizes development plans to meet the needs of each resident (both in the delivery of curricula and in the financing of the tuition). This is a key success factor, given each resident comes from a different context (i.e., charter schools, various forms within

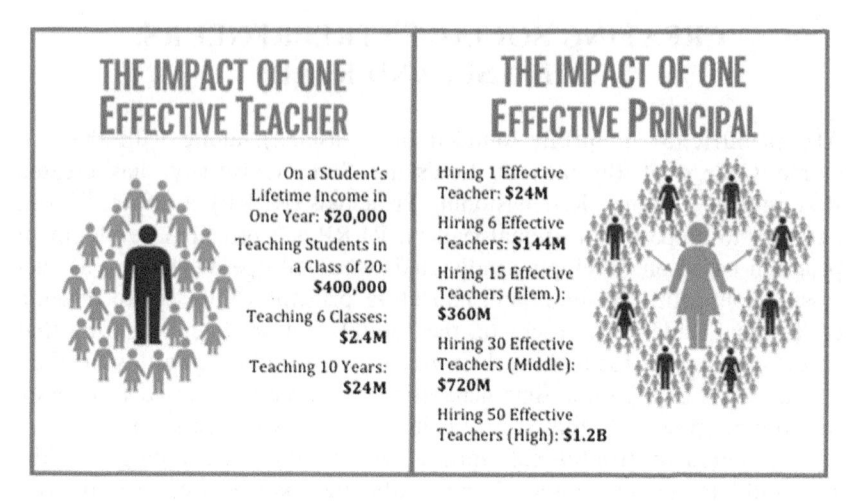

THE IMPACT OF ONE EFFECTIVE TEACHER	THE IMPACT OF ONE EFFECTIVE PRINCIPAL
On a Student's Lifetime Income in One Year: **$20,000** Teaching Students in a Class of 20: **$400,000** Teaching 6 Classes: **$2.4M** Teaching 10 Years: **$24M**	Hiring 1 Effective Teacher: **$24M** Hiring 6 Effective Teachers: **$144M** Hiring 15 Effective Teachers (Elem.): **$360M** Hiring 30 Effective Teachers (Middle): **$720M** Hiring 50 Effective Teachers (High): **$1.2B**

Fig. 1. From Potential to Exponential: The Return on Investment for One Effective Principal in One Year.

traditional school districts). The organizations that hire RLRP Residents are looking for leadership that will propel their strategic plans for their students. Additionally the organizations that are looking to AIE are doing so because of the large number of principals near retirement and the shrinking pool of *qualified* candidates to replace them.

RLRP provides an opportunity to produce new leaders who have the courage and skills to change school cultures, pushing instructional issues to the forefront of the reform agenda. By exposing participants to new philosophies and techniques, RLRP teaches its participants the necessity of integrating best practices of both business and education that drive schools to meet their charge of student success. RLRP is delivered over 14 months (two summers and the school year). The goal is to provide candidates with a solid foundation of theory, best practices, and technical know-how combined with opportunities to apply knowledge to solve real-life problems as they relate to student success. The measure of a Resident's success at the end of the 14-month program includes proficient portfolio of experiences and a passing score on the School Leadership Licensure Assessment.

At a recent Wallace Foundation conference (Louisiana, 2010), a presenter stated that soon private providers (for principal training) would put university departments of administration and supervision out of business because RLRP offers support far beyond the participant's enrollment. RLRP Alumni join a growing collaborative network that provides varying degrees of assistance. According to Peter Drucker (1999), "Knowledge has to be improved, challenged, and increased constantly, or it vanishes." AIE embraces Drucker's philosophy contending that a long-term focus on knowledge will provide school success.

RLRP's cohort structure reflects the development of a learning community. RLRP takes several best practices of business and nonprofit management and combines them with the best practices of education. The vision behind RLRP is to refocus public education so that large-scale student success is a reality. Through RLRP, the result of the partnership between AIE and LSU's E.J. Ourso College of Business, successful strides have been made toward this vision and these goals.

Embedded, sustained experiences, rather than short workshops, characterize a key element of RLRP's pedagogical approach. During internships, Residents complete "action research." They work with individual mentors to identify a project in the school that is more than just an oversight of traditional school management. AIE teaches Residents grant writing, how to obtain money from corporations, and how to leverage the per pupil dollars that come from the state. These experiences provide principals with the skills to obtain necessary resources to enable greater overall success. Maximizing Resident capabilities in these areas provides them with the knowledge not only for short-term success, but enhances their talent for long-term viability.

BUILDING SOCIAL ENTERPRISES

The RLRP program is designed to teach leaders how to run a school like a business. We believe competition is a good thing and that all schools should function autonomously with their profits dependent on the educational market. Just as CEOs are accountable to a board, it is also important for principals to report to a governing mechanism. Principals must manage money in a way they see fit to maximize student achievement. RLRP participants must know how to maximize community resources to fund school initiatives and to make up for budget shortfalls in tough economic times when states are freezing or even reducing educational budgets.

RLRP emphasizes that balancing a budget is not only about making cuts, as most traditional school systems do, but also increasing revenue.

This concept is not often found in traditional models of principal preparation (Cornwall, 2003). RLRP's model sees a principal as competing with other budget planners and executors for access to necessary resources. Rather than a bureaucratic decision-making process, followed in many traditional systems, RLRP encourages Residents to take action and develop innovative ways to increase revenue as one might see in the market. Most of the RLRP participants enter the program without much of a business background, so they benefit from classes provided by the Louisiana State University E.J. Ourso College of Business, one of the project partners. While emphasizing the creation of social enterprises, these classes deal also with everything from marketing to consulting. In the development of RLRP, we created a particularly helpful class called "Other People's Resources." Access to resources is fundamental to gaining a competitive advantage (Barney, 1991), and finding ways to gain control of these can greatly reduce a school's dependence on the uncertainties of operating only on state funding (Pfeffer & Salancik, 2003). Together these programs are taking important steps forward in educating and providing principals with necessary tools to become successful in a changing educational environment.

Throughout their residency (school year) RLRP participants are assigned to a Learning Team. These learning teams comprise three to five members of a cohort. Each Learning Team is given $1,500 in start-up money to finance a project(s).Managing this revenue teaches Residents financial skills with a focus on investment and implementation of an entrepreneurial endeavor. This provides a valuable leadership experience and readies them for using grant dollars as a way to initiate long-term investments. The "donation" works to help create an additional source of revenue and transfers into sustainability that will address meeting the mission of the school.

An example of an RLRP participant(s)-designed project was to launch a cyber café in a school. Teams used creativity and innovation in proposing a means to successfully complete the project. In a very insightful fashion, one of the team-leading Residents stated: "We want to get permission to open it up to parents." Thus, in stage one of the development, the cyber café was for students and then to be opened up to families. The following question was also raised, "Why go to Starbucks when there are so many perks of the local coffee shop that happens to be at school?"

Another team's vision was to begin to transform into a community economic development center. The center included classrooms with space for food prep and restrooms, so parents and community groups could have evening events or special classes. Further plans include eventually investing in a center for drop-out prevention as part of its service offering as well. Given time and guidance, teams find themselves creating great ideas and making entrepreneurial questions a regular part of educational leadership that they generally had not focused on throughout prior educational efforts.

THE ENTREPRENEURIAL PILLAR OF RLRP: LESSONS LEARNED

One of the most unique components of the RLRP program has been that from the beginning instilling an entrepreneurial approach to leadership was a core pillar of the curriculum. Certainly there was consensus that entrepreneurial leadership was needed in school reform, especially in a state as dire as Louisiana (see CABL, 2004). But despite this consensus, no one was exactly sure what the specific entrepreneurship curriculum needed to be. A temporal framework was approved by the State Department of Education (May, 2008) whereby the first year of the RLRP curriculum began with an intensive summer institute experience, and upon completion, students then progressed through two semesters of graduate coursework and coaching and mentoring during their residency or school year.

Traditional entrepreneurship students enter classes with a basic skill set learned through a core curriculum of business classes (e.g., accounting, finance, marketing, management). Essentially, they have a foundation of basic business acumen. This did not exist among the RLRP population of educators entering the program (most were not business majors and had limited experience outside of education). Given the unknown, in Year 1 RLRP followed what Popp (2011) now has termed the "add ideas, stir things up" approach to education reform. We did not consider this approach to have a negative connotation to it, rather we argued it to be one of the best strategies we could have employed − sometimes you just have to see what works for a given population.

This "formula for reform" has resulted in numerous successes, including the work of Joel Klein, former head of the Antitrust division of the Justice Department under President Clinton, who has been recognized as one of America's best education reformers by US News and World Report. As Chancellor of New York's Department of Education from 2002 to 2010, Klein led multiple reform initiatives on the premise that teachers are the most crucial component in a school system, and principals are the key change agents (Kingsbury, 2006). Klein attests that this approach necessitates change (Leadership for Change! Summit, January, 2012). The RLRP program shares this philosophy.

RLRP's entrepreneurial lesson number one is "Don't be afraid to make changes." We worked with the best entrepreneurship educators and subject matter experts available from around the country; the need for quality faculty goes without saying. They taught and mentored program participants on a variety of topics, from social entrepreneurship to entrepreneurial school leadership, to business planning and service learning. Continual assessment and feedback was gathered, and at the end of the first summer experience, some tough decisions had to be made: what worked and what did not, based on feedback and assessment results. Ultimately, we changed and rearranged components after this initial phase of the project. Some faculty members were not invited back, others were asked to teach different classes, and others were instructed to change their curriculum in their current classes. This process has happened after each subsequent summer experience, though the changes have been seemingly less severe over time (the core curriculum is now established).

As just mentioned briefly, from Day 1 the RLRP curriculum adopted an outcome focus. The LSU research team employed pre- and post−testing to assess progress. Additionally, it also conducted focus groups, supervisor and mentor evaluations, and site visits. Program participants also completed self-assessments to determine their level of entrepreneurial self-efficacy (ESE; items were from McGee, Peterson, Mueller, & Sequeira, 2009), educational entrepreneurial intentions (EEIs; Thompson, 2009, items were adapted to a school environment), their perceived behavioral control (PBC; Ajzen, 2002, items were adapted to a school environment), and their overall attitude toward venturing in an educational setting (ATV; McGee et al., 2009, items were adapted to a school environment). Our expectation, or working hypothesis, was that participant scores in each of these areas would increase over the course of the program. After all, Ronstadt (1985) noted that the implied objective of all entrepreneurial education is the production of more (and more skillful) entrepreneurs.

Yet, this hypothesis did not prove to be true, at least not initially. Table 1 contains the mean differences and descriptive statistics for each of the four focal variables as assessed immediately before and after the 2010 Summer Institute. Results show that the only significant change was in ESE, but the change was negative. These numbers were puzzling, depressing, and raised two important questions: (1) Why was there no

Table 1. Mean Differences and Descriptive Statistics: Pre and Post Summer Institute 2010.

Measure	Pre SI 2010 M	Pre SI 2010 SD	Post SI 2010 M	Post SI 2010 SD	Mean difference
ESE	5.04	.83	4.27	.71	.77*
EI	3.63	.89	3.55	.83	.08
PBC	4.93	.92	4.33	.69	.60
ATV	3.07	.36	3.43	.48	.36

Note: $N = 16$. diff = difference; ESE = entrepreneurial self-efficacy; EI = entrepreneurial intention; PBC = perceived behavioral control; ATV = attitude toward venturing.
*$p > .05$.

Table 2. Mean Differences and Descriptive Statistics: Pre Summer Institute 2010 − Post 2010 Coursework.

Measure	Pre SI 2010 M	Pre SI 2010 SD	Post Fall 2010 M	Post Fall 2010 SD	Mean difference
ESE	5.04	.83	5.87	.83	.83*
EI	3.63	.89	4.55	1.01	.92*
PBC	4.93	.92	5.23	.72	.30
ATV	3.07	.36	4.36	.88	1.29*

Note: $N = 16$. diff = difference; ESE = entrepreneurial self-efficacy; EI = entrepreneurial intention; PBC = perceived behavioral control; ATV = attitude toward venturing.
*$p > .05$.

significant improvement in EI, PBC, and ATV? And, (2) how is it possible that a five-week intensive training program can lower the efficacy perceptions of program participants?

The answer to these questions can be found in the entrepreneurship literature. For example, Krueger and Carsrud (1993) found that teaching individuals the true realities of entrepreneurship may actually lower the individual's desire to start a business. Basically, in five weeks of intensive training RLRP had overloaded the participants, and they needed time to reflect, absorb, and digest the material, or so it was hoped. Following Summer Institute the program participants have a short break and then begin graduate entrepreneurship coursework. Thankfully to RLRP's outcome measurement plan, data were collected again at the end of the Fall 2011 semester. Table 2 contains the mean differences and descriptive statistics for each of the four focal variables as assessed pre-Summer Institute and post-Fall 2010 coursework.

Results show positive changes in ESE perceptions, EEIs, and attitudes toward venturing in an educational setting. Thus, as the basic entrepreneurial skills and business language became more tacit over time, the true impact of the entrepreneurial component of RLRP began to emerge, and it was quite positive. No significant difference, positive or negative, however was found in the PBC measure. We speculate this is because regardless of improved self-efficacy perceptions, and positive intentions and attitudes, Residents still had a hard time seeing how they could break down the barriers to these types of behaviors in a traditional school setting. Ajzen (1988, 1991) posits that PBC is determined by one's total set of control beliefs (i.e., beliefs about the existence of factors that may facilitate or impede one's ability to carry out the behavior). In essence, we speculate that our Residents still did not perceive they would have the institutional support necessary to effect change, and in a Louisiana Public School that may very well be a true sentiment.

Overall, the partners were pleased with the progress and apparent impact the curriculum had on ESE, EI, and ATV. And, the partners remain optimistic RLRP can still teach and mentor Residents until they get to a point where they feel more confident in their ability to actually affect change, though it is worth noting that preliminary results from our more charter-school based cohorts do not appear to have the same PBC deficiency. Thus, the entrepreneurial lesson #2 is to expect a slump – efficacy perceptions can go down after training, but they should come back up over time.

CONCLUSION

Ultimately, the collaboration between AIE and LSU on the RLRP project provides key elements and suggestions for educators to consider. Creating social entrepreneurs and building social enterprises will be an important educational component of the future; providing excellent opportunities to train principals is fundamental in leading this progression. The data give insights to be mindful of the need to strive for success and to be ever cognizant of the need for continuous improvements on this project. A key take away is that it takes time for the impact of entrepreneurial education to emerge; the basic entrepreneurial skills and business language must first become tacit, and then entrepreneurial behavior will follow.

REFERENCES

Ajzen, I. (1988). *Attitudes, personality, and behavior*. Chicago: The Dorsey Press.
Ajzen, I. (1991). The theory of planned behavior. *Organizational Behavior and Human Decision Processes, 50*(2), 1–63.
Ajzen, I. (2002). Perceived behavioral control, self-efficacy, locus of control, and the theory of planned behavior. *Journal of Applied Social Psychology, 32*(4), 665–683.
Barney, J. (1991). Firm resources and sustained competitive advantage. *Journal of Management, 17*(1), 99–120.
CABL. (2004). *Statistics from the alliance for excellent education*. Baton Rouge, LA: Council for a Better Louisiana.
Cornwall, J. R. (2003). *From the ground up: Entrepreneurial school leadership*. Lanham, MD: R&L Education.
Drucker, P. (1999). *Innovation and entrepreneurship* (2nd ed.). Oxford: Butterworth-Heinemann.
Hanushek, E. A. (2010). Cry wolf! This budget crunch is for real. *Education Week, 29*(32), 32–40.
Isenberg, D. J. (2011). The entrepreneurship ecosystem strategy as a new paradigm for economic policy: Principles for cultivating entrepreneurship. Paper presented at the Institute of International European Affairs, Dublin, Ireland.
Kingsbury, A. (2006, October 20). Curing what ails the classroom. *U.S. News & World Report*.
Krueger, N., & Carsrud, A. (1993). Entrepreneurial intentions: applying the theory of planned behavior. *Entrepreneurship & Regional Development, 5*, 315–330.
McGee, J. E., Peterson, M., Mueller, S. L., & Sequeira, J. M. (2009). Entrepreneurial self-efficacy: Refining the measure. *Entrepreneurship Theory and Practice, 33*(4), 965–988.
Peterson, M. (2010, February 15). "Good to Great" hits grade school. *Business Week*, 56–58.
Pfeffer, J., & Salancik, G. (2003). *The external control of organizations: A resource dependence perspective.*. Stanford, CA: Stanford University Press.
Popp, T. (2011). Formula for education reform: Add ideas, stir things up. *The Pennsylvania Gazette, 109*, 30–38.
Ronstadt, R. (1985). The educated entrepreneurs: A new era of entrepreneurial education is beginning. *American Journal of Small Business, 10*(1), 7–23.
Thompson, E. R. (2009). Individual entrepreneurial intent: Construct clarification and development of an internationally reliable metric. *Entrepreneurship Theory and Practice, 33*(3), 669–694.
Weaver, K. M., Liguori, E. W., Hebert, K., & Vozikis, G. S. (2012). Building leaders in secondary education: An initial evaluation of an entrepreneurial leadership development program. *Journal of Higher Education Theory and Practice, 12*(1), 19–26.
Weber, K. (Ed.). (2010). *Waiting for "Superman": How we can save America's failing public schools*. New York: PublicAffairs.
Wolk, R. A. (2011). *Wasting minds: Why our education system is failing and what we can do about it*. Alexandria, VA: ACSD.

CHAPTER 9

LEARNING FROM THE EVOLUTION OF A UNIVERSITY–DISTRICT PARTNERSHIP

Karen L. Sanzo and Steve Myran

ABSTRACT

This chapter provides an overview of the development of a USDE SLP-funded leadership preparation partnership between a local school division and our university. We specifically describe our efforts to cultivate an authentic and purposeful partnership that would allow us to move beyond the limitations of the traditional leadership preparation programs that have been so widely criticized in the literature. This chapter describes the research and development efforts which involved iterative cycles of design, implementation, reflection, and redesign that helped to identify problems of practice and develop meaningful solutions to these identified areas of need. We also discuss four key elements of effective university–school partnerships that grew out of our efforts to build and refine an effective partnership.

A hallmark of the United States Department of Education (USDE) School Leadership Program (SLP) grant is the connectivity between various agencies to provide quality leadership preparation and development programs for aspiring and current school leaders. These collaborative efforts may involve districts, universities, city agencies, not-for-profit entities, foundations, private academic organizations, and others involved in the development of school leaders.

Our own USDE SLP grant was developed to (1) train aspiring leaders who will complete a leadership preparation and licensing program, (2) to prepare both aspiring and current school leaders to understand and use research-based educational strategies to guide and direct instruction, (3) to utilize contextually relevant, ongoing professional development, and (4) to update aspiring and current administrators' understanding of (a) supporting state-of-the-art data-driven decision-making practices and (b) effectively utilizing formative assessment practices. The goal of the program was to facilitate the district to "grow its own" leaders within the context of the school culture being served and to stabilize and strengthen the retention of school leaders who can successfully guide and direct instruction in a high-need LEA. This chapter describes the development and refinement of the district–university partnership.

Our SLP grant was developed from a partnership with a four-year foundation of a school district and university collaborating on professional development for school staff. We have sought in this chapter to provide a historical development of this partnership in order to help inform readers about the in-depth nature of partnership development. Hindsight provides perspective and can help inform other prospective partners seeking to engage in large-scale activities an understanding of the need to approach partnerships with deliberate intentionality, reflection, and an understanding of what is required to develop authentic partnerships. This chapter provides an overview of the development of that partnership and how lessons learned from the early years of this relationship contributed to School Leadership Program grant. We begin with a brief review of the literature around district–university partnerships, followed by a description of the evolution of the university–district partnership through the lens of activities we were engaged in around school district improvement. We provide lessons learned from our experiences with the hopes that others will benefit and use these as they develop their own partnerships.

CHANGING LEADERSHIP PROGRAMS

Leadership preparation programs designed to prepare staff for the challenges of administration positions (i.e., assistant principal, principal, curriculum leader) were once the sole domain of universities. Currently throughout the United States, school leadership preparation programs are being provided by other organizations, such as school districts, not-for-profit organizations, and for-profit providers. Changes in the way school leaders are prepared have been implemented for a variety of reasons, including more control over the way programs are developed and implemented, profitability perceived by some entities of these programs, as well as the result of complaints of traditional (university-based) preparation programs (Levine, 2005; Murphy, 2005; Walker & Qian, 2006). Critics lament that there is a strong disconnect between theory espoused in the classroom and the reality of the "on-the-job" work in the field (LaMagdeleine, Maxcy, Pounder, & Reed, 2009; Portin, Schneider, DeArmond, & Gundlach, 2003). Crow (2006) reports data from research studies on quality programs at the university level are scarce and there is poor programmatic quality control, leading to what Grogan, Bredeson, Sherman, Preis, and Beaty (2009) have cited as in part the catalyst for alternative preparation providers to proliferate.

While it is easy to bristle at some of the harsher complaints of critics about university-based leadership preparation programs, many Institutions of Higher Education (IHE) leadership preparation programs have not shied away from revising, and at times completely changing, their programs to address concerns from critics head on. At times, admittedly, these changes were politicized and foisted upon IHE's school leadership programs by state legislatures, as in the case with universities in Georgia. These programs were mandated by the state to "sunset" their original programs. New school leadership programs in Georgia were only able to offer accredited licensure degrees by changing their programs and partnering with school districts. Other universities throughout the nation have, or are, examining their own programs and making changes to address contemporary issues and needs of the school districts they serve.

Many universities have embraced change in their leadership preparation programs and have sought out ways to be innovative in the way they prepare aspiring school leaders and deliver instruction. Changes of this magnitude require many things, including faculty, input, and collaboration from school districts and current school leaders, as well as funding. One source of funding that has been available since 2002 is the USDE SLP. The USDE SLP emerged, in part, to address the critics and help prepare high-quality school leaders (Sanzo, Myran, & Clayton, 2011). Approximately 90 grants since the inception of the grant awards have been funded to support the preparation of aspiring and current assistant principals and principals. The grant money not only provides fiscal support to the funded grants, which Goodnough (2004) found in a study to be critical in partnership efforts, but the lesson learned and outcomes from the grants also inform the broader community of school leadership preparation providers. As indicated in the opening paragraph of this chapter, one of the key aspects of this program is the partnership between participating organizations within the grant.

DISTRICT–UNIVERSITY PARTNERSHIPS

There are many reasons why partnerships between school districts and IHE school leadership preparation programs make sense. For example, "well-articulated and coordinated programs with authentic university–district collaboration can bridge that theory to practice gap and work to provide authentic, in-depth, and meaningful experiences that will allow them to be much better prepared to become school leaders" (Sanzo et al., 2011, p. 295). At the university level, faculty members possess the requisite research skills and theoretical underpinnings to help develop effective and meaningful programs (Grogan & Andrews, 2002). They also can serve as change catalysts within districts to push unopposed assumptions and challenge the status quo (Sanzo et al., 2011). Sherman (2005) asserts that "[w]ithout a connection to the academy and a more global view of leadership, the result of stand-alone efforts is often a poorly designed program that tends to support only district views of leadership" (p. 711).

The inclusion of the district voice is just as important in the school leadership program partnerships (Peel, Peel, & Baker, 2002; Sanzo et al., 2011). "Although professors can design leadership preparation programs that focus on the theoretical underpinnings of educational administration, active engagement by practicing principals who serve as mentors to prospective candidates and novice school leaders provides authenticity" (Browne-Ferrigno & Muth, 2004, p. 471). Collaboration with school districts provides aspiring leaders authentic settings to learn in and the opportunity for "contextual relevance" (Sherman & Crum, 2009).

Undoubtedly, there can be difficulties implementing and sustaining a successful partnership between school district and university (Borthwick, Stirling, Nauman, & Cook, 2003). Evidence of successful partnership is scarce (Munoz, Winter, & Ricciardi, 2006; Simmons et al., 2007); however, the increasing attention to collaborative programs, such as the School Leadership Program grant, is providing more evidence for sustaining effective partnerships. One of the primary challenges identified to successful partnership is the inclusion of numerous people in the partnership (Borthwick et al., 2003; Miller & Hafner, 2008), clashing of beliefs and ideologies (Borthwick et al., 2003; Edens & Gilsinan, 2005), and the underlying reasons for the involvement of people and organizations in partnerships (Borthwick et al., 2003).

METHODS

Throughout the course of the partnership, university faculty were embedded in the collaborative efforts. Not only did we work together with the district in a concerted effort, we also engaged in substantive research efforts to identify problems of practice and develop meaningful solutions to address identified areas of need. These activities support the notion purported by Grogan and Andrews (2002) that faculty have the ability to conduct extensive and in-depth research that can then have practical applications in the PK-12 setting. Faculty can, in essence, help PK-12 teachers and administrators bridge the theory to practice gap and make the research meaningful and relevant. These research efforts were crucial to inform the development of the School Leadership Program grant proposal, and continue to be a primary avenue of research for us in our SLP efforts. Without focused, intentional research the ultimate work leading to the development of the SLP program would not have been possible. We present below a brief overview of design-based research to provide the reader a conceptual understanding of our work in the district.

Design-Based Research Methods

Research efforts since the beginning of the partnership in 2004 between Old Dominion faculty and Northampton County Schools' school leaders and teachers have drawn from the design-based research paradigm.

Design-based methods, according to Collins, Joseph, and Bielaczye (2004), were developed for educational settings to test and refine programs using theory, as well as formative data aimed at continuous program improvement. The knowledge gained via design-based research efforts is then utilized to iteratively improve the programs, with the goal of both producing new theory as well as identifying intervention to produce positive outcomes (Edelson, 2002).

Design-based research generally is conducted in a single-setting over a lengthy period of time. As evidenced by our work, these ongoing collaborative efforts were not activities that took place overnight. Rather, this represents a concerted effort among partners to make ongoing, substantive school improvement based upon theory, research, and practical application. We have used iterative cycles of design, implementation of intervention, examination of result, and redesign. The interventions utilized in these processes, in adhering to design-based research principles, have been contextually relevant.

DEVELOPMENT OF THE PARTNERSHIP

Given the importance of the iterative cycles of design, implementation, reflection, and redesign, a description of the development of the partnership with the school division involved in SLP project provides a clearer understanding of lessons learned from this work. Below is an overview of the development of the district–university partnership.

Background

Our USDE School Leadership Program grant is a collaboration between Northampton County Public Schools and Old Dominion University, both in Virginia. The partnership between the district and university was established in 2004 after the district superintendent contacted the then Dean of the College. A memorandum of agreement was developed with the intent to identify collaborative grants and other funding opportunities to help the district with a number of key school improvement needs. Initially small teams of educators from both the university and school system worked together to identify district needs and create supportive authentic activities. Given the lack of such programs that make authentic connections between schools and universities (Blumenfeld, Fishman, Krajcik, Marx, & Soloway,

2000), our efforts were geared toward identifying and refining genuine and effective ways of collaborating between public schools and universities.

The partnering district is a geographically isolated rural county in Virginia. With an agrarian economy, the county faces difficult financial challenges and is arguably one of the most economically disadvantaged counties in the state. The per capita income for the county is roughly half the state average. The district is a high-need school district with a diverse student body: African American (48%), White (37%), and Hispanic (13%). The district student population is approximately 2000 students, of which (60%) are economically disadvantaged.

Identifying Priorities

An initial task in our emerging partnership was to clearly identify the priorities of the school district, as well as to ensure that the priorities met the capacity of the university personnel involved in the initiative. One of the ways the university learned about the district and the priorities was by being closely involved in a variety of professional development activities with staff in a wide array of areas. These early efforts ranged from test score data disaggregation training to professional development in mathematics instruction.

Through these first-hand experiences university faculty worked shoulder to shoulder with school personnel. We were able to gain a depth of understanding about the complexities and challenges school personnel face that we would not have been able to learn by simply engaging in once a month conversations or general meetings. These experiences were critical to the understanding of the district needs, as well as enabling university personnel to obtain a level of buy-in from district staff that could not have been obtained otherwise.

Within the first year of the partnership we were able to secure state grant dollars that supported the stabilization of hard-to-staff teaching positions. The funding supported Instructional Support Team (IST) teachers in each elementary school and in building a distance learning lab (which has been central to the ongoing collaboration of multiple departments and programs in the university with the district). Over the next several years, a number of Teacher Quality grants were won that continued to build partnership momentum.

As the partnership grew, we were able to strengthen the level of trust and authenticity of the collaboration, which in turn gave university faculty involved in the partnership efforts access to the various stakeholders and vice versa. The increased level of trust enabled the partners to critically examine the types of projects and activities the district was engaged in and compare these district priorities and needs. While the first several years of the partnership had resulted in a notable influx of grant funding and greater human and financial resources, the team observed a number of disconnects between the different levels of the organizations involved. Observations and feedback suggested there were different conceptual understandings of the purpose and goals of the partnership. Without trust, the partners would not have been able to have direct, honest conversations about the various initiatives within the district and to examine whether or not certain activities, even though they were garnering funds from external sources, were in line with the direction of the district. The team was able to assess strengths and weaknesses of the different projects and develop clearer and more strategically linked goals and objectives.

University personnel had a unique opportunity to work directly with teachers and school administrators, as well as central office leaders. This provided access to all stakeholders within the district and to hear the diverse voices and opinions from across the district about the school system's initiatives and direction. This feedback, at times solicited and at other times unsolicited and provided spontaneously throughout the partnership activities, revealed a great deal of frustration among teachers. Teachers expressed their perceptions about an overwhelming number of disparate activities under way in the distract. Teachers felt there were too many improvement initiatives and they lacked the understanding about how these were linked. These teachers were overwhelmed by the volume of activities and felt pulled in many different directions. In contrast many central office administrators believed there was continuity and clear focus on the various initiatives and did not always understand why the teachers were concerned about what was under way.

As such it was increasingly apparent that while many aspects of the partnership were successful, how these various efforts were strategically linked and how they helped build the organizational capacity to address the real needs of the school district needed to be clarified and strengthened. It seemed that the initial partnership effort successes were having a counter effect – too much funding success led to an influx of activities requiring staff to participate in more professional development. We hesitate to say the district was participating in more initiatives than when this partnership originally started. Rather, the initiatives were increasing in intensity and stratification, impacting more teachers in diverse ways than in years past.

For example, related arts teachers were required to participate in professional development on math and science. The challenge was to demonstrate the connections of the initiatives across instructional disciplines, as well as incorporate these activities into the district framework without overloading staff with new priorities.

In an effort to address this issue we conducted a survey of school personnel and central office administrators. We inquired about the different "perceived" initiatives across the district.

– Teachers were asked to: "list all the school improvement or professional development initiatives you are required to attend to and for which you may be evaluated on"
– Principals and other school level administrators were asked to: "list all the school improvement or professional development initiatives you or your teachers are required to attend to and for which you and your teachers may be evaluated on"
– Central office administrators were asked to: "list all the school improvement or professional development initiatives the teachers and administrators in your schools are required to attend to and for which they may be evaluated on."

The survey also incorporated an open-ended question: "what other feedback would you like to share about the various school improvement efforts currently under way in the district?" to provide an opportunity for additional input.

Clarifying Priorities

After summarizing the results we found that teachers listed 31 distinct district program initiatives they believed they could be assessed on in their annual evaluation. These were at every level of the larger organization from building level to district level as well as partnership initiatives and state-mandated programs. In many cases the teachers did not know the impetus or the purpose of the initiative, and viewed it as a disconnected and burdensome obligation. Teachers tended to list different related expectations or elements of the improvement efforts separately, revealing they may not have been provided adequate opportunity to develop a big picture of understanding how the individual elements within a school improvement initiative were strategically and conceptually related. This may be attributed to a lack of effective communication between the different levels of partnership efforts as well as teachers feeling they could be assessed on the specific elements of the various school improvement efforts and were concerned with their annual evaluation. While principals and other building-level administrators listed somewhat fewer separate initiatives, they too tended to list specific elements of the various school improvement efforts separately. The summary of the central office administrators' survey responses revealed a very different perspective, with a list of just nine school improvement initiatives, outlined within broader categories.

As such at the building level, teachers, in particular, felt the combined pressure of many efforts to improve the school. Similarly, principals and other building-level administrators felt pressure to assure their teachers were fulfilling their specific responsibilities to the varied initiatives, helping to make school leaders what Mintrop and Trujillo (2005) called "conduits of pressure." This pressure can result in difficult working relationships between teachers and administrators and, among other challenges, may lead to "additional organizational fragmentation" (Mintrop, 2004, p. 66).

Both teachers and building-level administrators complained in the open-ended question about too many different initiatives, the educational fad of the day, and the lack of opportunities to stay with an initiative long enough to gain effective use of it. As DeVita (2007) points out, efforts to bring about meaningful change have rarely been effectively organized and result in a hodge-podge of reform efforts that have proven unsuccessful.

Initially, when we presented these findings to the central office leadership team, they were very surprised at the results. They expressed that it was clear to them how the individual elements of the larger strategic initiatives were linked and did not understand how, at the building level, this clear focus was lost. We discussed the various organizational challenges of translating the larger strategic goals to the level of practice and how the partnership might refine its efforts to help address this disconnect.

In order to gain a more detailed understanding of the lack of continuity of the various improvement efforts, we deconstructed the three combined lists and looked for the particular areas where there was the greatest miscommunication about how the individual elements fit together in clear and focused ways. One of the important insights of this activity was the group's realization that some of the conceptual and strategic links of the different programs were merely assumed. That is, some of the efforts were tacked on to address a specific need at the time, and after more careful examination, within the larger context of the overall vision for school improvement, it was evident that some initiatives did not fit, or in some cases may actually have been counterproductive to the overall vision.

A central issue in this partnership was the dominant training-and-coaching model which focuses on expanding teachers' skills which are not adequate to the current climate of school improvement and reform; school improvement and reform initiatives can often project a vision of teaching and learning that the teachers themselves have not experienced (Little, 1993). As such, structural changes without clear understanding about how these changes support instructional goals (Elmore, 2002) and actually exemplifies these in the improvement effort itself do not impact student performance. What is often missing is instructionally focused leadership that can help move beyond simple structural change and facilitate changes in the instructional core and foster a more dynamic and supportive learning environment for students.

Next Steps: Building the Leadership Capacity

Authentic partnerships are deliberate, reflective, and time-intensive. Sometimes they are messy and require the partners to back track, regroup, evaluate, analyze, and redo certain components of the activities they are engaged in. The USDE SLP funded grant depicted in this chapter, the Generational Educator's Network for the Future, or GEN F, grew out of these earlier partnership efforts and represent the efforts of deliberate, hardworking partners that were not afraid to dig below the surface and identify the true needs of the school district. Specifically, this grant was informed by the growing understanding of what we identified through the result of our analyses of our ongoing work with the district partners as the *Four Pillars of Effective University–School District Partnerships* (Myran, Crum, & Clayton, 2010):

1. Take a Developmental View
    a. An Iterative and Additive View of Growth
    b. Transformative Growth
2. Finding the Balance between Theory and Practice
    a. An Alternative Approach to Professional Development

b. Integrating Partnership Activities into Division Initiatives
   c. Authentic Research
3. The Need to Develop and Maintain an Effective Communication System
4. The Need for Instructionally Focused Leadership Practices

Below is a brief description of each of the pillars. A more detailed description of the pillars can be found in *Four Pillars of Effective University–School District Partnerships inEducational Planning* (see Myran et al., 2010). In addition to the description, we also discuss how earlier lessons learned informed our grant development efforts and how these efforts informed the ultimate grant proposal that received funding from the USDE.

Take a Developmental View: This pillar acknowledges what research has shown us, in that school improvement does not happen overnight (Copland, 2003; Streshly & Bernd, 1992). A developmental view of school improvement recognizes that new understanding takes time and deep engagement to develop into well understood and generalizable teaching practices. This kind of change requires a developmental view that understands that an organization's improvement efforts will need to go through a number of developmental phases and each phase will require different types of support and encouragement (Myran et al., 2010).

Early in the partnership some of the initiatives that resulted from our collaboration were rushed. We also failed to look from "the balcony" and see how the different pieces of the puzzle fit together. Through this recognition we understood the USDE SLP GEN F program needed to be developed slowly and take into account all of the ongoing district initiatives. In this manner we sought to develop a program with our partner that dovetailed with current district goals and objectives, rather than creating new and competing activities that would put undo strains on the school district staff. For example, the internship was designed to run throughout the length of the program and to focus specifically on the overarching instructional goals of the program which complemented district initiatives. Major course projects were all specifically aimed at school and district improvement needs.

Finding the Balance between Theory and Practice: In our early partnership efforts we struggled to find ways to successfully integrate the theoretical principles espoused in higher education and research literature with the reality of day-to-day school practices. Initially, early partnership professional development efforts were the traditional "sit-and-get" activities. The staff involved in these sessions demonstrated a high level of resistance to this approach along with little retention and ability to implement the practices that were demonstrated.

We co-designed the GEN F program to specifically address the need to bridge the theory to practice gap. For example, all of the course activities had direct relevance to the needs of the school district. We utilized what we called "pragmatic anchors." These anchors served as "conceptual building blocks to developing deep substantive understandings from one's own contextualized, first-hand experiences." During the Human Resources course, the members of the aspiring leadership cohort did not just read about recruitment, they facilitated the first teacher recruitment fair for the division in over fifteen years and for the first time in over a decade all instructional staff positions were filled at the start of the next academic year (as opposed to having to use numerous long-term substitutes and noncertified staff in instructional positions). These experiences allowed the members of the grant cohort to build usable knowledge (Glaser, 1998).

The Need to Develop and Maintain an Effective Communication System: Communication is an important component in university–district partnerships (Teitel, 2003). We were aware of the concerns and fears of some PK-12 educators that our role as university personnel was to "fix" the problems at the school (LePage, Bordreau, Maier, Robinson, & Cox, 2001; Clarken, 1999; Day, 1998; Lieberman & McLaughlin, 1992; Simpson, Payne, Munro, & Hughes, 1999). Because of our presence in the school district and ongoing communication with the district staff (we had been working in all of the buildings and had interacted with all of the staff during this time period) for at least four years prior to the development, funding, and implementation of the USDE SLP grant, we were able to counteract many of these concerns. However, we still found initial challenges in communication that had to be addressed.

During the first six months of grant implementation, we found the need to specifically identify a line of communication between the district liaison, the project director (at the university), and the lead program evaluator. The district had two primary points of contact for the grant for different purposes. It became necessary early on to clarify the one person the project director would speak to in order to ensure smooth lines of communication and no confusion in terms of grant implementation. We also found it critical to specifically detail how communication would take place between the primary points of contact (district, university, and program evaluator) to ensure all partners were "in the loop" regarding each grant activity. In this way we were able to overcome initial communication concerns, allay any residual (or new fears) about district intrusion to "fix" problems versus collaboratively solve problems, and ensure program evaluation data was being collected in the most nonintrusive and efficient manner.

The Need for Instructionally Focused Leadership Practices: The GEN F program was developed to counter Elmore's (2002) lament of many educational reform efforts that often there are structural changes, but no clear understanding about how these support instructional goals. Instructionally focused leadership practices emphasize all aspects of learning and are critical in today's schools. These include higher-order cognitive skills and promoting self-efficacy (Bandura, 1986; National Science Foundation, 1992; Pintrich, 1989; Pintrich & De Groot, 1990; Schunk, 1989), in addition to the more traditional forms of instructional leadership such as supervision and evaluation. School leaders need to help teachers look beyond "teaching to the test" and help facilitate the use of research-based instructional practices that focused deeply and pervasively on learning. Throughout the development of the GEN F program with the partners and the implementation process upon funding, the need to focus on solid instructional leadership practices was at the heart of every discussion. This resonates throughout the program.

CONCLUDING THOUGHTS

One of the critical elements of the GEN F program was that it grew out of our deliberative efforts to learn from our earlier partnership experiences. The goal of the program was to facilitate the district to "grow its own" leaders within the context of the school culture being served, and to stabilize and strengthen the retention of school leaders who can successfully guide and direct instruction in a high-need LEA. These goals were identified as a result of carefully listening to teachers and school-level and central office leaders. Ultimately the partners developed the primary grant objectives to (1) train aspiring leaders who will complete a leadership preparation and licensing program, (2) to prepare both aspiring and current school leaders to understand and use research-based educational strategies to guide and direct instruction, (3) to utilize contextually relevant, ongoing professional development, and (4) to update aspiring and current administrators' understanding of (a) supporting state-of-the-art data-driven decision-making practices and (b) effectively utilizing formative assessment practices.

The GEN F partnership did meet its objectives; however, an important observation is that these objectives were not met quickly, taking time, effort, and patience on the part of all the partners involved. In our work, we (1) have collaboratively developed the GEN F with the school division, (2) set pragmatic goals for the program, with data collection designed to inform our progress toward those goals, (3) created proximal assessment "way points" to assess data and make suggestions for program improvements, and (4) measured the more summative effectiveness and produce scholarship for wider dissemination. Because there is scarce evidence in the literature of successful partnership (Munoz et al., 2006; Simmons et al., 2007) these concluding thoughts provide some important reflection points for school divisions and universities to consider as they work to build or refine partnership efforts.

Through these efforts we found that an authentic partnership that has clear communication paths and is well organized can bridge the theory to practice gap and provide in-depth, meaningful experiences for future school leaders. We found that including the district voice, identifying priorities within the real world context of practice, establishing trusting relationships, considering the importance of authentic learning settings, embedding faculty in the world of practice, and utilizing the principals of design-based research methods to test and refine program efforts all helped to sustain a meaningful and productive partnership.

We also noted a number of challenges that required careful deconstruction of the underlying issues in order to develop solutions that could actually penetrate the complexities of well-established school norms. These included the presence of multiple stakeholders from different levels of the two organizations, who often held competing or disconnected beliefs, ideologies, and conceptual understandings of the purpose and goals of the partnership. Specifically we noted a lack of understanding among teachers and school leaders about how the various partnership efforts were strategically linked and how they helped to build the organizational capacity of the division. That these conceptual and strategic links were often only assumed, and not specifically explained, mentored for, and demonstrated is a challenge that other developing partnerships should be attuned to.

Similarly we noted that the dominant training-and-coaching model which tends to focus on knowledge dissemination is out of step with the vision of teaching and learning that contemporary school improvement efforts attempt to realize and can lead to surface level and structural changes that ultimately don't support instructional and pedagogical goals. In this way we worked toward developing approaches to professional development that were authentic to a research-based vision of teaching and learning and supported by instructionally focused leadership.

Our experience with the GEN F partnership highlights that developing authentic partnerships are deliberate, reflective, and time-intensive, and often messy and require the partners to back track, regroup, evaluate, analyze, and redo certain components of the activities they are engaged in. We found that when we took a developmental view, worked to find an appropriate balance between theory and practice, built and maintained effective communication systems, and focused on instructionally centered leadership practices, our work had a better chance of both penetrating the complexities of school cultures and being sustained over time.

REFERENCES

Bandura, A. (1986). *Social foundations of thought and action: A social cognitive theory.* Englewood Cliffs, NJ: Prentice-Hall.

Blumenfeld, P., Fishman, B., Krajcik, J., Marx, R. W., & Soloway, E. (2000). Creating useable innovations in systemic reform: Scaling-up technology-embedded project-based science in urban schools. *Educational Psychologist, 35*(3), 149–164.

Borthwick, A. C., Stirling, T., Nauman, A. D., & Cook, D. L. (2003). Achieving successful school–university collaboration. *Urban Education, 38*(3), 330–371.

Browne-Ferrigno, T., & Muth, R. (2004). Leadership mentoring in clinical practice: Role socialization, professional development, and capacity building. *Educational Administration Quarterly, 40*(4), 468–494.

Clarken, R. H. (1999). University/school collaboration: A case study. Annual Meeting of the American Association of Colleges for Teacher Education. ERIC Document Reproduction Service No. ED429-080, State Dept. of Education, Special Education, Lansing, MI.

Collins, A., Joseph, D., & Bielaczyc, K. (2004). Design research: Theoretical and methodological issues. *The Journal of the Learning Sciences, 13*(1), 15–42.

Copland, M. A. (2003). Leadership of inquiry: Building and sustaining capacity for school improvement. *Educational Evaluation and Policy Analysis, 25*(4), 375–395.

Crow, G. M. (2006). Complexity and the beginning principal in the United States: Perspectives on socialization. *Journal of Educational Administration, 44*(4), 310–325.

Day, C. (1998). Re-thinking school–university partnerships: A Swedish case study. *Teaching and Teacher Education, 14*(8), 807–819.

DeVita, C. (2007). Why leadership, why now? *New York Times.* Retrieved from http://nytimes.com/ref/college/l4l-devita.html

Edelson, D. C. (2002). Design research: What we learn when we engage in design. *The Journal of the Learning Sciences, 11*(1), 105–121.

Edens, R., & Gilsinan, J. (2005). Rethinking school partnerships. *Education and Urban Society, 37*(2), 122–138.

Elmore, R. F. (2002). Hard questions about practice. *Educational Leadership, 59*(8), 22.

Glaser, R. (1998). Education for all: Access to learning and achieving usable knowledge. *Prospects, 28*(1), 5–20.

Goodnough, K. (2004). Fostering collaboration in a school district–university partnership: The teachers researching inquiry-based science project. *Teaching Education, 15*(3), 320–330.

Grogan, M., & Andrews, R. (2002). Defining preparation and professional development for the future. *Educational Administration Quarterly, 38*(2), 233–256.

Grogan, M., Bredeson, P. V., Sherman, W. H., Preis, S., & Beaty, D. A. (2009). The design and delivery of leadership preparation. In M. Young, G. Crow, J. Murphy & R. Ogawa (Eds.), *The handbook of research on the education of school leaders* (pp. 395–416). New York, NY: Routledge.

LaMagdeleine, D., Maxcy, B. D., Pounder, D. G., & Reed, C. J. (2009). The contest of university-based educational leadership preparation. In M. Young, G. Crow, J. Murphy & R. Ogawa (Eds.), *Handbook of research on education of school leaders*. New York, NY: Routledge.

LePage, P., Boudreau, S., Maier, S., Robinson, J., & Cox, H. (2001). Exploring the complexities of the relationship between K-12 and college faculty in a nontraditional professional development program. *Teaching and Teacher Education, 17*(2), 195–211.

Levine, A. (2005). *Educating School Leaders*. New York, NY: Schools Project.

Lieberman, A., & McLaughlin, M. (1992). Networks for educational change: Powerful and problematic. *Phi Delta Kappan, 73*(9), 673–777. Retrieved from ERIC database.

Little, J. W. (1993). Teachers' professional development in a climate of educational reform. *Educational Evaluation and Policy Analysis, 15*(2), 129–151.

Miller, P., & Hafner, M. (2008). Moving toward dialogical collaboration: A critical examination of a university–school–community partnership. *Educational Administration Quarterly, 44*(1), 66–110.

Mintrop, H., & Trujillo, T. (2005). Corrective action in low performing schools: Lessons for NCLB implementation from first-generation accountability systems. *Education Policy Analysis Archives, 13*(48). Retrieved from http://epaa.asu.edu/epaa/v13n48/. Accessed on 13 September 2006.

Mintrop, H. (2004). *Schools on probation: How accountability works (and doesn't work)*. New York: Teachers College Press.

Munoz, M., Winter, P., & Ricciardi, D. (2006). Inter-organizational research collaboration in education: A district–university partnership model. *ERS Spectrum, 24*(1), 13–17.

Murphy, J. (2005). Unpacking the foundations of ISLLC standards and addressing concerns in the academic community. *Educational Administration Quarterly, 41*(1), 154–191.

Myran, S., Crum, K., & Clayton, J. (2010). Four pillars of effective university–school district partnerships. *Educational Planning, 19*(2), 46–60.

National Science Foundation, W. C. (1992). To Strengthen American Cognitive Science for the Twenty-First Century. Report of a Planning Workshop for the Cognitive Science Initiative at the National Science Foundation, April 20–21, 1991, Washington, DC.

Peel, H. A., Peel, B. B., & Baker, M. E. (2002). School/university partnerships: A viable model. *International Journal of Educational Management, 16*(7), 319–325.

Pintrich, P. R. (1989). The dynamic interplay of student motivation and cognition in the college classroom. In C. Ames & M. Maehr (Eds.), *Advances in motivation and achievement: Motivation enhancing environments* (Vol. 6, pp. 117–160). Greenwich, CT: JAI Press.

Pintrich, P. R., & De Groot, E. V. (1990). Motivational and self-regulated learning components of classroom academic performance. *Journal of Educational Psychology, 82*(1), 33–40.

Portin, B., Schneider, P., DeArmond, M., & Gundlach, L. (2003). *Making sense of leading schools: A study of the school principalship.* New York: Wallace Foundation.
Sanzo, K. L., Myran, S., & Clayton, J. K. (2011). Building bridges between knowledge and practice: A university–school district leadership preparation program. *Journal of Educational Administration, 49*(3), 292–312.
Schunk, D. H. (1989). Self-efficacy and cognitive skill teaming. In C. Ames & R. Ames (Eds.), *Research on motivation in education* (Vol. 3, pp. 13–44). San Diego: Academic Press-Goals and cognitions.
Sherman, W. (2005). Preserving the status quo or renegotiating leadership: Women's experiences with a district-based aspiring leaders program. *Educational Administration Quarterly, 41*(707), 707–740.
Sherman, W. H., & Crum, K. S. (2009, Winter). Designing the internship in educational leadership as a transformative tool for improved practice. *International Journal of Educational Reform, 18*(1), 63–81.
Simmons, J., Grogan, M., Preis, S., Matthews, K., Smith-Anderson, S., & Walls, B. (2007). Preparing first-time leaders for an urban public school district: An action research study of a collaborative district–university partnership. *Journal of School Leadership, 17*(5), 540–569.
Simpson, M., Payne, F., Munro, R., & Hughes, S. (1999). Using information and communications technology as a pedagogical tool: Who educates the educators? *Journal of Education for Teaching, 25*(3), 247–262.
Streshly, W., & Bernd, M. (1992). School reform: Real improvement takes time. *Journal of School Leadership, 2*(3), 320–329.
Teitel, L. (2003). *The professional development schools handbook: Starting, sustaining, and assessing partnerships that improve student learning.* Thousand Oaks, CA: Corwin Press.
Walker, A., & Qian, H. (2006). Beginning principals: Balancing at the top of the greasy pole. *Journal of Educational Administration, 44*(4), 297–309.

CHAPTER 10

THE RURAL ALASKA PRINCIPAL PREPARATION AND SUPPORT PROGRAM: A COMPREHENSIVE APPROACH TO STRENGTHENING SCHOOL LEADERSHIP IN RURAL ALASKA

J. Kelly Tonsmeire, Kathy Blanc, Al Bertani, Susan Garton, Gary Whiteley, Lexie Domaradzki and Carol Kane

ABSTRACT

This chapter highlights the collaborative efforts of committed partners engaged in four distinct yet inter-related programs designed to build leadership capacity across schools serving rural Alaska. The Rural Alaska Principal Preparation and Support (RAPPS) program has built a comprehensive system of leadership development programs that develop aspiring leaders, induct and coach new principals, promote the professional learning of practicing principals, and support the school improvement efforts of the state education department. Each program is described in detail with special attention devoted to the unique elements of the program designs, including summer institutes; cohort models; distance learning offerings; targeted coaching; blended learning models using webinars; critical friends' conversations; and a festival of ideas. Lessons learned are highlighted, and impact and evaluation results are also detailed.

The Rural Alaska Principal Preparation and Support (RAPPS) program is a comprehensive, five-year US Department of Education-funded effort to strengthen school leadership in 16 remote and high-need Alaskan school districts. As a proving ground, Alaska provides a full spectrum of school environments. The 509 public schools in Alaska range from large comprehensive high schools in our urban centers to small K-12 schools in districts that span 40,000 square miles with schools accessible only by small aircraft. Many of our school leaders work in some of the most challenging situations that can be found in the United States.

The project serves 141 low-performing, predominantly Alaska Native schools in a huge roadless area of Alaska, where the annual principal and teacher turnover rates can approach 40 percent. In this chapter we seek to detail the unique aspects of the RAPPS program that helps build capacity in current and aspiring school leaders to lead effective change, support best instructional practices, and improve the educational outcomes for students in underperforming schools.

OVERVIEW OF THE RAPPS PROGRAM

The RAPPS program is designed to create a new generation of school leaders for rural Alaska by preparing at least 55 new principals to serve in Alaska's high-need rural schools, and by working in collaboration with our statewide partners to provide a continuum of support for new and practicing principals working in RAPPS districts. The University of Alaska Anchorage (UAA) plays the lead role in our aspiring principals program by providing a distance-delivered, rural-focused cohort within the UAA Educational Leadership Program. RAPPS has provided scholarships and support to 73 aspiring principals over the last four years.

Another key component of the RAPPS comprehensive leadership development program is inducting new principals into school leadership. All principal interns from the RAPPS UAA program, and all first and second year principals in our 141 partner schools are eligible to receive face-to-face training, and onsite and online coaching through the Alaska Administrator Coaching Project (AACP).

A third component of the RAPPS program is professional development for practicing principals, especially those whose schools have not made adequate yearly progress or whose districts are in corrective action with the State of Alaska, Department of Education and Early Development. RAPPS professional development is aligned with ongoing school improvement efforts so that statewide professional learning opportunities are focused and coherent. Major professional development activities are sponsored by the Alaska Staff Development Network. These include an intensive, annual, week-long summer institute for over 100 administrators, and follow-up webinar series throughout the school year which have been attended by over 1,700 educators.

The RAPPS partnership is led by the Alaska Staff Development Network with strong support from the UAA Education Leadership Program, the AACP, the Alaska Department of Education and Early Development, and an instructional design team of expert consultants. A project management team composed of key leaders from project partner organizations and project consultants and evaluators meet every two weeks by teleconference to monitor progress in all project components.

PREPARING A NEW GENERATION OF SCHOOL LEADERS FOR RURAL ALASKA

The principal preparation program at the UAA is an accredited program based upon the *Interstate School Leaders Licensure Consortium (ISLLC) Standards for School Leaders* (The Council of Chief State School Officers, 2008). The principal preparation program is a master's level program offered in the Department of Educational Leadership. Candidates who apply to the program must have a four-year education degree, a 3.0 grade average, and teaching experience. Candidates must provide a current teaching certificate for entry into the program and must complete three years of teaching before qualifying for the Type B certificate, the principal's certification in Alaska.

Completion of the program with a master's in education (MED) or a graduate certificate takes a minimum of two years. About a third of all candidates take three years to complete the program. All candidates are employed full time as teachers, principal/teachers, or school central office administrators and are required to complete a field-based, year-long internship under the joint direction of a field mentor (principal) and a university supervisor.

UNIQUE ASPECTS OF THE UAA RAPPS PROJECT

Because the RAPPS project was designed to serve high-need, rural Alaskan districts, candidates were recruited from the 16 partnering districts named in the grant proposal. Superintendents were asked to nominate potential principals from the practicing educators employed in their respective districts. Nominated candidates were required to meet the same admission requirements as all other aspiring principals, but with the UAA formal admission complete, RAPPS nominees were assigned to an RAPPS cohort and an RAPPS advisor. Scholarships were awarded to support each candidate with the first attendance at a Summer Institute. Four cohorts were planned to meet the goal of training and placing 55 principals by the end of five years.

The RAPPS cohorts were a departure from the UAA cohort model which grouped graduate students by geographic (urban) location. Fairbanks, Mat-Su, Anchorage, and the Kenai School Districts were the existing cohort locations. Since these cohort locations were all on the road system, travel was relatively easy, and instructors could travel from UAA to the districts. These cohorts used a hybrid delivery, a combination of face-to-face classes and distance delivery. The curriculum was tailored to the district by using district administrators as adjunct instructors for one or more of the required courses in the graduate program. This model was not appropriate for the RAPPS project since the partnering districts represented an enormous geographic area without a road system. There were 141 rural schools in the initial grant proposal. Nearly all these schools required travel by small plane or snow machine or both. The varied contexts and challenges of the RAPPS districts demanded a program different from the urban cohorts.

All beginning RAPPS cohort members were required to attend a summer institute, a four-day meeting in Anchorage that provided foundational knowledge for aspiring principals, expert presentations by educational consultants, and active learning with administrative teams from the RAPPS districts. The summer institutes developed coherence among the cohort members. Networking began spontaneously as the cohort members shared email addresses and other contact information. Summer institutes had an attendance of 30–35 RAPPS candidates, consisting of new cohort members and returning second-year candidates.

Distance delivery of courses is a necessity since RAPPS candidates teach in isolated villages. Satellite transmission of Internet-based courses has been generally reliable, although ground storms, heavy snows, and equipment failure may interrupt connectivity. The Eluminate software used by UAA is the vehicle for providing synchronous sessions with audio, video, chat, and whiteboards. While these sessions are often intimidating to new distance students, RAPPS candidates proved to be active participants from the first session. Courses have once-a-week sessions in Eluminate, from 5:00 to 8:00 PM. The Blackboard Discussion Board is used for keeping in touch between the weekly sessions. All written assignments are published in the Discussion Board to increase the vicarious learning and to provide peer review and discussion of assignments among RAPPS participants.

The curriculum in the UAA program required modification because the rural districts serve primarily indigenous people with varied languages and cultures. Culturally responsive strategies, articulated in the Alaska Department of Education and Early Childhood Development Standards for Culturally Responsive Teaching, became a regular component of classes. RAPPS courses emphasized Alaskan contexts whenever possible. Courses in instructional leadership used traditional curriculum theory texts but also introduced *Alaska Native Education* by Barnhardt and Kawagley. Other courses used Alaska-based case studies. Alaska-based cases are absent from published collections of case studies designed for use in educational administration programs. As a result, RAPPS students were asked to write case studies based upon village experiences. These case studies reflect the growing use of place-based educational units or "relevant" education in the villages. A collection of these case studies will be an enduring product from the RAPPS project which will provide relevant topics for study in future rural cohorts.

VALUE ADDED

We found through our work that several value-added components contributed to the success of the UAA principal preparation program. These included the use of summer institutes, coaching, unique professional development designs. For example, our Summer Institutes were located in Anchorage and utilized national consultants to support RAPPS districts who remained a part of the Instructional Design Team and the Management Team. The result was coherence as a collaborative team, proactive planning to address issues, and full involvement of district leaders. Participants benefitted from assigning a coach for the duration of the internship AND for the candidate's first and second year as a principal. Coaches visited candidates in the field, made frequent phone and email contact, and were a continuing source of support for the intern.

Additional value-added components were the use of outreach programs by the Alaska Staff Development Network, continuing communication and coordination with all partners, UAA coordinators working with the internships, and the integration of evaluators into the management team. National speakers and writers offered webinars for RAPPS candidates without tuition. District leaders met by audio conference with the RAPPS Management Team each quarter to give voice to any concerns or needs to be addressed in the next summer institute. The UAA coordinator proved convenient and efficient to have one main contact at the university for recruitment, monitoring of progress, administering of RAPPS scholarships, reporting progress to the program evaluators, and serving as the UAA advisor for candidates. Finally, RGI evaluators became a regular participant in the RAPPS Management Team, and contributed to the overall coordination of the program.

LESSONS LEARNED IN THE ASPIRING LEADERSHIP PROGRAM

Recruiting

In order to achieve a goal of 15 graduates per year, superintendents nominated 30–40 candidates for each cohort. Nearly half of those nominated declined to join the RAPPS program due to personal reasons, generally a family commitment or a health concern which prevented participation. Others did not complete the admission process or did not meet the grade point requirements for admission. Once the admitted candidates began completing courses, attrition was greatly reduced; nonetheless, a cohort of 20 or more was required to produce 15 graduates.

RAPPS Cohort Model

The cohort model for rural districts is successful in providing connectedness among cohort members. With each successive year of the RAPPS project, candidates demonstrated more networking within and among RAPPS districts. The UAA RAPPS advisor plans a study of all RAPPS candidates to develop a better understanding of the factors of most impact in the rural cohort model. Factors to be studied will include the advisor's role in maintaining the cohort, the impact of the Summer Institute, the impact of the coaching provided to interns, the availability of enrichment through webinars offered by the Alaska Staff Development Network.

Summer Institutes

RAPPS candidates who attended a summer institute were more likely to continue in the program than those who did not attend a summer institute. At the summer institute, RAPPS candidates met the UAA instructors, met the RAPPS advisor, met other RAPPS candidates, enjoyed learning with small/large groups, and practiced relevant skills. At the end of each institute, RAPPS candidates evaluated the RAPPS institute presenters and sessions with very positive ratings. Those candidates who were admitted but who chose not to attend the institute did not advance in the RAPPS program.

Course Delivery

Distance delivery of the RAPPS courses proved to be effective. Once enrolled in an RAPPS section, few candidates dropped. A current research study attempts to determine pedagogical approaches which are most effective in creating an online learning climate for synchronous classes like these for RAPPS candidates. This study involves a sample of 34 RAPPS students. Early reports indicate the use of small group assignments in breakout rooms is effective in engaging learners. This is a sanctioned study at UAA and will be reported in professional literature in fall, 2012.

Revised Curriculum

Case studies are relevant and meaningful to RAPPS candidates. Because Alaska-based cases do not exist in published texts for principal training programs, the RAPPS candidates have written cases based upon village experiences. These cases will be compiled and published for future rural cohorts. Candidates have responded positively to the use of *Alaska Native Education* as a text for the program. Students have also responded positively to materials from the online resource: the Alaska Native Knowledge Network (ANKN). The differentiated curriculum made a positive difference for the RAPPS candidates, especially for the Alaska Natives in the program. The use of Alaska Native materials, such as the *Alaska Native Education* text validated the rural Alaska experience and gave voice to indigenous traditions and cultures.

The success of the RAPPS project is not due to the university preparation program or any other single partner. The success is due to an unprecedented collaborative approach with many intersecting points of responsibility. The university, the district partners, the Department of Education, consultants, and leadership through the Alaska Staff Development Network — all of these partners came together as a committed team. The team maintained coherence and strength over the years through consistent participation of the key players. The lack of turnover was remarkable and a boon to the project.

THE ALASKA CONTEXT: LEADERSHIP LEARNING FOR EARLY CAREER PRINCIPALS

Coaching Program Design

The AACP was created in January 2005 to positively influence student achievement and increase retention of early career principals. AACP is primarily funded through the Alaska Department of Education and Early Development as one of the Department's mentoring initiatives. AACP provides coaching to new administrators throughout Alaska. Statewide, more than half of the first- and second-year principals enrolled in AACP have obtained their administrative endorsement from outside of Alaska.

Administrative interns participating in the RAPPS UAA program have been served by AACP coaches beginning in 2008 through funds provided by the RAPPS grant. The RAPPS project, in concert with AACP and the UAA–EDL program provide collaborative leadership learning content to support the one-year internship of rural administrators during fall and spring semesters.

Annually since the inception of the RAPPS grant, UAA RAPPS interns have been assigned an AACP coach during the intern's final fall and spring semesters. Identified outcomes include AACP Coaching tools and resources used with AACP early career principals, which compliment the UAA/EDL course expectations. Individual intern coaching may include but is not limited to collegial conversations and site visits, emails, and participation in webinars. RAPPS interns are strongly encouraged to enter the AACP program when they are hired as new administrators, and thereby participate in a three-year supportive relationship with their principal coach.

PROGRAM DESIGN – SOURCES AND CONSIDERATIONS

The role of the principal has changed significantly over recent years – from a manager of the school to a leader that is expected to develop the "human capital" into a responsive culture that addresses the achievement gap and improves the delivery of instruction. Implicit in the new role as a leader are the skills, abilities, and practices necessary to collaborate with teachers, analyze achievement data, identify and set school goals, influence the delivery of instruction, and manage the change process.

The AACP initial and ongoing program design was gathered from three critical areas. The first step in program development was a review and analysis of reports about school leadership development and design. The second source for elements to include in the AACP program was an examination of The *Interstate School Leaders Licensure Consortium* (ISLLC) Standards for School Leader. The third step was utilizing the framework developed by Gordon Donaldson in the book *How Leaders Learn: Cultivating Capacities for School Improvement* (2008). Additionally, we examined seven reports and one comprehensive curriculum (Darling-Hammond, LaPointe, Meyerson, Orr, & Cohen, 2007; Hess & Kelly, 2005; Levine, 2005; Nathan & Plotz, 2008; Southern Regional Educational Board, 2008; The Wallace Foundation, 2008) and identified the skills, abilities, and practices for developing successful school-level leaders. We organized the skills, abilities, and practices from each report into Leadership Development Attributes and Curricular Implications to include in the AACP program design. We intentionally selected reports that approached leadership development from different perspectives.

Table 1. The Six Program Components.

Coaching	A two-year relationship with a coach utilizing Cognitive Coaching strategies
Cohort Structures	Developing and deepening relationships with colleagues
Curricular Coherence and Relevance	The processes and products used during Institutes have a direct and immediate application ("Take and Bake" materials)
Performance Learning	Rehearsals are a problem-based learning strategy that encourages practicing an upcoming conversation
Research-based Content	Content focused on leadership AND teaching, and learning
Professional Growth System	Individualized three-part goal-setting system

The AACP program content and processes were readily adjusted based upon feedback from early career principals through focus group discussions, case studies, and an annual survey. The program adjustment process was not bound by a lengthy course approval process or bureaucratic regulations that inhibit a quick response to program feedback. In other words, we could immediately respond to the needs of our audience – the early career principals. The greatest and most immediate challenges as reported by the early career principals: (1) evaluating and supervising adults, (2) making Adequate Yearly Progress (AYP) and improving achievement for all students, (3) micro political nature of the job, (4) paperwork, and (5) student behavioral expectations and how that translates into developing school-wide and classroom-level expectations (Table 1).

A synergy exists when focused professional development (institutes) are combined with targeted principal coaching. The AACP is focused around six critical components as noted below. A coaching relationship, cohort structures, a coherent and relevant curriculum, performance learning, research-based materials, and a goal-setting process contribute to the success of early career principals.

FOCUSED PROFESSIONAL DEVELOPMENT (INSTITUTES)

The AACP provides seven days per year of professional development to early career principals for the first two years of employment. The AACP is not a comprehensive leadership development program. In designing and adjusting the three Institutes, we constantly take into consideration the five challenges as defined by novice principals, the Leadership Development Attributes and Curricular Implications from the national reports on school-level leadership, the ISLLC Standards, and Donaldson's Core Knowledge Areas. The Institutes are designed to be engagement-based professional development experiences where active learning is encouraged. The Institutes have an overall facilitator, as well as principal coaches facilitating their respective early career principals in groups of six to eight. The novice principals are organized into Learning Teams by school districts and complete all three Institutes as a team with their respective principal coach. Learning while doing and by doing is emphasized over presentation of material to a passive audience.

The major institute themes:

- Institute One: Instructional Literacy, Interpersonal Communication, Classroom Observation Protocols for Teacher Feedback, and Step One of Goal Setting;
- Institute Two: Organizational Literacy and Leadership, Teacher Collaboration, and Protocols, and Step Two of Goal Setting;
- Institute Three: Assessment Literacy, School-level and Classroom-level Assessment Practices, and Step Three of Goal Setting.

The six program components can only be achieved in a supportive environment. AACP coaches and staff recognize that early career principals are beginners in a complex and challenging profession. It is important to remember the multiple programs, processes, and information they are expected to master. Effective professional development takes place in a supportive and collegial environment where principals can practice new skills and solicit feedback from colleagues and principal coaches. *We facilitate with the belief that building assets (individual development) is more powerful than operating from a deficit model.* Our definition of Instructional Leadership is a combination of the beliefs and the actions necessary for shaping the culture of a school around teaching and learning. Another benefit of the Institutes for rural principals is that it provides an opportunity for them to network with other principals working in small, K-12 schools. These informal social networks greatly help to reduce the isolation new principals encounter in rural Alaska.

In addition, the RAPPS project extends the learning opportunities for RAPPS interns and first and second year principals by providing no cost distance delivered professional learning opportunities throughout the school year. Interns, first and second year AACP principals, and AACP coaches attend these webinar series. RAPPS also provides consultants to augment the instruction at the AACP Institutes. This cross training between the AACP Institutes and the RAPPS professional development helps to keep the professional learning aligned among the various state efforts with rural districts.

TARGETED COACHING

The AACP arranges a confidential relationship between a coach and an early career principal. If the principal enters as an RAPPS intern and continues as a first- and second-year administrator, they are eligible to receive three years of coaching. The coaching is focused on assisting each principal to implement the practices, strategies, and skills learned and refined during the three Institutes. Coaches use the Professional Growth System (PGS) with each early career principal. The PGS is an individualized three-step goal-setting process used to identify specific areas for the targeted coaching. The goal-setting process includes a timeline and sources of formative feedback for early careers principals to adjust their goal and improve performance.

The coaches use skills and processes learned through training provided by the Center for Cognitive Coaching. Coaches focus on leading early career principals through Planning, Reflecting, or Problem-resolving Conversations. The use of the AACP Leadership Conversation Guide is an important tool used by coaches during coaching conversations either face-to-face or over the phone. The conversation guide provides shape and structure for the coaching conversations. The success of each conversation requires a skillful coach and a willing and engaged principal.

Principal coaches for RAPPS interns and new principals have all served as principals in Alaska. RAPPS coaches all have many years experience with the special challenges found in rural areas of the state. The long-term relationship of new administrators with their experienced coach reduces the isolation reported by new rural principals. Regular communication with their coaches gives interns and new administrators a confidential, apolitical, and seasoned contact to advise and assist them on an regular basis.

COACHING SUMMARY

The model developed by AACP for leadership learning by early career principals has demonstrated success. Early career principals served by AACP recognize that instructional leadership is more than espousing beliefs; it also encompasses the actions necessary in shaping the culture of the school around teaching and learning. Thoughtful use and strategic implementation of the skills, abilities, and practices learned by early career principals through focused professional development experiences are less likely to happen without focused coaching support. This personal connection is especially important for AACP strives to develop early career principals with a leadership framework that will assist and improve their performance in their professional endeavors in Alaska.

PROFESSIONAL LEARNING FOR PRACTICING PRINCIPALS

Alaska School Leadership Institute

A major component of the RAPPS Project has been the week-long annual Alaska School Leadership Summer Institute (ASLI). Designed as a residential experience convened in Anchorage, Alaska, it draws together over 120 practicing educational leaders including teacher leaders, assistant principals, principals, central office administrators, and superintendents. It is held in conjunction with the summer institute for the RAPPS aspiring principals cohort at UAA so that the aspiring principals can interact with their district leadership and so the project can maximize the use of RAPPS national-level consultants for instruction.

The following section will detail the process used to design the institute program; the design components and content emphases over the life of the program; and unique program features to enhance professional learning.

CONSULTATIVE DESIGN PROCESS

An Instructional Design Team assumes primary responsibility for planning and implementing the annual ASLI program. The Team is comprised of nationally recognized consultants with specialized expertise working with school- and district-level leaders; selected partners including the University of Alaska–Anchorage and the AACP; and the anchor organization for the RAPPS Project – the Alaska Staff Development Network. Working virtually through phone and Skype conferences, the Instructional Design Team uses an iterative, consultative process to build the program for each of the annual institutes.

Each year, Research, Grants, and Information Corporation (RGI) has conducted a comprehensive evaluation of all aspects of ASLI. These evaluations have included: daily surveys assessing the value and impact of all content presentations, learning design elements, and unique program features; in-depth interviews with selected participants and partners; and an overall program evaluation at the close of the institute. The results of these evaluations have become the starting point for building the design for the following year.

Using the results of the institute evaluation, the Instructional Design Team establishes a content focus for the year and considers learning design elements for structuring the actual institute design. Following principles of adult learning and professional learning standards (Learning Forward, 2011), the Instructional Design Team develops an initial draft of the institute program and then engages in several rounds of consultation to refine and fine-tune the program. This iterative, consultative process takes several months and is described in the paragraphs that follow.

With a philosophy that focuses on meeting the learning needs of our primary clients (school and district leaders), the Instructional Design Team engages representatives from across participating districts in three deliberate consultations. These 60–90 minute consultations are conducted via phone conference with as many as 16–18 representatives participating. They are intended to accomplish three specific objectives: (1) solicit background, challenges, and recommendations; (2) stress-test proposals for content and process decisions; and (3) build direct ownership into the design process.

In addition, the RAPPS Management Team plays an important consultative role in the institute design process. Comprised of representatives from all project partners – Alaska Staff Development Network, University of Alaska–Anchorage, AACP, and the Alaska Department of Education and Early Development – the RAPPS Management Team engages in bi-weekly phone conferences to manage the work of the RAPPS project. The RAPPS Management Team provides an all important program coordination and quality assurance function during the design process. Over the years, they have offered valuable advice and counsel from their respective "support" seats at the table.

Finally, the Instructional Design Team has been committed to building and sustaining a coherent program of learning from year to year. Focusing on a few high leverage strategies for improving student learning and organizational performance, the Instructional Design Team have helped build knowledge, develop skills, and motivate individuals and teams to improve and transform learning in their schools and districts. All in all, the design process is (1) highly collaborative engaging participants as well as partners; (2) data driven using multiple sources of information; and (3) custom designed to meet the needs of educational leaders working in rural schools across Alaska.

EVOLUTION OF INSTITUTE DESIGN COMPONENTS

Over the life of the program, the institute has evolved in a significant number of ways. In an effort to remain responsive to participant needs, changing conditions at the school, district, and state levels, and emerging developments in research and practice around leadership, the institute has changed in content emphases, learning design, special features, and length of the program. Each of these changes will be elaborated in the section that follows.

In designing the first institute (2009), school and district participants and project partners played a significant role in determining the content of the institute program. Through the iterative design process described earlier in this section, the following content themes served as anchors for the institute in the first year. These themes included:

- collaboration based on a model of professional learning communities;
- individual leadership actions for producing second-order change;
- strategies, protocols, and tools to analyze data at the district and school levels;
- curriculum standards, instructional practices, and assessments.

All learning sessions were designed as large group plenary sessions with a specific content theme dedicated to each of the four days of the institute program. Learning sessions were structured as 75–90 minute blocks involving presentations, small group work, and individual reflection. Participants were organized into role-alike home groups that promoted networking across schools and districts. In addition, each home group was facilitated by a team member from one of the partner organizations. Facilitators were prepared for their roles through a half-day training session that preceded the actual institute.

Using the knowledge taxonomy developed by Marzano, Waters, and McNulty (2003), the 2009 institute program was deliberately focused on developing participant knowledge around the "what" of specific leadership actions. The "what" is described as declarative knowledge — knowing what to do as a leader. This knowledge element served as the foundation for building a design that could expand and evolve during each succeeding institute.

Planning for the second institute (2010), the design team repeated the process using the evaluation results from the previous year, consultations with school and district leaders, and conversations with partner organizations to build the new design. With 100% of the ASLI 2009 participants indicating their continuing interest in another institute program, the design team also faced the challenge of how to build on the work from the previous year as well as bring fresh new ideas to the institute design. This challenge was addressed by maintaining coherence around the content themes as well as introducing new content and design elements.

The institute design for 2010 maintained a continuing content focus around the following themes:

- Professional development and professional learning for collaboration;
- Results-driven collaboration using AIMS Web student assessment data;
- Linking assessment and Instruction through formative evaluations.

Learning sessions also assumed a new form with some sessions structured as a large group and others structured to accommodate about half of the group. Once again participants were organized into role-alike home groups, and these home groups were facilitated by team members from the partner organizations. All sessions were scheduled as 75–90 minute learning blocks.

In addition, the 2010 institute design introduced several new features. A pre-institute day was organized to accomplish several objectives. One objective was to orient new participants to the content and design of the institute program. The design team produced a day-long orientation program to help participants connect with content from the previous year and learn something about how the institute operates. Another dimension of the pre-institute day included half-day and day-long workshops on hot topics and current issues for Alaska's rural education leaders. While the orientation program was mandatory, the workshops were voluntary. Over 60 individuals participated in the orientation and workshops in 2010.

The 2010 institute program also saw the introduction of two new features – critical friends conversations (CFCs) and the festival of ideas (FOIs). CFCs were designed to provide a structured conversation about problems of practice. Role-alike quartets were formed to help participants serve as critical friends for one another in exploring potential solutions to problems of practice. FOI was designed for participants to share emerging best practices with one another across school and districts boundaries. Both of these new features will be described in detail in the next section of this chapter.

Building on the knowledge taxonomy developed by Waters et al. (2003), the 2010 institute program continued to develop participant knowledge around the "what" – knowing what to do as a leader while adding experiential knowledge – the "why" – knowing why this is important. Viewing the annual institutes as inextricably interwoven across multiple years, the knowledge taxonomy provides a research-based design approach to building the knowledge, skills, and dispositions important to the multiple roles of educational leaders.

The 2011 Institute Program Planning followed the model developed in earlier years – reviewing evaluation results from the previous year, engaging in consultations with school and district leaders, and discussing with partner organizations to build the design for the third institute program. With 94% of the ASLI 2010 participants indicating their continuing interest in another institute program, the design team assumed responsibility for continuing to maintain a high-quality program by ensuring program coherence while expanding on the content themes to deepen and broaden leaders' knowledge and skills.

Content themes for the 2011 Institute continued build on the "what" and "why" knowledge elements from previous years by focusing on the following:

- Coherence and Sustainability
- Implementation Issues
- Protocols and Processes

A major shift in the 2011 institute design included the use of role-alike learning groups that had district administrators, school principals and site administrators, and teacher leaders learning in cohorts across the course of a day. In effect, content sessions were customized to meet the needs of the different role groups engaged in the institute program.

Once again a pre-institute program was offered the day before the official institute began with a day-long orientation for new institute attendees, a special day-long pre-institute workshops on the newly developed Alaska STEPP program for School Improvement, and two half-day workshops focused on culture and community engagement and emerging trends in teacher evaluation. All of the special pre-institute workshops featured

Alaskan school- and district-level practitioners as members of the presentation teams.

The highly rated CFCs were reprised once again as part of the 2011 Institute with role-alike quartets discussing and advising one another about problems of practice. Using a structured protocol, each day began with these highly personal and professional conversations. During the 2010 Institute, several FOI projects were integrated into working sessions around the content themes. This enabled presenters to demonstrate application of Institute learning and themes in rural Alaskan schools.

Finally, the 2011 Institute continued to evolve within the knowledge taxonomy developed by Waters et al. (2003). The Institute focus shifted to the aspects of procedural knowledge – knowing how to do something – and contextual knowledge – knowing when to do something. When combined with the other elements of the knowledge taxonomy, each year built on the previous year seeking to expand and refine the knowledge, skills, and dispositions of Alaska's school and district leaders.

UNIQUE PROGRAM FEATURES

With the evolution of the Alaska School Leadership Institute over the first three years of the program, several unique program features have anchored the design while other new features were introduced to enhance the quality of the program. Each of these unique features is highlighted below with short descriptions.

Role-Alike Home Groups

From the first year of the institute in 2009, the design has always included organizing participants into role-alike home groups. These groups had participants usually starting their day together across the program. Typically, they would be comprised of eight to nine role-alike members facilitated by a member of one of the partner organizations. The role-alike home groups played a critical role in building human networks across schools and districts for the institute. In the rural environments of Alaska, these networks helped to address the issues of isolation that are faced by almost all of the institute participants. They provided a vehicle for culturing role-alike networks throughout the institute while also nurturing relationships that could be sustained electronically across the school year.

Critical Friends Conversations

The Institute Design Team had always worked to integrate "real-life" problems of practice into the institute design. While the content-themed learning sessions offered multiple opportunities for inviting "real-life' problems of practice into discussions, it was also deemed important to structure these conversations as person-to-person dialogues between and among practitioners. In order to accomplish this goal, the Design Team proposed a light touch protocol to serve as the structure for these CFCs. Working in role-alike quartets, each participant had an opportunity to present a problem of practice while seeking advice from their colleagues serving as critical friends for them. Over the course of the program, each person had half-an-hour "on the couch" where they benefitted from the wisdom and counsel of their colleagues. The structured protocol followed this basic format throughout the institute.

Step 1 Presentation of the Problem of Practice or Dilemma (5 minutes)

- Overview of the Dilemma
- Frames a Question for the Group to Consider
- Presents Artifacts as Appropriate

Step 2 Clarifying Questions (3 minutes)

- Group Asks Questions for Clarification Purposes
- Questions that Have Brief, Factual Answers
- Presenter Responds with Brief, Factual Answers

Step 3 Discussion of the Dilemma (15 minutes)

- Group Members Talk to One Another about the Dilemma Presented
- Potential Questions
  + *What did we hear?*
  + *What didn't we hear that we think might be relevant?*
  + *What assumptions seem to be operating?*
  + *What questions does the dilemma raise for us?*
  + *What do we think about the dilemma?*
  + *What might we do or try if faced with a similar dilemma?*
  + *What have we done in similar situations?*
- Group Members Make Suggestions – Sometimes – Group Works to Define the Issues More Thoroughly and Objectively
- Presenter Doesn't Speak – Only Listens and Takes Notes during Step 3

Step 4 Presenter Reflection (7 minutes)

- Presenter Reflects on What He/She Heard
- Presenter Shares What He/She Is Now Thinking
- Presenter Highlights Specific Ideas/Comments that Resonated

In addition, the Design Team, RGI Research Team, and Partner Organizations collected all of the topics that surfaced as problems of practice. This information was collated and then reviewed as another potential data source for future institute planning. It is worthy to note that the CFCs have remained the most highly rated element of the institute since they were introduced in 2010.

FESTIVAL OF IDEAS

As a teaching, learning, and school improvement context, Alaska presents several unique challenges. The rural and isolated nature of schools, the small size of many schools embedded within large geographic areas, second language learning issues, complex cultural issues working in Native communities, and the very nature of the multiple roles of school and district leaders in these challenging conditions — all present circumstances that are significantly different than many other contexts across the United States. Influenced by these contextual conditions, the Institute Design Team has worked diligently each year to "Alaskanize" the institute content and design to meet the needs of educational leaders in their respective contexts.

One major mechanism for "Alaskanizing" the institute has been the introduction of an FOI designed to identify emerging best practices from the classroom, school, and district levels across Alaska. While the implementation of FOI has differed each year of the institute, the basic intent and format has remained consistent. Each year we have solicited volunteers as well as sought nominations to feature as part of the program.

Participants have been invited to self-nominate, be nominated, or solicited to describe an emerging best practice that will have significance for classrooms, schools, and districts across the rural schools that populate Alaska. Using a highly structured selection process, members of the Institute Design Team and Partner organizations screen nominations and solicitations for inclusion into the institute program. FOI selections then participate in a one-hour videotaped interview to capture the essence of their story. Each interview uses the following protocol to guide the inquiry process.

1. Background of the Emerging Best Practice
   a. What are the demographics of the district or school?
   b. What were your improvement priorities for the 2009–2010 year?
   c. What specific problem were you trying to solve?
   d. How did you identify your emerging best practice to address the problem?
   e. What is the research base for your emerging best practice?

2. Description of the Implementation Efforts
   a. How did you initiate the implementation of emerging best practice?
   b. What were your implementation challenges?
   c. How did you bring people along to own the emerging best practice?
   d. Were there specific phases to your implementation?
   e. How have you been able to sustain momentum with your implementation?

3. Indicators of Impact and Improvement
   a. What impact and improvement were you seeking with your implementation?
   b. What evidence of impact and improvement can you provide?
   c. What impact did the best practice have on your staff and students?

4. Description of Key Supports Leading to Success
   a. What leadership actions did you take to ensure successful implementation?
   b. What resources did you use to ensure successful implementation?
   c. Who were the other leaders that helped to ensure successful implementation?
   d. What role did central office play to help ensure successful implementation?

5. Summary of Key Lessons Learned
   a. What lessons did you learn while implementing your emerging best practice?
   b. What would you want others to learn from your implementation experience?
   c. What would you do differently if you could do it over again?

6. Artifacts from Implementation of the Emerging Best Practice
   a. What print artifacts are available to support your FOI story?
   b. What non-print artifacts are available to support your FOI story?
   c. Can your artifacts be sent in electronic form?

The videotaped interview serves as the basis for developing PowerPoint materials, artifacts as support materials, and finally a DVD to summarize the emerging best practice. All of these materials are then used for two specific purposes: (1) presentation materials for participants to tell their stories as part of the institute program; and (2) as web-based case materials to be used by leaders across Alaska as well as other rural settings across the United States. FOI has also spawned interest networks where participants seek out one another to explore how ideas can be replicated to improve student learning, staff learning, and organizational performance (Table 2).

DISTRICT TEAM PLANNING TIME

In order to maximize the impact of team participation during the institute, each day also included meeting time dedicated to District Team Planning Time. These daily meeting times were devoted to applying new learnings from across the institute, integrating content into district initiatives, and

Table 2. Example – FOI Summary: *Focus on PLCs in Rural Settings.*

Title	Description	District
Starting a PLC in a Small School	Learn how Koliganek School handled the challenges of building a PLC in a rural, small school setting with limited staff	Southwest Region School District
Transforming Your Administrative Meetings into a PLC	How should district leaders make the best use of the limited time that principals spend together? LKSD turned their "sit-and-get" administrative meetings into PLC teams – and found that they started getting more meaningful work accomplished	Lower Kuskokwim School District (LKSD)
Place-Based Education: A PLC at Work	Russian Mission School uses a PLC to develop place-based activities; find out how teachers and community members move the classroom outside to learn from each other	Lower Yukon School District

ultimately building plans for the new school year. The District Team Planning Time became a strong "transfer mechanism" for moving content from the institute to implementation at the school and district levels. It also helped enhance communication, promote reflection, and strengthen team relationships.

ASLI SUMMARY

ASLI continues to serve as the foundational program for practicing school and district leaders engaged in the Rural Alaska Principals Preparation Program. It brings together the largest group of school and district leaders for learning in a face-to-face setting on an annual basis. The content, design, presentations, and mix of institute activities continue to receive high ratings from participants. Perhaps most importantly, it has developed as a community of practice that networks school and district leaders in the transformational work of improving student learning and enhancing organizational performance.

RAPPS BLENDED LEARNING MODEL

The ASLI provides the anchor for designing additional professional learning opportunities that are offered via distance delivery throughout the school year. Alaska Staff Development Network has a long and rich history of offering 40–50 webinars a year to support the ongoing learning needs of Alaskan educators. While many of these webinars are designed to meet the current and emerging professional needs of educators across the state, they also created a somewhat fragmented menu of offerings. Beginning with the first ASLI in 2009, a series of webinars were developed that aligned directly to the content themes of the Alaska School Leadership Institute.

These webinars were intentionally designed to reinforce content from the precious Institutes as well as preview new content that was being planned for future Institutes. These efforts to promote coherence, build alignment, and sustain implementation efforts are strongly reinforced through this blended learning model that includes face-to-face interactions via the Institute with virtual interactions through webinars. Teachers are strongly encouraged to participate in RAPPS webinars along with their principals (Fig. 1).

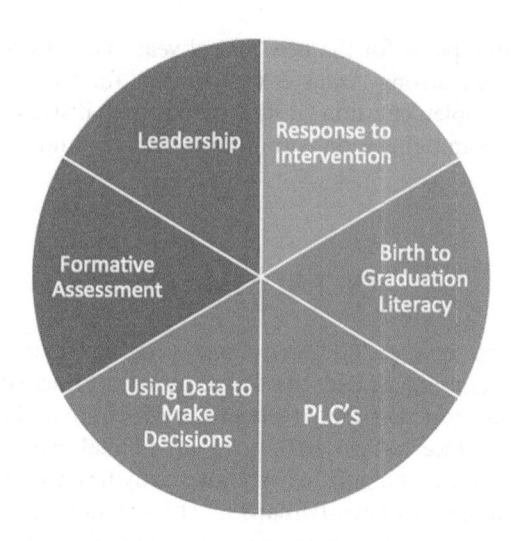

Fig. 1. Focus Areas for RAPPS Webinars.

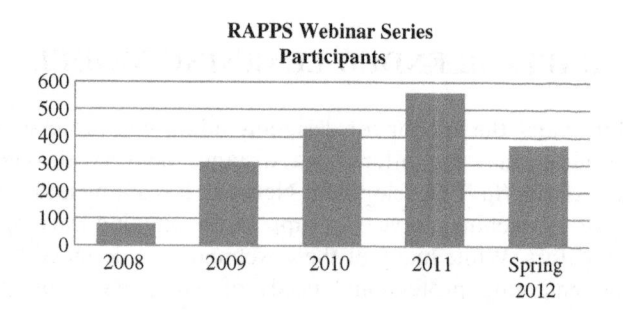

Fig. 2. Number of RAPPS District Staff Enrolled in Webinar Series.

Over 1,700 educators have participated in RAPPS webinars over the course of the project. Distance-delivered professional learning through RAPPS provides equity in the quality and number of learning across the state. These webinars are all recorded and the recordings are available to RAPPS districts to use at no cost. All of the webinar resources, the FOI artifacts, and the materials from the Alaska School Leadership Institute are posted on the RAPPS website http://www.rappsproject.org (Fig. 2).

CONCLUSION

RAPPS not only focuses on best practice for preparing new administrators, it also provides a continuum of support for new and practicing principals. RAPPS project partners work collaboratively to align content and customize professional learning for the unique needs of school leaders in rural Alaska. Collaboration between the Alaska Staff Development Network, the AACP, the Alaska Department of Education and Early Development State System of Support, and the UAA Educational Leadership Program allows RAPPS to leverage existing school improvement and professional development efforts to reach more educators. Project evaluations show that RAPPS participants value the professionalism and place-based relevance of our professional learning opportunities. Working together, the RAPPS partners have had a tremendous impact on all aspects of school leadership and student learning in Alaska. The RAPPS program results in improving school leadership and student learning in rural Alaska will be felt for years to come.

REFERENCES

Darling-Hammond, L., LaPointe, M., Meyerson, D., Orr, M., & Cohen, C. (2007). *Preparing school leaders for a changing world: Lessons for exemplary leadership development programs.* Stanford, CA: Stanford Educational Leadership Institute.

Donaldson, G. (2008). *How leaders learn: Cultivating capacities for school improvement.* New York: Teachers College Press.

Hess, F., & Kelly, A. (2005). *Learning to lead? What gets taught in principal preparation programs.* Cambridge, MA: Harvard University, Kennedy School of Government.

Levine, A. (2005). *Educating school leaders.* New York: The Education Schools Project.

Marzano, R. J., Waters, T., & McNulty, B. (2003). *School leadership that works: From research to results.* Alexandria, VA: Association for Supervision and Curriculum Development.

Nathan, J., & Plotz, J. (2008). *Learning to lead.* Minneapolis: Center for School Change, Humphrey Institute, University of Minnesota.

Southern Regional Educational Board. (2008). *SREB leadership curriculum modules: Professional learning framework and module summaries.* Atlanta: Southern Regional Education Board.

The Council of Chief State School Officers. (2008). *Educational leadership policy standards: ISLLC 2008.* Washington, DC: Author.

The Wallace Foundation. (2008). *Becoming a leader: Preparing school principals for today's schools.* New York: Author.

CHAPTER 11

ACCELERATING LEADERSHIP EXCELLENCE: NYC LEADERSHIP ACADEMY'S SCHOOL LEADERSHIP COACHING MODEL

Tierney Temple Fairchild

ABSTRACT

As states and districts increasingly focus on school leadership training programs, one less discussed yet vital component is the support mechanisms that can accelerate school leadership performance. This chapter highlights the unique school coaching model developed by NYC Leadership Academy (Leadership Academy), a national organization focused on improving student outcomes through effective leadership practice. Using a standards-based, facilitative approach to coaching early-career leaders in high-need schools, the Leadership Academy has developed a rigorous process for training and developing a cadre of coaches to provide intensive coaching support to school leaders that focuses on strengthening their leadership performance. The chapter discusses the methods and results of the Leadership Academy's coaching model for the 139 principals leading high-need schools as part of the U.S. Department of Education's School Leadership Program (SLP) and offers insights into school leadership coaching as a distinct professional practice in education.

> I have found leadership coaching to be one of the most valuable strategic structures that I have experienced as a principal. My coach has supported me in developing my own personal strengths and overcoming my weaknesses, along the dimensions of leadership that are my priorities. We spent a good deal of time getting to know the school together, and she helped me develop the confidence and the skill to manage the complex set of conditions and events that occur in the course of a school year.
>
> – Milo Novelo, Principal

Research demonstrates that school leaders play a critical role in driving school improvement; highly effective school leaders do so by creating the conditions necessary for teachers to excel in the classroom and improve student achievement (Hallinger & Heck, 1996; Leithwood & Jantzi, 1999; Leithwood, Seashore Louis, Anderson, & Wahlstrom, 2004; Seashore et al., 2010). This is particularly true for chronically low-performing schools. Established by Mayor Michael Bloomberg and former Schools Chancellor Joel Klein in 2003 with the support of the business community, the Wallace Foundation, and other leading foundations, the NYC Leadership Academy (Leadership Academy) works to prepare and support the type of highly effective school leaders who serve as change agents to lead schools out of distress. Through high-quality leadership preparation, coaching, and support programs, the Leadership Academy develops and trains leaders to cultivate learning environments that expect high achievement for all students as well as the adults responsible for educating them. This chapter provides an overview of the philosophy and practices associated with the Leadership Academy's school leadership coaching model.

Today, the Leadership Academy counts one in six of New York City's 1,600 public school principals among its alumni, and it has coached and supported more than 1,000 principals across the city. Over nearly ten years, it also has grown into a national organization that works to improve the quality of school leadership development by providing strategic advice to state and local school systems, universities, and other nonprofits seeking to improve schools by adapting the Leadership Academy's approach to leadership development.

At the core of the Leadership Academy's work is an innovative leadership development model that is experiential, standards-based, and aligned to school system policies and reform strategies. In recognition of the vital role that on-the-job development and support play in leadership performance, coaching for school leaders is a central component of the Leadership Academy's work. For the Leadership Academy, school leadership coaching[1] is a professional practice integral to building the leadership capacity necessary to accelerate student achievement and transform schools. Through a federal School Leadership Program (SLP) grant, the Leadership Academy has been able to strengthen its coaching model by developing a comprehensive, three-year coaching program for graduates of its Aspiring Principals Program (APP) who lead high-need schools.[2]

The chapter is organized as follows: first, the author sets the context for coaching by discussing how school leadership can influence student achievement. The second section provides detail on the Leadership Academy's approach to leadership development. The third section discusses coaching as a vital component of leadership development, including the role of executive coaching in the private sector. The specifics of the SLP grant are presented in section four as the chapter turns to how coaching at the Leadership Academy enhances leadership performance. The chapter concludes with a brief discussion of the growing importance of coaching as a professional practice in education leadership.

LINK BETWEEN SCHOOL LEADERSHIP AND STUDENT ACHIEVEMENT

School leadership matters in transforming schools: it influences student learning, including the closure of persistent achievement gaps between racial and economic subgroups (Chenoweth & Theokas, 2011; Williams et al., 2005). School leaders respond to the contexts in which they work, influencing staff motivation and the conditions that affect school climate to improve teaching and learning (Leithwood, Harris, & Hopkins, 2008). In fact, high-quality leadership ranks second only to teaching in the school-related factors impacting student achievement (Leithwood et al., 2004). Researchers "have not found a single case of a school improving its student achievement record in the absence of talented leadership" (Seashore Lewis et al., 2010, p. 9), suggesting that while individual variables have an effect on student achievement, school leaders are often uniquely positioned to create synergy across the many variables that benefit students.

How much difference can a talented leader make in a school? Quite a bit, according to one meta-analysis, which found that 25 percent of the variation in student achievement could be explained by principal leadership skills (Marzano, Waters, & McNulty, 2005). From this analysis involving 69 studies, over 2,800 schools, 1.4 million students, and 14,000 teachers, researchers identified 21 categories of leadership behaviors, or "responsibilities," offering new insights into the nature of school leadership and its relationship to student achievement.

As growing research shows the effect of educational leadership on student achievement, the work of organizations like the Leadership Academy that train and support school leaders with the goal of increasing their ability to improve students' academic outcomes becomes even more critical. A recent RAND study (Burkhauser, Gates, Hamilton, & Ikemoto, 2012), for instance, underscores the particular challenges faced by first-year principals and the lack of trend data on what makes a principal successful. New principals face a myriad of challenges stemming from their need to assimilate to a school's culture, quickly assess its environment, and implement strategies that can improve student performance. As this RAND study points out, "first-year principals are responsible for all of the duties that an experienced principal must attend to, including academic performance" (p. 2).

It is not surprising that in an era of increased accountability, which has changed performance expectations for principals, states and districts would want to offer more support to school administrators, especially those leading chronically underperforming schools out of distress. A growing body of research on principal leadership in the 21st century (Elmore, 2000; Fullan, 2001; SREB, 2001; Hargreaves & Fink, 2006), coupled with increased accountability for principals, has spurred innovative alternatives to traditional educational leadership preparation and support. States and local school systems, universities, as well as a number of nonprofits have developed new offerings for aspiring and current school leaders (Cheney, Davis, Garrett, & Holleran, 2010). Some programs combine the management thinking found in business schools with the instructional leadership that underpins administrative preparation programs. Others draw on enquiry-based pedagogical methods, experiential learning, and coaching and/or mentoring support to meet the current needs of administrators, especially those in underperforming schools. In addition, more states are offering alternative certification for administrators, expanding opportunities for programs pursuing school leadership as a critical lever for school improvement.

THE LEADERSHIP ACADEMY APPROACH

The Leadership Academy began with a groundbreaking mission to provide comprehensive leadership development and support programs for aspiring and current New York City public school leaders. After nearly 10 years of working with aspiring principals, sitting principals, and district staff in New York City and with school systems, universities, and nonprofits across 23 states, the Leadership Academy has developed and refined a rigorous, standards-based, experiential learning model focused on building a pipeline of school leaders capable of turning around chronically underperforming schools.

The Leadership Academy's work focuses on three inter-related levers impacting school leader performance: leadership preparation for aspiring principals; leadership coaching and support for current school leaders; and an advisory practice that helps state and local school systems, universities, and other education-focused nonprofits.

At the core of these inter-related elements is the Leadership Academy's multifaceted Leadership Development Model, which embraces standards-based leadership development and the promise of enquiry-based and experiential learning and drives all of its program design and delivery. The Model's essential components are:

- *Research-based Leadership Standards* – Leadership Academy programs begin with behaviorally-based standards for leadership performance. These research-based competencies are used to guide program design and curriculum development, focus participant learning and growth, and assess program and participant effectiveness.
- *Experiential Learning* – Drawing on adult learning theory, all programs bring experiential learning to participants in order to best engage them in their development.
- *Teaming* – Whether through planned development activities or informal facilitated retreats, all Leadership Academy programs recognize the importance of school teams as integral to school improvement.
- *Context-specific Programming* – Recognizing that there is a set of conditions that enable leaders to be effective within the school system where they will serve, Leadership Academy aligns programs with school system initiatives, policies, and priorities as well as the specific school context in order to create deeper, more relevant learning experiences for current school leaders.

- *Mutual Accountability* – The Leadership Academy measures program effectiveness by holding each practitioner in the relationship (e.g., coach/coachee and participant/faculty) accountable for achieving standards and expectations of leadership performance.
- *Ongoing Improvement through Evaluation/Feedback* – With a commitment to organizational learning, the Leadership Academy continually assesses and improves its programs through summative and formative evaluations and external research studies.

The Leadership Academy's Leadership Development Model also views effective and supportive relationships as central to improving leadership performance. The emphasis on teaming and ongoing facilitative interactions between program participants and faculty, mentor principals who guide field-based preparation for aspiring leaders, coaches for current principals and fellow program participants ensure that school leaders are not isolated as they learn and apply their skills in challenging contexts.

Developed and facilitated by expert leadership development practitioners, Leadership Academy programs prepare and strengthen the abilities of aspiring and current school leaders to accelerate student learning. Program designers and faculty, the majority of whom are former school leaders and superintendents who have had strong track records of success as administrators, are trained to apply data-rich, research-based methods to help school leaders improve school performance. They do this by enabling teachers to work collaboratively to improve teaching and learning, using multiple sources of data to inform their decision making and cultivating school cultures that support teachers, students, and families.

The strengths of the Leadership Academy's model are well exemplified by its APP, a nationally recognized program[3] that prepares aspiring New York City public school leaders to become visionary, highly effective principals able to lead schools in a unified effort that orients around accelerating student learning and academic growth, with an emphasis on developing the skill required to transform high-need schools. Employing teamwork, simulations, and job-embedded learning opportunities, APP is a highly selective program that has accepted on average 16 percent of those who apply and graduates only those who meet standards.

The program includes three distinct and related components: six-week summer intensive, which employs teamwork and simulations; a year-long apprenticeship alongside an experienced mentor principal; and a year of coaching support and job-embedded leadership development opportunities.

Evaluation results demonstrate that principals trained and supported through the APP are making a difference (Corcoran, Schwartz, & Weinstein, 2012), particularly in serving high-need schools. In the 2012 peer-reviewed journal article, researchers at NYU's Institute for Education and Social Policy (Corcoran et al., 2012) compared 109 schools led by APP graduates with 331 schools led by other new principals using a variety of statistical analyses. Acknowledging that the Leadership Academy "has succeeded in recruiting and training a large number of new principals to serve in some of the city's most challenging schools" (p. 248), the study's other notable findings show that:

- APP graduates were placed in schools in which less experienced teachers were teaching students with more educational need as well as higher concentrations of minority students and students eligible for free and reduced lunch.
- The "most striking difference" between schools led by APP graduates and those led by comparison principals was that APP graduates were placed in schools that were substantially lower performing than other schools citywide and than comparison schools (p. 242).
- Nonetheless, all methods of analysis conducted by the researchers show that schools led by APP graduates performed at least as well as comparison schools (p. 250). And, according to the study's most robust method of analysis, APP-led schools actually improved more rapidly in both ELA and Math than comparison schools (p. 246), cutting the gap in ELA achievement by nearly half by the principals' third year.

COACHING SUPPORT: A VITAL COMPONENT OF LEADERSHIP DEVELOPMENT

The Leadership Academy's commitment to school leadership coaching grew out of its experience developing aspiring principals. Its faculty recognized early on that in order to best support APP graduates, the majority of whom lead high-need schools, they would need to continue offering development opportunities once principals were placed in schools. With funding from the Wallace Foundation, the Leadership Academy was able to develop and invest in coaching support for its newly placed principals, creating a coaching component that is now vital to its work.

Since 2008, the NYC Department of Education (NYCDOE) has made Leadership Academy 1:1 coaching available to all new NYC public school principals. The NYCDOE provides each new principal with up to 72 hours of coaching annually, which may be used for individual coaching or coupled with retreats for school teams. New principals who seek additional coaching or those beyond their first year can pay for these services using their school-based budgets. With these various offerings, the Leadership Academy has provided coaching support services to well over 1,000 New York City school leaders system-wide.

The Leadership Academy believes that providing real-time support to principals is essential, so that leaders can strengthen teaching and learning and enhance school climate. Most programs invest heavily in the tools and skills to prepare principals for their assignments, yet it is the application of that knowledge on the ground that is most challenging, especially for those assigned to lead troubled schools. One year of support can be critical to giving a leader the confidence and feedback he or she needs to prepare the environment for change. It also can help ensure that the investments in training pay off. One year, however, may not be enough to develop the skills necessary to transform complex environments. Leadership Academy, therefore, believes that both new and experienced principals and the schools they lead, particularly high-need schools, can benefit from more intensive coaching for at least three years.

Coaching: A Growing Practice

What is coaching? Peterson and Hicks (1996) describe coaching as "the process of equipping people with the tools, knowledge and opportunities they need to develop themselves and become more effective" (p. 14). Rather than view coaching as a means of developing people, they see a coach serving as a "catalyst for development" of a leader over an extended period of time. A coach might work across a number of experiences, meeting with individuals one-on-one, guiding from afar, and fostering learning opportunities with others in the organization.

In the private sector, executive coaching typically is reserved for the most senior levels of an organization. Leaders may seek one-on-one guidance from trusted external consultants for executives with development needs that cannot otherwise be met by leadership development programs or peer coaching. Coaches, carefully selected, work confidentially and carefully on identified weaknesses for a concentrated period of time (e.g., six months) to produce desired changes in behavior to support a leader's success (McCauley, Moxley, & Velsor, 1998). Some view the need for coaching as an indication of underperformance; however, those that understand its benefits know it can be a powerful tool to improve individual, and therefore organizational performance.

Executive coaching in the education sector is still relatively new. Policymakers, education officials, and practitioners are increasingly realizing that principals need a broader toolkit – strategies, skills, and knowledge – to lead schools effectively. A growing number of school systems mandate or endorse mentoring, induction, or internships for school leaders, particularly those early in their careers. In 2006, the Education Commission of the States (ECS) conducted a policy scan that found more than a dozen states had policies that provided mentoring and internship opportunities for K-12 school leaders (Hancock, 2006). In January, the National Conference of State Legislatures reported an additional 12 states between 2007 and 2011 that had added mentoring or induction laws. While the language of "coaching" may yet to be common nomenclature in the K-12 sector, laws like that of New Mexico S.B. 85 which provides "intensive support for principals at schools in need of improvement" demonstrates that the need for coaching support is finding its way into the policies that govern schools.

Unlike the private sector, however, school districts often must overcome additional obstacles to realize the benefits coaching support can provide. For instance, districts typically do not have the sophisticated human capital systems or the financial resources of their private sector counterparts. Some educators also inaccurately view coaching as a program to help those "in trouble." Moreover, there is no unified consensus regarding what a high-quality coaching program must entail, nor how such programs should be evaluated.

The positive news is that with more states requiring mentoring and induction programs for early-career teachers and administrators, more attention will be given to how programs and services are developed and assessed. Even though a recent report by the New Teacher Center (2012) showed 27 states requiring induction or mentoring for teachers and only 16 states with administrator requirements, the trend seems to be moving toward more, rather than less, support for administrators. Considering the important role administrators play in the growth of teachers, it logically follows that investments in principals' leadership success would positively impact teacher retention and development. As the report notes, "Through professional development and direct coaching, school and district administrators need an opportunity to build leadership capacity while creating school conditions that support teacher development and student learning" (Goldrick, Osta, Barlin, & Burn, 2012, p. 4).

COACHING TO ENHANCE LEADERSHIP PERFORMANCE

As a grantee of the U.S. Department of Education's School Leadership Program (SLP), the Leadership Academy has been able to expand its preservice APP program to include early-career coaching support for 139 principals leading high-need schools. Each of these principals received at least one year of enhanced support and many principals received two full years of enhanced Leadership Academy coaching. This length of support was particularly important for principals of high-need schools as they faced more significant challenges, more distressing contexts with greater urgency for improvement. A five-year grant that includes a study of student outcomes, principal retention, and other impact measures, the SLP coaching program has helped the Leadership Academy refine its coaching model so principals can strengthen their leadership practice, deepen their knowledge, and expand the capacity of their school teams to lead school improvement efforts. See Appendix A for the SLP Coaching Model Chart, which explains the inputs, activities, and expected outcomes from this coaching program.

The three-year coaching commitment allows coaching to reach beyond the principal to the entire school community. In year one, coaches primarily focus on principal development, while over the next two years support often extends to school teams with an emphasis on distributive leadership. Coaches can build on the trust they have developed to engage in coach-facilitated retreats for the school team. At the same time, principals continue to receive customized feedback and support. Beyond 1:1 coaching, the program includes sessions for the cohort on emerging issues in the field and to address areas of common need, intervisitations (coaches visiting each other's coaching sessions), and targeted school data analysis support, an area of support the Leadership Academy has found facilitates alignment with school plans and is especially critical for principals in high-need schools.

High-quality coaching programs pay careful attention to the coach-coachee relationship, including the selection, development, and placement of the coaches themselves (Bloom, Castagna, Moir, & Warren, 2005). The Leadership Academy knows that for the principals to value and benefit from the coaching relationship, coaches must be confidential and trustworthy. Principals must be able to share professional and personal experiences, concerns, and fears without hesitation; likewise, coaches must be active listeners, skilled at asking the questions that will facilitate reflection, deeper thinking, and growth.

The importance of these relationships is one reason why the Leadership Academy selects coaches that were successful experienced principals, yet who are no longer serving in that capacity. Developing such a cadre of coaches ensures that they have both the experience and the time to focus on the coaching relationship. This also facilitates knowledge of the political climate and other contextual issues, while maintaining confidentiality and a healthy distance. The matching of coaching and principal is a thoughtful process as well, one that considers experiences, expertise, personalities, and development needs.

Once a coach has been matched to a principal, the Leadership Academy provides the coach with a customized school profile to ensure the coaching is as targeted and contextual as it needs to be at the outset of the engagement. Data on school performance, student achievement, demographics, and human capital are compiled in a brief report to offer coaches a snapshot of the school's history over a four-year period. Grounded in the school's context, the coach uses these data to better understand the challenges the school leader may be facing. Attending to these important elements on the front-end of the coaching experience provides greater assurance that the coaching program will have the opportunity to be successful.

While many leadership and executive programs bring experiential and standards-based learning to participants, few include the type of coaching support system that is central to the Leadership Academy's approach. The Leadership Academy's coaching model uses a facilitative, job-embedded learning process that enables principals to develop or strengthen leadership behaviors essential to improving school and student outcomes. Aligned to its leadership development model, it includes the following:

- *Facilitative Learning Process* – The Leadership Academy believes that leaders learn best when they are guided and not told; coaching support, therefore, facilitates learning through enquiry, reflection, and feedback, using clear performance standards to guide the work. Coaches offer confidential support that is not evaluative.
- *Competency-based Coaching* – As in other Leadership Academy programs, coaching focuses on helping leaders assess and improve leadership behaviors that support leadership performance.

- *Responsive to District Needs* — The Leadership Academy provides coaches with ongoing training in school system policies and initiatives so they can play an important role in supporting principals as they respond to district priorities and requirements as they implement their schools' education plans. Coaches, therefore, are trained in new school policies and able to help principals analyze a wide range of school and student-level data to spur school improvement.
- *Tailored Support* — The Leadership Academy believes that coaching in the field must be rooted in the principal's reality and so coaching services may need to be flexible in the short-term to support long-term development. Coaches use a principal's work-based circumstances to craft learning opportunities. Through the analysis and interpretation of school data and the leadership development needs of principals, coaches help guide principals toward school improvement and professional development.

To ensure quality and consistency in the application of this model, the Leadership Academy developed and maintains a database of participants and an online learning community for coaches. The database is used for program development, support, and evaluation and tracks participant and school data, including coaching and leadership. Coaches have access to an extranet which provides a place for information and resources as well as enquiry and collaboration. On this site, for instance, the Leadership Academy's School Leadership Support team posts reports, district policies, and other vital documents that allow coaches to stay grounded in research and respond to changes in the principals' environments. Coaches may pose questions and challenges in a forum, post to a blog, co-create articles, provide feedback to each other, or manage private coaching documents in protected folders. Whether through data collection, engaging in feedback, or providing information and resources, the Leadership Academy offers numerous supports for coaches and, in turn, for coaches to support their principals and each other.

Continuous Support and Feedback

Just as the coaches provide support and feedback to principals, the coaches also receive multiple opportunities for feedback about their coaching practice and ongoing professional development to strengthen their knowledge influence and potential impact. The Leadership Academy considers these program elements essential to ensuring that an investment in coaching pays dividends for the leader, the school staff, and the student body. In addition to this resource investment, coaching requires the cultivation of trust. The establishment of a trusting coaching relationship is critical and requires that all parties – including the district – value the coaching experience and its potential to improve leadership performance and, thus, student achievement. As one Leadership Academy coach described, "The basis of the coaching relationship is trust. Trust is our ability to be clear from the beginning [about] what we [as coaches] commit to deliver, what we expect from [the principals] and how we will work together. You commit to me to do the follow up and that is important. I can't commit to their growth if they're not committed to themselves."

> Trust is fundamental to the development of a coaching relationship; without it no effective coaching relationship can exist. Since every principal is different, both the process of establishing trust and the time it may take to develop it varies from principal to principal.
>
> The trust conversation begins during my initial visit when the principal and I review the coaching agreement. It presents an opportunity to clarifying our respective roles, set the expectations and commitments – what do I as the coach commit to deliver and what do I need the principal to commit in order for us to produce the desired outcomes and achieve the identified goals. Assuring confidentiality is another important element in the development of a trusting coaching relationship. I always look for ways to maintain trust by delivering on promises and holding each other accountable to the goals we set.
>
> There are instances when I have assessed that the trust building process is taking longer than anticipated. In those instances I usually name it directly. By naming it, it gives us a chance to talk about it and discuss what may be preventing the principal from trusting the coaching relationship. That has worked for me.
> — Sonia Bu, NYC Leadership Academy Coach

Competency-Based Support

The Leadership Academy's coaching model is anchored in a partnership between a coach and principal aimed at addressing a set of school leadership competencies found in the organization's Leadership Performance Planning Worksheet (LPPW). Developed by the Leadership Academy and rooted in the day-to-day behaviors most critical to effective leadership, the LPPW grounds the coaching experience. The approach relies on a thought partnership between coach and principal to facilitate behavior changes that are tied to leadership and school performance. When a coach sees something problematic, he/she might ask the principal, "Have you thought about it this way? Or, what do you think will happen if ...?" It is not technical assistance. Rather, the coach fosters a trusting relationship that nonetheless asks the school leader to observe his or her practice dispassionately to identify whether leadership actions met standards.

Coaches are trained and adept at asking difficult questions to ensure that the purpose of the work is front and center. This skilled facilitation by the coach enables the principal to engage in critical and targeted reflection about her/his practice, and to develop concrete opportunities and action steps to further her/his leadership capacity. The majority of coaching takes place at the principal's school and involves ongoing observation of the principal's leadership practice in a variety of settings and contexts.

The Leadership Academy uses the competencies contained in its LPPW to anchor and assess coaching work. Originated as part of a Wallace Foundation initiative to find ways of developing and supporting school leaders so that they could accelerate student achievement, the LPPW presents 39 critical leadership behaviors, which are organized into eight leadership dimensions (Scott, in press). These behaviors were identified through research on instructional leadership, principal development and evaluation, and the LPPW tool was piloted over two years in urban, suburban and rural school districts in the United States. Introduced in 2008, use of the LPPW expanded quickly to sites across 11 states in three years and has been tested with early-career principals as well as assistant principals, aspiring principals, teacher leaders, superintendents, and other district administrators. These applications have allowed the Leadership Academy to refine its development programs, tools, and applications through a growing learning community focused on effective leadership.

The LPPW enriches the coaching process by providing a developmental framework and common language that allows principals to self-assess their leadership competencies and behaviors and, working with their coach, to identify areas of development strength and need. These 39 behaviors and eight leadership dimensions are shown in Fig. 1.

The Leadership Academy's coaching model helps principals develop their leadership skills through a facilitated, job-embedded learning process aligned to LPPW competencies. The coach acts as confidential advisor, creating conditions that allow principals to reveal what they do not know without fear of judgment or professional vulnerability. They are able to use the LPPW as a self-assessment tool, rating behaviors as either

Accelerating Leadership Excellence

Identifies 39 core leadership behaviors organized into 8 leadership dimensions

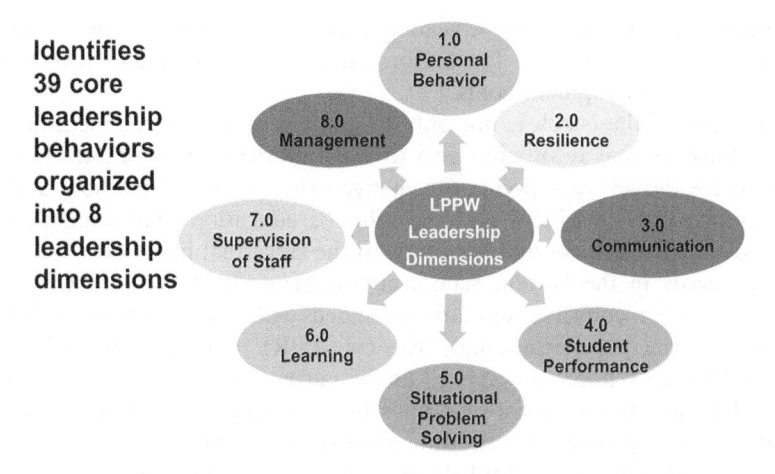

- 1.0 Personal Behavior
- 2.0 Resilience
- 3.0 Communication
- 4.0 Student Performance
- 5.0 Situational Problem Solving
- 6.0 Learning
- 7.0 Supervision of Staff
- 8.0 Management

Fig. 1. LPPW Leadership Dimensions.

"approaching the standard" or "meeting the standards" so they can isolate which dimensions need attention. See Appendix B for a sample LPPW dimension.

While working on a set of leadership behaviors, coaches ground their work in the school's education plan. They seek to support principals in addressing the conditions that inhibit teaching and learning and ultimately in meeting and exceeding district-based performance goals. Typically at the start of an engagement, principals and coaches create a Coaching Compact, an agreement that outlines the coach and principal expectations and desired outcomes. The coach learns as much as he/she can about the school, its environment, and the principal's vision and effectiveness so that he/she is providing thoughtful feedback from the start of the engagement.

The LPPW provides the leadership dimensions for self-assessment and principals rate themselves in these dimensions on an Individual Growth Plan (IGP), which contains a self-assessment tool and section to identify the areas that will constitute the focus of the coaching work. Conversations between the coach and the principal include what skills are most important in their current placement so that the IGP reflects a plan for the principal in the context of the school. Throughout the year, the principal and coach use the IGP as a guidepost for assessing leadership growth and to refine development planning. At the end of the engagement, a post-assessment IGP, which also uses the LPPW dimensions, is administered to evaluate the success of the coaching experience in helping the principal build leadership capacity for performance improvement and meet their professional development goals.

The job of the coach is not only to address specific needs identified in the self-assessment results but also to use multiple sources of data to find out where the leverage points for change exist, both in the school and in the principal. The LPPW and the school's education plan (e.g., School Improvement Plan) act like bookends to the skills that most meet the principal's needs in the current school environment. In New York City, for instance, these conversations are grounded with data from the district-required Principal Performance Review (PPR). Coaches are skilled in understanding school data as well as the current demands of the job, and thus, they are able to assist principals in ensuring they have the necessary leadership competencies to meet the goals of their PPRs.

The Leadership Academy believes that when coaches are responsive to district policies and priorities they can more effectively help principals meet the challenges of their complex roles. Coach Kevin McCormack explained, "I've had them linking their Individual Growth Plan with the PPR very closely, and then using that to drive a deeper conversation around leadership skills and the LPPW dimensions and enhancing those skills that they want to develop around resilience or communication or any of the dimensions that they chose." By aligning their work to the needs of the school and district, the coach ensures that their work is relevant and that their leadership development goals support district strategies for school improvement.

While the Leadership Academy uses a framework with tools, assessments that are grounded in leadership competencies, they also realize that coaching is more art than science. Coaching cannot follow a blueprint for action; rather, coaches must be flexible in the ways in which they guide principal development. A strong coach offers support that is rooted in the principal's reality. This might mean, for instance, that the coach decides to focus on immediate, short-term (transactional) needs in service of growth and development for longer-term (transformational) support.

> We set goals at the start of the year with principals and try to work through them. They might want to raise reading scores 5 percent. But we are flexible.....If they have a problem they need to discuss, we talk about that, like "my superintendent stopped in last week and did a walkthrough and I need to talk about that." It's all about helping them.
>
> I'll try to connect the conversations back to their goals at some point. What's important to me is getting to what's important to them. There may be an opportunity for a

> teachable moment but you can't plan them. Good coaches are active listeners so when those opportunities present themselves, we use them to open another opportunity or help them see another way to address or attack a problem to be a better principal.
> — Kevin McCormack, NYC Leadership Academy Coach

> Coaching is a unique experience with and for each of my principals. While my coaching is always guided by our competency-based facilitative coaching framework and approach, each coaching session is different in its implementation. I differentiate each session to meet the needs and learning style of the principals. The differentiation may also be generated by the presenting issue, the mood of the principal at that moment, and/or my purpose for the session. For example, do I need to create a platform from which to push the principal's thinking or do I need to provoke anxiety in order to produce the "aha" learning moment for the principal?
> — Sonia Bu, NYC Leadership Academy Coach

A skilled coach will encourage the type of candid feedback and communication that allows the principal – or the principal's staff – to reveal needs that may fall outside of the typical coaching activities but that may be essential to address before a principal even sees the behaviors that need to change. Assisting a principal with an immediate crisis might give the coach insight that will help the principal evaluate why it happened and how they can build the skills necessary to avoid such "fires" in the future. The coach's role is to find opportunities to bring clarity to the leader's thinking, to pull back and reflect on situations, and to help the principal learn how to be a better leader.

When Leadership Academy coach Kevin McCormack was assigned to a principal of a new school, he watched as she doubled her staff in one year as the school grew. She was struggling in her efforts to institute a culture of accountability. He remembers reminding himself to "be comfortable in the silence" as she shared her frustrations with her staff and their seeming lack of commitment. "It's not about me solving the problem; it's about me asking the right questions to get her to rethink the problem," he explained. After listening actively, he paused and asked her, "What do you think your role has been in this?" She sat back in her chair, reflected and admitted she had never considered the role she may have played in not building the community she knew was right for children.

Coaching experiences are especially rewarding when visible change follows a powerful realization. In Kevin's case, his principal began to address communications concerns, establishing a new website, reaching out to teams to help enhance student work, and being positive with all staff members, especially those that were a little resistant. "Coaching is about the principal's willingness to be open and receptive to having someone question them," he said. "To have a coach come in and challenge a principal in those areas can be difficult for the principal."

The coach is always looking for the teachable moments that will make a difference in a leader's current and future performance. Coaches use many sources of data from the principal, the district, and school team to stay grounded in the reality of the school context. The tools and data offer important frameworks for decision-making, and yet ultimately there is no recipe. Coaching must be customized to meet the individual and immediate needs of that school leader while at the same time building skills that will ensure the leader's long-term success.

Dual Development Focus

Most coaching programs emphasize the coaching experience itself. The Leadership Academy's approach views the coaching relationship as dependent on a skilled set of coaches also committed to their own growth and development. Effective coaching, therefore, includes a set of experiences between coach and principal, and programming for the coaches as well.

For the principals receiving coaching support, the Leadership Academy offers a set of experiences designed for one-on-one, school team, and group capacity building. The engagement between coach and principal is typically a one-on-one relationship, averaging six hours per month. Part of this time may be used for analysis of data, reflection of practice, and guidance for action, and part may be for job-embedded learning experiences.

While coaching is anchored in the relationship with the principal, it may extend beyond to strengthen and sustain leadership throughout the school. For instance, through the SLP project, the Leadership Academy focused on improving principal retention and student outcomes for more than 50 early-career APP principals leading high-need schools. In addition to the one-on-one support for principals, which emphasizes analysis and interpretation of school data in particular, coaching services also provided whole school support to promote capacity building across the school community.

Specific opportunities for whole school support also include retreats and just-in-time sessions. School teams often use retreats to work through school-wide issues or build capacity in a particular area. These off-site experiences align with the instructional focus of the principal and bring specific skills or facilitation to more of the school community. Just-in-time sessions are Leadership Academy-led meetings designed to address common needs of the cohort and issues emerging in the field such as teacher effectiveness, time management, or building powerful partnerships. One goal of these sessions is to help the principal develop the leadership capacity of their teams, and so typically the principal is invited to attend the session along with one or two members of his/her staff.

In order to best serve the needs of principals, professional development for coaches is deep and ongoing at the Leadership Academy. It focuses on school data analysis and increasing the ability of coaches to design professional development in response to issues that emerge in the field for themselves and the principals. In order to ensure quality in the field, feedback is regularly provided to coaches so that they can fine-tune their coaching practice and guide program improvements. Some of the ways in which the program team supports coaches include:

- *Coaching Competencies.* These are clear, behaviorally-based standards for effective coaching that emphasize the importance of authentic feedback.
- *Coaching Conferences.* Approximately every six weeks, the program team meets with each coach to discuss individual principals, identify high-priority cases, surface professional development needs, review coach-specific program evaluation data, and solicit feedback.
- *Team Meetings.* These meetings, also every six weeks, provide opportunities for professional development (speakers, working groups, consultancies). They may emphasize problem-based learning, address operational issues, or provide opportunities for peer-to-peer work and support.
- *Field Observation.* These less frequent (three times per year) low-inference observations are aligned to coaching competencies and focus on exploring coaching decisions.
- *Professional Development.* Coaches also receive ongoing professional development and resource development experiences, informed by formal and informal coach feedback. These experiences are delivered using a variety of modalities – small group, 1:1 support, intervisitations – to meet individual needs and ensure coaching quality and consistency.

One final dimension of coaching support is the peer-to-peer assistance that the Leadership Academy coaches offer each other. In a field that is relatively new and an arena wherein policies and laws frequently change, the need for peer support is clear. As one NYCLA coach explained, "It's been an enormous growth opportunity for me to be able to coach with another person and watch them interact with the principal and also be able to interact with the principal myself. The process allows us – even with the principal right there – to be able to trade ideas back and forth with the other coach, trying to wrestle with the particular problem that the principal has."

The Leadership Academy is committed to coaching as a professional practice and, as such, continues to strengthen the opportunities it provides for peer-to-peer feedback and support. Currently, they offer the following structured supports:

- *Working Groups.* These groups are self-formed by coaches based on interests and needs for coaching support.
- *Intervisitations.* In this opportunity, coaches can visit each other in the field and reflect on practice. They may be matched based on a needed skill or interest area. While voluntary, there are reflection sheets and many coaches take advantage of this twice per year.
- *Session Facilitation and Design.* Coaches work in teams to design a just-in-time session for early-career SLP-supported principals based on issues that have emerged in the field (e.g., application of new budget mandates or focus on supervision issue common among participants). These design groups develop and then one or more coaches facilitate the session.
- *Identification of Colleagues with Subject Matter Expertise.* The Leadership Academy has developed an official coaching specialization in budget and school data. It also draws on other coaches for specific expertise in subjects such as special education or transfer schools (i.e., schools for undercredited or overage students). Coaches work closely together and are knowledgeable about the types of expertise each of their peers offer.

In an ideal world, the impact of coaching would have a clear and measurable outcome: gains in student achievement. Like many variables affecting student achievement, however, coaching may have tremendous influence but the influence is indirect and difficult to isolate. While the Leadership Academy sees value in exploring the relationship between principal coaching and student gains, it considers changes in leadership behaviors as the primary metric of its coaching program evaluation, focusing on principals' development of competencies known to influence student achievement.

The IGP serves as an anchor in the coaching experience, providing pre- and post-assessment data for principals and their coaches. Each principal–coach pair targets a selection of leadership behaviors based on their pre-assessments of the principal's strengths and weaknesses. The subsequent coaching, then, focuses on improving the principal's targeted behaviors. The post-assessment enables each principal–coach pair to evaluate the progress the principal has made in these behaviors. The Leadership Academy relies on the notion that with improved leadership performance in this set of competencies comes improvements in student achievement.

Measures of school improvement are essential in evaluating coaching success; however, they cannot be the sole metric used to assess coaching effectiveness. That is why the Leadership Academy uses many forms of evaluation to assess the success of a coaching relationship. How was the coaching support received? How committed was the leader to their plan for leadership performance improvement? How did the principal's practice change? How did the principal progress toward the goals of the engagement? How much did the principal change the learning environment and move student achievement? These are essential questions for those focused on strengthening leadership practice that enhances student learning.

The Leadership Academy views principal feedback about the coaching experience a critical indicator of coaching success. In 2010–2011, coached principals reported an average rating of 3.8 (on a four-point scale with 4 = significantly) when asked about the extent to which the coaching they received increased leadership capacity at their schools. They also reported an average rating of 3.9 (on the same scale) when asked about the extent to which they were satisfied with the support they received from their Academy coach. Ninety-three percent of the responding coached principals reported that their coaches significantly pushed their thinking. Over 80 percent of coached principals attributed their development in the LPPW leadership dimensions directly to their work with their coach.[4]

As more states and districts embrace support systems for school leaders, there is an important opportunity for the field to define leading indicators for coaching success. Such indicators would tie to leadership behaviors and competencies known to influence leader performance and student achievement. Metrics would extend beyond student achievement, which, while the ultimate performance measure, is difficult to tie to a coaching experience.

LEADERSHIP COACHING AS PROFESSIONAL PRACTICE

> Through coaching I support principals [as they] navigate a very complex system with often-competing priorities and demands on their time, attention and expected outcomes. Coaching also helps principals reconnect with what they care about (what brought them to become educators and principals) in order for them to re-focus their attention on improving instruction and increasing students performance and outcomes. I see myself as a mirror that reflects for the principals their strengths, their passion and their commitment to their students and learning community.
> — Sonia Bu, NYC Leadership Academy Coach

High-quality coaching is about building a leader's capacity to analyze, assess, develop, and improve the behaviors that drive performance.

Effective coaching is systematic, utilizing tools and models of reflection and support that promote leadership growth and development. Yet, coaching is also flexible, capitalizing on real-time opportunities to strengthen abilities in context. Short-term needs may take precedent so that long-term growth can be achieved.

The Leadership Academy's coaching model, while well developed, is continuously improving as it strives to meet the needs of principals in the field. In an era of heightened accountability, coaches must understand and help their principals grasp the urgency around accountability measures. At times, they may need to help solve complex problems or immediate challenges with critical stakeholders. Yet, they must maintain their roles as coaches, confidentially supporting and facilitating without compromising objectivity.

It is for this reason that coaching at the Leadership Academy is a professional practice that requires feedback and learning loops like the relationship between coach and principal, and the network of coaches. Like the medical rounds model applied to the K-12 context as networks of superintendents form communities of practice to diagnose and solve problems to improve instruction (Elmore, 2007), the Leadership Academy views opportunities for skilled feedback and practice as essential to developing leaders that can transform schools. This commitment to the principal as learner as well as leader is similar to the type of iterative and developmental feedback found in formative assessments used to improve classroom learning, which research has found to support learning gains (Black & William, 1998).

With evidence that early-career principals in high-need schools experience higher turnover and their schools continue to suffer (Burkhauser et al., 2012), more attention may need to be paid to the impact coaching has on leader performance. Like many of their Rainwater Alliance peers, the Leadership Academy has demonstrated that leadership matters in transforming schools. With continued research and support from their peers, partners, and supporters like the USDOE's School Leadership Program and the Wallace Foundation the Leadership Academy is now focused on identifying how leadership contributes to leadership performance.

NOTES

1. In this chapter, "coaching" refers to the practice of supporting and guiding transformational development in principals, through confidential one-on-one sessions, observation, retreats, and other development activities. Some organization

may use the term "mentoring" for similar relationships and support of leadership performance.

2. For purposes of the SLP grant, the NYC Leadership Academy defines a "high-need" school as a school that is eligible for Title 1 funding (high free/reduced lunch rates) and meeting one or more of the following criteria: non-screened, new or small school; low-performing (schools with statistics unsatisfactory compared to citywide averages); concentration of student subpopulations (higher concentration of students with IEPs or ELL than citywide averages); complex organizational challenges (schools with statistics unsatisfactory compared to citywide averages, such as schools in restructuring or corrective action).

3. The Leadership Academy is recognized as an exemplar-level program within the Bush Institute's Alliance to Reform Education Leadership and is featured in the U.S. Department of Education's Doing What Works program, an online library of resources providing tools to implement research-based instructional practices in schools (http://www.bushcenter.com/newsreleases/2011/12/presidentgeorge-w-bush-meets-with-new-york-city-education-leaders. Accessed on March 20, 2012; http://dww.ed.gov/School-Turnaround/Improved-Leadership/see/?T_ID521&P_ID544&c152407&c252407&c352407. Accessed on March 21, 2012).

4. Leadership Academy internal survey data.

REFERENCES

Black, P., & William, D. (1998). Assessment and classroom learning. *Assessment in Education: Principles, Policy & Practice, 5*(1), 7–74.

Bloom, G., Castagna, C., Moir, E., & Warren, B. (2005). *Blended coaching: skills and strategies to support principal development.* Thousand Oaks, CA: Corwin Press.

Burkhauser, S., Gates, S., Hamilton, L., & Ikemoto, G. (2012). *First-year principals in urban school districts: How actions and working conditions relate to outcomes.* Santa Monica, CA: RAND Education.

Cheney, G. R., Davis, J, Garrett, K, & Holleran, J. (2010). *A new approach to principal preparation: Innovative programs share their practices and lessons learned.* Fort Worth, TX: The Rainwater Charitable Foundation.

Chenoweth, K., & Theokas, C. (2011). *Getting it done: Leading academic success in unexpected schools.* Cambridge, MA: Harvard Education Press.

Corcoran, S., Schwartz, A., & Weinstein, M. (2012). Training your own: The impact of New York City's aspiring principals program on student achievement. *Educational Evaluation and Policy Analysis, 34*(2), 232–253.

Elmore, R. F. (2000). *Building a new structure for school leadership.* Washington, DC: The Shanker Institute.

Elmore, R. F. (2007). Professional networks and school improvements. *School Administrator,* 20–24.

Fullan, M. (2001). *Leading in a culture of change.* San Francisco, CA: Jossey-Bass.

Goldrick, L., Osta, D., Barlin, D., & Burn, J. (February, 2012). *Review of state policies on teacher induction.* Santa Cruz, CA: New Teacher Center.

Hallinger, P., & Heck, R. H. (1996). Reassessing the principal's role in school effectiveness: A review of empirical research, 1980–1995. *Educational Administration Quarterly, 32,* 5–22.

Hancock, J. (2006). *Mentor programs for leaders: A policy scan.* Denver, CO: Education Commission of the States.

Hargreaves, A. & Fink, D. (2006). *Sustainable leadership.* San Francisco, CA: John Wiley & Sons, Inc.

Leithwood, K., Harris, A., & Hopkins, D. (2008). Seven strong claims about successful school leadership. *School Leadership and Management, 28,* 27–42.

Leithwood, K., & Jantzi, D. (1999). The relative effects of principal and teacher sources of leadership on student engagement with school. *Educational Administration Quarterly, 35,* 679–706.

Leithwood, K., Seashore Louis, K., Anderson, S., & Wahlstrom, K. (2004) How leadership influences student learning. St. Paul, MN: Center for Applied Research in Education, University of Minnesota and Ontario Institute for Studies in Education, University of Toronto. Retrieved from http://www.wallacefoundation.org/knowledge-center/school-leadership/key-research/Documents/How-Leadership-Influences-Student-Learning.pdf. Accessed on March 10, 2012.

Marzano, R., Waters, T., & McNulty, B. (2005). *School leadership that works: From research to results.* Alexandria, VA: Association of Supervision and Curriculum Development.

McCauley, C., Moxley, R., & Velsor, E. (Eds.). (1998). *Handbook of leadership development.* San Fransisco, CA: Jossey Bass.

Peterson, D., & Hicks, M. (1996). *Leader as coach: Strategic for coaching and developing others.* Minneapolis, MN: Personnel Decisions International.

Scott, L. (in press). The Leadership Performance Planning Worksheet (LPPW): A development tool for early career school leaders. In J. Shen (Ed.), *Tools for improving school principals' work* (pp. 169–200). New York, NY: Peter Lang Publishing.

Seashore Louis, K., Wahlstrom, K. L., Michlin, M., Gordon, M., Thomas, E., Leithwood, K., …, Moore, S. (2010). Learning from leadership: Investigating the links to improved student learning. St. Paul, MN: Center for Applied Research in Education, University of Minnesota and Ontario Institute for Studies in Education, University of Toronto. Retrieved from http://www.wallacefoundation.org/knowledge-center/school-leadership/key-research/Documents/Investigating-the-Links-to-Improved-Student-Learning.pdf. Accessed on March 1, 2012.

Southern Regional Education Board (SREB). (2001). *Preparing a new breed of school principals: it's time for action.* Atlanta, GA: Bottoms, G & O'Neill, K.

Williams, T., Perry, M., Studier, C., Brazil, N., Kirst, M., Haertel, E., …, Levine, R. (2005). *Similar students, different results: Why do some schools do better? A large-scale survey of California elementary schools serving low-income students.* Mountain View, CA: EdSource.

APPENDIX A: NYC LEADERSHIP ACADEMY SLP COACHING MODEL

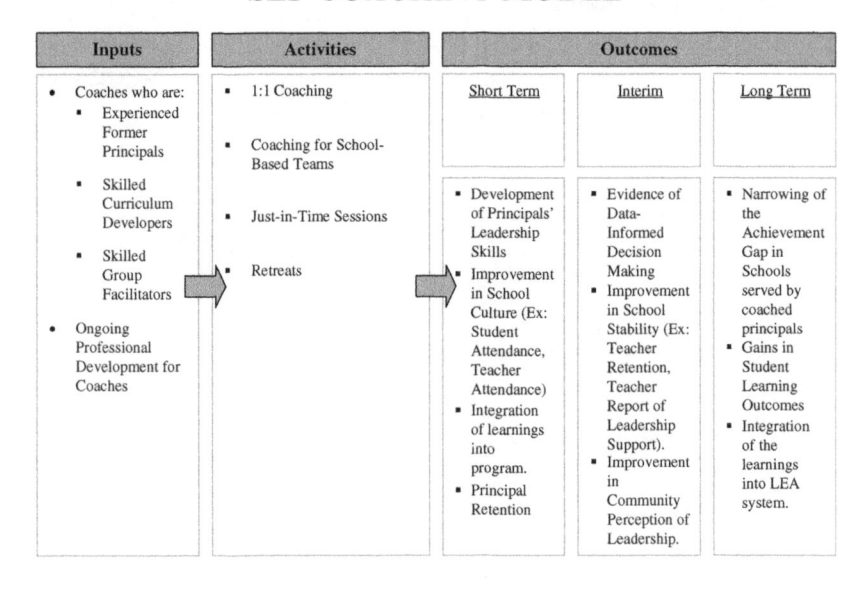

Inputs	Activities	Outcomes		
		Short Term	Interim	Long Term
Coaches who are: • Experienced Former Principals • Skilled Curriculum Developers • Skilled Group Facilitators • Ongoing Professional Development for Coaches	• 1:1 Coaching • Coaching for School-Based Teams • Just-in-Time Sessions • Retreats	• Development of Principals' Leadership Skills • Improvement in School Culture (Ex: Student Attendance, Teacher Attendance) • Integration of learnings into program. • Principal Retention	• Evidence of Data-Informed Decision Making • Improvement in School Stability (Ex: Teacher Retention, Teacher Report of Leadership Support). • Improvement in Community Perception of Leadership.	• Narrowing of the Achievement Gap in Schools served by coached principals • Gains in Student Learning Outcomes • Integration of the learnings into LEA system.

APPENDIX B

NYC Leadership Academy
The Leadership Performance Planning Worksheet

Dear School Leader,

Welcome to the Leadership Performance Planning Worksheet (LPPW), a tool designed to help early-career school leaders improve student progress through effective instructional leadership.

Developed by the NYC Leadership Academy in consultation with The Wallace Foundation and the state education departments of Delaware, Missouri and Kentucky, the LPPW reflects a thorough review and synthesis of principal leadership standards used nationally, including ISLLC. It is grounded in the belief that focused work on a subset of clearly defined school leadership competencies helps early-career school leaders promote student success. The LPPW contains eight leadership dimensions — (1) Personal Behavior, (2) Resilience, (3) Communication, (4) Student Performance, (5) Situational Problem Solving, (6) Learning, (7) Supervision of Staff, and (8) Management — and identifies core leadership behaviors critical to each. These core behaviors address the day-to-day challenges of school leadership and are responsive to a wide range of principal performance standards. The goal of the use of the LPPW is to ground the coaching (mentoring) relationship in concrete skill and knowledge development and set actionable goals.

School Leaders:

- Review the LPPW with your coach (mentor) early in the school year to identify the leadership dimensions you need to strengthen to improve student learning within the context of your school. You and your coach (mentor) should discuss your leadership behaviors and the outcomes they generate.

- Together with your coach (mentor), develop purposeful, evidence-based, leadership support and development strategies for your work together.

- Make the LPPW a living document by discussing and charting your leadership growth and progress regularly.

Coaches/Mentors:

- At the beginning of the school year, communicate to the school leaders you coach (mentor) that the LPPW review process is an opportunity for growth, and create an environment that enables them to be reflective and open about their strengths and weaknesses.

- Use the LPPW throughout the year to establish a common language for your coaching (mentoring) relationship and to focus your work together on concrete knowledge and skills development.

Copyright © 2010 by NYC Leadership Academy, Inc., Long Island City, NY. All rights reserved.

Accelerating Leadership Excellence 235

Student Performance

Leadership Dimension	Behaviors That Meet the Standard
4.1 Plans and sets goals for student performance ○ Meets Standard ○ Approaches Standard	⇨ Leader sets goals that are within the zone of proximal development for students, teachers, and the organization.
4.2 Recruits and retains qualified staff ○ Meets Standard ○ Approaches Standard	⇨ Leader develops and implements plan to attract and retain qualified teachers and staff.
4.3 Ensures continual improvement for students, teachers, and the organization ○ Meets Standard ○ Approaches Standard	⇨ Leader possesses working knowledge of current curricular initiatives, approaches to content, and differentiated instructional design including the options offered by technology. ⇨ Leader understands, articulates, and implements effective instructional strategies and evaluates their effectiveness. ⇨ Leader focuses staff meetings on instructional issues.
4.4 Demonstrates understanding of the relationship between assessment, standards, and curriculum ○ Meets Standard ○ Approaches Standard	⇨ Leader facilitates the analysis and alignment of assessment tools and the curriculum. ⇨ Leader aligns school's organizational structure, resources, and instructional priorities to address learning standards and leverage student learning.
4.5 Reports student achievement results transparently ○ Meets Standard ○ Approaches Standard	⇨ Leader gathers and uses multiple indicators of student success that reveal patterns, trends, and insights. ⇨ Leader creates systems to make school data accessible and understood by staff, families, and students.

Progress Update **4.0**

Areas for Improvement

Next Steps

Student Performance

Leadership Dimension	Behaviors That Meet the Standard
4.6 Uses student performance data to make instructional leadership decisions ○ Meets Standard ○ Approaches Standard	⇨ Leader uses student performance data to guide decisions about instruction. ⇨ Leader provides staff with framework for looking at student work to identify instructional next steps for teachers and students.
4.7 Implements a systemic approach for struggling learners and special populations and critically reviews all approaches for effectiveness ○ Meets Standard ○ Approaches Standard	⇨ Leader monitors intervention strategies for effectiveness and adjusts them to accelerate learning. ⇨ Leader includes specialized knowledge and skills into general practice.
4.8 Continually reads and interprets the environment to identify patterns in student performance indicators ○ Meets Standard ○ Approaches Standard	⇨ Leader uses a multi-dimensional environmental analysis of student performance indicators. Diagnosis is ongoing.

Progress Update **4.0**

Areas for Improvement

Next Steps

CHAPTER 12

THE INTEGRATION OF PRACTICAL, COGNITIVE, AND MORAL APPRENTICESHIPS FOR LEADERSHIP LEARNING: THE EVOLUTION AND INITIAL IMPACT OF FULL-TIME INTERNSHIPS

Susan Korach and Maureen Sanders

ABSTRACT

This chapter presents an integrated model of principal preparation featuring full-time internships and enquiry-based coursework. The development of the full-time internship component is the result of an award of a US DoE School Leadership Program grant in 2008 to expand and enhance the Ritchie Program for School Leaders, a collaborative principal preparation program between University of Denver and Denver Public Schools. The integration of Shulman's (2005) model of practical, cognitive, and moral apprenticeships for professional education provided the foundation of the design and implementation of full-time internships through this collaborative partnership for principal preparation.

Collaboration among interns, host principals, district leadership, and university faculty provides the focus, means, and structures of learning. This chapter describes the evolution of the Ritchie Program for School Leaders through features and initial impact of full-time internships and offers lessons learned about mentoring aspiring leaders.

"Professional education is about developing pedagogies to link ideas, practices, and values under conditions of inherent uncertainty that necessitate not only judgment in order to act, but also cognizance of the consequences of one's action." (Shulman, 2005, p. 19)

Applying Shulman's definition of professional education to the obligation of preparation programs focuses the purpose around preparing aspiring leaders to act ethically and effectively. He promotes a pedagogy for professional education that supports aspiring leaders as they "engage in practice" with "a sense of personal and social responsibility" (Shulman, 2005, p. 18). To optimize this learning, the context of the profession and the preparation of professionals should be interconnected and enable generative knowledge development. According to Franke, Carpenter, Levi, and Fennema (2001), knowledge becomes generative when one sees the need to integrate newly gained knowledge with existing knowledge to continue learning and to solve new and unfamiliar problems. The rapid pace of change in the 21st century requires educators to become generative in their thinking and their practices. In order to meet the educational needs of aspiring leaders, professional learning must be embedded in the context of practice so educators can continually connect their theoretical knowledge with the practical knowledge that they gain from their families, students, and communities.

There are no technical solutions to the issues of teaching and learning. In fact, the educational system is filled with technical innovations, but the complex and interrelated nature of problems require a sophisticated continuous improvement orientation to uncover the layers of cause and effect and determine actions. An integration of the school, district, and university systems has the capability to promote generative learning and provide coherence to a system beset with educator overload and multiple fragmented innovations. Learning experiences that are connected to the real work of improving schools significantly add to the depth and breadth of knowledge and skills that prospective teachers and leaders obtain and use (Martin, Ford, Murphy, & Muth, 1998).

The Carnegie Foundation for the Advancement of Teaching conducted a ten-year study to understand how aspiring leaders are prepared for practice in the professional fields of law, engineering, the clergy, teaching, nursing, and medicine. One result of this study was the conclusion that professional education is

> ... a synthesis of three apprenticeships — a cognitive apprenticeship wherein one learns to think like a professional, a practical apprenticeship where one learns to perform like a professional, and a moral apprenticeship where one learns to think and act in a responsible and ethical manner that integrates across all three domains. (Shulman, 2005, p. 3)

University-based principal preparation has historically consisted of models that isolate the cognitive and practical dimensions of leadership development. Program participants often learn theories and methods within university settings that they are then expected to apply within schools with little interaction between university faculty and school practitioners (Murphy, 1992; Murphy & Vriesenga, 2004). These models have been criticized and deemed ineffective by those within and outside of the field (Hess, 2003; Levine, 2005; McCarthy, 1999; McCarthy & Forsyth, 2009; Murphy, 2002; Murphy & Forsyth, 1999). Research has shown the connections between leadership preparation and the practice of the principal (Darling-Hammond, Meyerson, LaPointe, & Orr, 2009) and the relationship between principal preparation and school outcomes (Braun, Gable, & Kite, 2008; Martorell, Heaton, Gates, & Hamilton, 2010; Orr & Orphanos, 2011). Effective leadership programs offer a coherent curriculum that links theory and practice, and productive pedagogy that emphasizes problem-based learning, action research, and field-based projects with robust internships that are well-designed and supervised, are grounded in both theory and practice, and allow participants to engage in leadership roles (Darling-Hammond et al., 2009). The components of exemplary principal preparation indicate the need to provide developing leaders experiences where they can integrate theory and practice within an authentic and accountable leadership context.

This chapter presents an integrated model of principal preparation featuring full-time internships and enquiry-based coursework, grounded in instructional leadership to improve student achievement within a school. The development of the full-time internship component is the result of an award of a 2008 US DoE School Leadership Program grant to expand and enhance the Ritchie Program for School Leaders, a collaborative principal preparation program between University of Denver and Denver Public

Schools. Collaboration among interns, host principals, district leadership, and university faculty provides the focus, means, and structures of learning in this program. This chapter describes the evolution of the Ritchie Program for School Leaders and the features and initial impact of the addition of full-time internships.

RITCHIE PROGRAM FOR SCHOOL LEADERS

In 2002, the University of Denver and Denver Public Schools worked together to refocus their work to improve the preparation and performance of principals. The school district recognized that the principal was the key lever to supporting and improving teacher practice. District leaders believed that in order to close the achievement gap, improve student achievement, and hold all adults accountable for higher expectations they must become engaged in the process of developing their own aspiring leaders. The district and the university began to craft a principal preparation program to provide a coherent and coordinated system for leadership development based on the district's existing needs and goals. The Ritchie Program for School Leaders evolved from an examination of the core values and practices of the district and the standards and promising practices of urban school leadership. This analysis of the district's strengths and needs led to a call for collaborative action that linked the development of principal knowledge and skill with the work within the principal preparation program (Korach, 2011).

The vision of the Ritchie Program for School Leaders was to develop relentless, courageous, and effective instructional leaders who are knowledgeable, highly skilled, and committed to building learning communities designed to accelerate the achievement and success of each and every student. The program's commitment to values essential for ethical and responsible leadership in urban settings is reflected in the interactions of theories of action science, dialogue, self-organized learning and learning organizations, systems, change, and culture (Argyris & Schön, 1978; Deal & Peterson, 1999; Fullan, 2001; Freire, 1972; Harri-Augstein & Thomas, 1991; Senge, 1990; Wheatley, 2001), and operationalized within the program's coursework, projects and experiences. The goal was that the aspiring leaders would develop the skills and ways of thinking to become highly effective principals within the district. The Ritchie Program featured the following components that are consistent with the characteristics of

Integration of Practical, Cognitive, and Moral Apprenticeships 241

practices associated with effective school leader preparation programs (Darling-Hammond et al., 2009):

- A multi-day retreat immersed the cohort in experiential activities, authentic leadership work, and theories of systems, culture, and change and fostered relationships for the year-long journey of leadership learning
- Four quarters of university coursework integrated leadership theory, effective practice, and district context through weekly six-hour seminars facilitated by a teaching team of three Ritchie facilitators (one facilitator is a Denver Public School (DPS) employee).
- Five action research projects allowed participants to apply program content, engage them in the reform work at the district school, and contribute to the school's capacity to improve.
- Four quarters of an internship within a district school required participants to gather data and apply learning in addition to performing their existing job responsibilities with the support of the school principals serving as mentor principals.

Participants were individually responsible to demonstrate leadership knowledge and skills as they negotiated the demands of their job with the expectations of the program. Each participant received additional support and advocacy from one of the Ritchie facilitators to integrate theory and practice and collaborate with the mentor principal. The emphasis of the program was to develop not only effective leadership skills, but also the dispositions and habits of mind that are integral to ethical and responsible leadership as a principal in an urban setting.

RITCHIE PROGRAM EVALUATION AND IMPROVEMENT

Since the goal of this program was to prepare principals capable of accelerating the achievement and success of all students in district schools, it was important to execute program evaluation that followed graduates into their practice as leaders. The multidimensional evaluation plan was designed in alignment with the theoretical base of the program and reflected Guskey's (2000) model of critical levels of professional development evaluation.

Table 1. Ritchie Program Evaluation Plan

Evaluation Level	Data Sources	Use
Participants' reactions	2005–present – Ritchie Program case study consisting of document review, surveys, interviews with program graduates, mentor principals, faculty, and district administration 2007–present – School Leadership Preparation and Practice Survey (formerly the UCEA/LTEL Survey of Leadership Preparation and Practice) – perception of program graduates about their learning, leadership skills relative to quality program features (Davis, Darling-Hammond, LaPointe, & Meyerson, 2005)	Annual revision of program content and delivery Annual alignment with district expectations of principals National comparisons Identification and prioritization of needs for funding
Participants' learning	Project protocols and rubrics Mentor principal evaluation	Ongoing program adjustments and feedback to participants
Organization support and change	An evaluation of the principal preparation program was conducted by an external entity (Palaich, Kramer-Wine, Anthes, & Walker, 2008); Interview protocol for program faculty, district leaders, program graduates, and current program participants based on high-quality program features (Davis et al., 2005)	Validation of internal program review Validation of results from School Leadership Preparation and Practice Survey (formerly the UCEA/LTEL Survey of Leadership Preparation and Practice) Support for 2008 US DoE School Leadership Program grant request

Each year results were shared with district leadership and program faculty and influenced programmatic change and district priorities for funding. Table 1 summarizes the main components of the evaluation plan.

Each phase of the evaluation plan influenced both the content and delivery and the program and identified needs for further research. Initial findings from the Ritchie Program case study and the administration of the School Leadership Preparation and Practice Survey (formerly the UCEA/LTEL Survey of Leadership Preparation and Practice) revealed that the Ritchie Program graduates rated it most highly on program features based on best practices research and studies of exemplary leadership preparation programs as compared to graduates in a nonpurposeful sample of 17 leadership preparation programs (Orr, 2010). However, there were two areas where the results from the graduates of the Ritchie Program for School Leaders were lower compared to that of the average of the national sample: the areas of managing school operations efficiently and supervision by knowledgeable school leaders. Participants in the Ritchie Program completed the requirements of the internship in addition to the workload of their current district or school job. The areas for growth identified by the survey revealed that the internship aspect of the program could be improved. Not only was there no job-embedded learning opportunities for the interns, but also the principal of each participant's school automatically became the mentor principal. Some mentor principals were able to alter participant workloads and maximize their opportunities to practice leadership but others were not engaged at all. Ritchie facilitators individualized expectations and assisted participants' in simulating and extending the learning from inadequate leadership experiences. However, the lack of opportunities for all participants to authentically practice leadership and the convenience method of designating mentor principals created inequitable experiences for leadership learning. The concerns regarding the quality of the internship were confirmed when the "Evaluation of the Ritchie Program for School Leaders" (Palaich et al., 2008) revealed that graduates desired more deliberate and purposeful pairings with mentors and additional time to practice the work of a school leader (p. 9).

The need for intensive job-embedded training experiences for aspiring principals is well documented in the literature (Bottoms, O'Neill, Fry, & Hill, 2003; Davis et al., 2005; Levine, 2005). The Carnegie Foundation concluded that mentoring programs were effective ways to prepare and support principals in their careers (Malone, 2002). A study of schools in Colorado with large numbers of students in poverty scoring higher than the average Colorado student identified the importance of leadership mentoring with the consistent finding that successful principals with fewer than five years of experience had access to an experienced leader within their district (Anderson & DeCesare, 2008). In response to the internal program evaluation and research on best practices in school leadership preparation, the district crafted a grant proposal to substantially enhance the internship and mentoring components of the Ritchie Program through a one-year fully paid, job-embedded internship with a district principal. The award of the US DoE School Leadership Program grant in 2008 made full-time internships and mentor principal training for the Ritchie Program a reality.

FULL-TIME INTERNSHIP DESIGN

In addition to building on the experiences and research on the existing program, the work of the Southern Regional Education Board, Wallace Foundation, and New York City Leadership Academy (Bottoms et al., 2003; Fry, Bottoms, & O'Neill, 2005; Gray, Fry, Bottoms, & O'Neill, 2007; Southern Regional Education Board, 2006a, 2006b; Spiro, Mattis, & Mitgang, 2007; Stein & Gewirtzman, 2003) influenced the design of the Ritchie Program's full-time internship. The main goals of the full-time internship were to more deeply embed the learning experiences from the Ritchie Program projects into the internship and provide interns with authentic leadership responsibilities. The job of the full-time intern was focused on learning the work of a school principal and developing effective leadership practices. Before the existence of the full-time internship, program participants had to rely on simulations to integrate the cognitive, practical, and moral apprenticeships (Shulman, 2005). The opportunity to focus all efforts on learning how to think, act, and be a leader with the support of a mentor principal was designed to promote a process of transformation where participants became school leaders through the process of preparation. Bloom, Castagna, Moir, and Warren (2005, p. 85) describe the transformative process as progressing through three stages:

1. We gain new knowledge, skills, or ways of acting in incremental steps.
2. As we experience success with these new ways of doing things, we begin to change our way of thinking, we imagine a new context for these incremental changes, and we begin to reframe our sense of possibilities.
3. As our new knowledge, skills, and ways of acting become transparent to us — integral to who we are — and as we see the world differently, our learning is fully integrated. We are transformed.

Before the full-time internship existed, Ritchie interns were able to consistently engage in the first step of this process by completing the action research projects at their schools and engaging in simulations and leadership learning in the seminars. Participating in the program as full-time interns made the final two stages of the transformative process more obtainable. In order to practice transformative leadership, leaders must be able to apply new knowledge, skills, and strategies independently, reflect on actions, and learn new ways (Bloom et al., 2005). This integration of ways of doing, ways of thinking, and ways of being is the foundation of the *blended coaching* model developed at the University of California, Santa Cruz's New Teacher Center (Strong, Barrett, & Bloom, 2003). The role of the mentor or coach in this process is critical because an external perspective often serves as the catalyst for changes in thinking and support for the creation of new ways of being. The complexity of this vision for the full-time internship and the support of a mentor is a dramatic change from most traditional internship designs. The expectations of the full-time internship required the development of a process to select both a school site where the intern will be able to fully engage in leadership learning and make contributions to school improvement and a mentor principal who will nurture and support this learning.

Site Placement and Mentor Selection

Once candidates are accepted in the Ritchie Program through the University of Denver, they begin a two-week process with DPS to determine the site for their full-time internship. This process begins with their application for the full-time internship that identifies their skill set, interests, and experiences (Appendix A). Simultaneously, principals interested in becoming a mentor principal for a full-time intern complete an application (Appendix B). The mentor application process considers prior mentor experience and demonstrated success with an intern, and these applications are reviewed and ranked by DPS Instructional Superintendents and Assistant Superintendents. There have always been more mentor principal applications than Ritchie interns, and only the top applicants move on to the next stage of the process. All potential mentor principals receive the Ritchie intern applications. Potential mentor principals and Ritchie interns participate in a matching/interview event where all intern applicants are interviewed by the panel of prospective mentor principals. Following this interview process, the prospective mentor principals identify their top three choices and negotiate the selection of their intern through a draft process. In addition to this process, school characteristics and needs and the skill set of the intern are considered to finalize a match. Once the match is made the Ritchie intern begins to connect with the mentor principal and the school before the Ritchie Program begins with coursework in the summer. Site placement and mentor selection is a technical aspect of the full-time internship design. The professional development and training for mentor principals and Ritchie interns address the more adaptive issues of the complex and engaged practice of mentoring aspiring leaders through a full-time internship.

Professional Development

The practices of many internship programs consist of time logs and task checklists. The Southern Regional Education Board study, "The Principal Internship: How Can we Get It Right?" reported that 61 percent of mentors indicated that their responsibility was to help interns complete a list of tasks determined by the university rather than help them with projects or master leadership competencies (Fry et al., 2005). Traditional internship practices within principal preparation programs greatly influenced the thinking of mentor principals. Most district principals participated in internships consisting of time logs and checklists, so the training of mentor principals for full-time interns became a priority. It was important to be very explicit about the role of the mentor and provide training opportunities where mentors and interns were able to process this new learning together. The expertise of the New York City Leadership Academy (NYCLA) was sought to provide professional development for mentor principals and to become thought partners for the Ritchie Program facilitators as they enhanced the program with the full-time internship. Mentors and interns attended semiannual trainings focused on mentor competencies to foster transformational growth and strategies and tools for giving feedback. They were able to practice these strategies and have facilitated conversations with program faculty and NYCLA trainers.

In addition to shifting the mental models of traditional internship experiences, it was important to develop an evaluation tool to guide the feedback from mentor to intern. Instead of an activity or time log, an evaluation tool that described leadership behaviors based on the NYCLA Performance Standards was developed. Each quarter the interns complete a self-rating and receive ratings from their principal and a peer on the Aspiring Leader Evaluation form. The interns analyze the results of this 360 evaluation and set goals with their mentor principal and Ritchie facilitator. One significant characteristic of this document is the requirement for those completing the evaluation to provide low-inference evidence of their rating so the intern can see the specific behaviors that are influencing the judgment of their performance. In addition to serving as an evaluative tool for the performance of aspiring leaders, it also identifies the areas that the intern has not yet gained experience.

These structures and processes have created a solid infrastructure for the full-time internship, and evaluation data have revealed the need for greater clarity about what effective mentoring looks like in action.

INITIAL RESULTS AND IMPLICATIONS

The full-time internship component of the Ritchie Program has had a significant impact on the career paths of program graduates. Since 2008, 40 Ritchie Program participants have benefitted from a full-time internship and 25 are currently serving as assistant principals, eight are principals, four are district leaders, one left the district, one is a teacher, and one is still seeking an assistant principal position.

Each year Ritchie Program mentors and interns were asked to complete a brief survey regarding the mentor–intern partnership. Survey items focused on mentor engagement, learning opportunities, mentor effectiveness, and benefits of the mentor–intern relationship. There were also questions that assessed how mentors determined intern activities and ways to improve the relationship. The results of these surveys revealed that mentors and interns were satisfied with the full-time internship model. Both mentors and interns offered benefits of the full-time internship. Mentors mentioned mutual learning, relationship building, and helping to grow solid leaders; and interns cited an ability to do meaningful work, the flexibility to try new things, reflection, and seeing the work done. Mentors stated that they took one of the following approaches for their work with the interns: treating the intern like an administrator but with additional support, having the intern shadow the mentor, or meeting with the mentor to discuss the most appropriate activities for the mentorship. These stated approaches demonstrated the range of conceptualizations of the role of the mentor from being an administrator to shadowing and discussing leadership. It was clear that many mentor principals were still operating from the understanding that that their role was to support the first stage of transformation (Bloom et al., 2005) and help the intern learn knowledge, skills, or ways of acting.

Survey results (JVA Consulting, 2012) revealed a discrepancy between mentor and intern perceptions of the learning opportunities provided by mentors. This result supported the descriptive data about the approaches of the mentors. In general, mentors felt that they provided interns with a high frequency of learning opportunities. Mentors were asked to rate, using a five-point Likert-type scale (1 = not at all and 5 = to a great extent), the extent to which they provided various opportunities to the intern (from a pre-determined list of seven opportunities). Mentors' combined ratings of all learning opportunities were quite high (mean = 4.45, standard deviation = 0.64). This rating indicates that mentors felt confident in the extent to which they provided opportunities to the interns. Interns, on other hand, rated their extent of learning opportunities somewhat lower. This was true for every item individually, as well as for the combined mean; interns' average ratings were 4.14 (SD = 0.88). Upon reviewing the disparity between ratings, it was clear that mentors and interns had a slightly different perspective with regards to learning opportunities. Specifically, the largest disparity between mentor and intern ratings were seen for items that assessed the degree to which learning experiences assisted in the developing of skills in the area of systems (mean difference = 0.50), the assigning of meaningful school-based work (mean difference = 0.49), and delegating authority to the intern (mean difference = 0.41).

These results have supported the qualitative feedback from mentors and interns about the range of quality of mentoring and inequities regarding access to authentic leadership experiences. Since the full-time internship was proposed to provide interns with real-time leadership experiences to help them become effective principals and engage in a process of transformative leadership, results demonstrating a disparity between mentor and intern perceptions of learning experiences and responses identifying inequities prompted deeper investigation. Interns identified a few mentors who were highly effective at balancing challenge and support as they helped interns learn ways of doing, ways of thinking, and ways of being. The practices of one of these effective mentor principals were examined through self-report and intern description. The following section describes learning from the implementation of the full-time internship component of the Ritchie Program for School Leaders. It begins with the district perspective of leadership development and concludes with a description of effective mentor practice using the specific actions and behaviors of a highly effective mentor principal and one of her interns.

District Perspectives and Effective Mentor Practice

The experiences of instituting a full-time internship for the Ritchie Program and the results of the annual evaluations have identified growth opportunities for the district. Prior to this work, the district viewed that school performance should be considered the main criteria for placing interns in schools. They had not developed criteria that considered the capabilities of the mentor for coaching leadership development in decisions regarding the matching of interns with mentor principals. The data from the Ritchie interns was clear; many interns were not being provided with the sets of leadership experiences that they needed to be the most effective as a new principal. In fact, it was discovered that the mental model of some existing mentors was they were preparing these interns for assistant principal positions rather than principal positions.

The need for explicit language and a tool to promote personal accountability for the roles and responsibilities of mentor principals, Ritchie interns, and Ritchie facilitators emerged from the initial years of implementing the full-time internship. The resulting document, Ritchie Compact (Appendix C), explicitly states specific dispositions and actions for the collaborative work of providing rich leadership learning opportunities and effective feedback for Ritchie interns. This compact was instituted in 2012 and will be reviewed and signed by all parties at the beginning of the program to serve as a contract for accountability. These expectations will be revisited and evaluated on a quarterly basis.

In addition to institutionalizing a compact that clearly defines the roles and expectations of mentors, interns, and facilitators, the identification of mentors' best practice has emerged from a case study of a highly effective mentor. One mentor principal, Mary Cole, has been extremely successful with every one of her interns. Since 2008, she has had five interns; three of whom are currently principals and two are assistant principals. A careful examination of her practices revealed that a culture of learning was embedded within her school and the mentoring interactions activated triple loop learning (Hargrove, 2003) and integrated ways of doing, ways of thinking, and ways of being.

Leadership Development and School Culture

Introducing a leadership intern into a school is critical to his/her ability to enact leadership within the school. The announcement that a school is receiving an intern should be met with celebration and introduction to the school community. Since interns are placed in schools in the spring, it is possible for mentor principals to arrange a time for the intern meet and greet the faculty and be introduced with a title like Principal in Training or Assistant Principal. At this time, the staff should be informed that the intern will have specific duties and responsibilities as well as be supported in the role as a learner for the principalship. The intern should also be formally introduced to the school community through a process like a written introduction to families in the school newsletter. From the time of selection, it is important for the intern to be a part of the school email list and receive all school correspondence. The intern should be involved in all conversations with the leadership team about plans for the upcoming school year. Mary stated that she explicitly invites the intern to ask questions about anything and through these questions she is able to gain insight about the aspiring principals' strengths and areas of growth. The work of each intern is personalized and is focused on *buckets of responsibility* (e.g., discipline, school culture, middle school students, and teachers) with the freedom and latitude to lead and make decisions in these spheres. Effective mentoring requires time to build relationships. The integration of cognitive, practical, and moral apprenticeships is readily apparent in Mary's description of this relationship:

> I feel that it is vital for each of us to have a sense of who we are and how we think and lead, so that, we can establish trust and effective forms of communication. For example, I want the intern to understand that I expect them to be an active learner and make mistakes. I tell them if you are not making mistakes, bumping into problems, or faced with challenges, then you are not learning and challenged enough. I also tell them I will be there to support them through the challenge and pick them up. For me, it is crucial that I spend time upfront in the late spring and summer forming the mentoring relationship, so that, the aspiring principalship work throughout the school year will maximize the intern's leadership development, enhance my leadership development, and benefit the school community. (M. Cole, personal communication, June 4, 2012)

This description reflects the culture of learning within the school and the reciprocity between the learning of the mentor principal and intern with an explicit focus on school improvement. The relationship between the intern, mentor, and program facilitator requires an inquiry stance (Cochran-Smith & Lytle, 2009) built from the belief that partners are "legitimate knowers and knowledge generators," relationships should be "reciprocal and symbiotic," and educational practice is "relational, theoretical, practical, and political" (p. 89). Connections between the learning in the program and the practices at the school enhance the learning of the intern. One of Mary's interns reported that the school has school-wide learning agreements and staff are trained on a consistent practice of the Ritchie Program, Garmston and Wellman's (1999) seven norms of collaborative work. These norms of collaborative work are a set of skills that are practiced by participants in the Ritchie Program to support dialogue, engage productively in conflict, and problem solve. The common language and practice between the program and the school allowed this intern to internalize these norms into his own leadership practice. This integration of expectations and processes within the preparation program and practice at the school provides consistency and common values to practice leadership and reflect on actions.

The work of the intern is negotiated through frequent and consistent interactions. One intern described, "We would meet daily in the course of our work and 2–3 times a week to talk about bigger picture issues in terms of school leadership and my development." Interns should be given opportunities for authentic leadership tasks, "I was given a very large role in laying out a plan to improve school culture. I was allowed do design policies, professional development, and to make decisions around these issues" (B. Jones, personal communication, May 24, 2012). Assigning the role of the intern can be a delicate issue because it often disrupts predictable patterns of responsibility. For example, an intern was assigned the role of a team leader that was typically assigned to the principal of the school. One teacher expressed disappointment because she did not want to take the time to get to know the intern and doubted his subject matter expertise. It was important for the mentor principal to communicate trust in the capabilities of the intern by maintaining the assignment. At the end of the year, the teacher who had resisted this change communicated that she learned new skills regarding classroom culture and benefitted from helping the intern grow in his understanding of the needs of second language learners (M. Cole, personal communication, June 4, 2012).

Continual growth and evaluation is a trait of an effective organizational culture, so it is important for consistent application of the Aspiring Principal Evaluation tool to pinpoint key areas for growth, goals, and strategies for improved leadership practice. The intern should seek feedback and engage in conversations with all staff regarding his/her growth areas. Mary and her interns complete the evaluation tool every six weeks as a "roadmap to leadership improvement and actionable next steps" (M. Cole, personal communication, June 4, 2012). Trust and value of continual improvement provide for foundation for the effectiveness of this tool. Using this explicit framework and rubric of leadership actions objectifies reflections and allows the mentor to promote a balance between advocacy and inquiry. This balance comes from the requirement that both the intern and the mentor principal provide evidence to support their analysis and ratings. Mary reported the importance of preparation before these reflective conversations:

> It is essential that prior to going into the reflective conversation that I gather data points and plot a course of action or vision for the conversation. Without this step, the debrief of the rubric is not purposeful in changing key leadership actions and ultimately raising achievement within the school. The observable data points provide concrete examples for us to collaboratively discuss effective leadership practice. The use of data combined with the aspiring principal's self assessment, allows us to determine if the leadership practice is leading to growth in both the intern's leadership development and the impact on individual teachers and students. Ultimately, the pre-work sets up a reflective conversation, where the intern feels invested and empowered through constructive feedback and next steps to improve practice. (M. Cole, personal communication, June 4, 2012)

It is important to note that as this effective mentor principal describes mentoring processes, the learning culture within the school becomes visible. Mary consistently reinforced the importance of the impact of every leadership action on improved staff and student performance. This emphasis and consistency assists the intern's development of skill in connecting thought and actions with the desired outcome of improving teaching and learning. The pattern of these reflective conversations is aligned with the final stage of transformational coaching (Bloom et al., 2005, p. 85):

> As our new knowledge, skills, and ways of acting become transparent to us – integral to who we are – and as we see the world differently, our learning is fully integrated.

Reflective practice becomes a new way of being for the interns, "it is now impossible for me to not think of the broader implications of my actions and seek feedback" (B. Jones, personal communication, May 24, 2012).

The description of effective mentor principal practices from the introduction of the intern to the school community and designation of role to the evaluation of leadership actions provide a model and structure for the work. In addition to predictable and explicit practices, effective mentoring requires the mentor to personally engage in a reflective process and possess dispositions of a learner.

Dispositions of Effective Mentor Principals

According to conversations with interns who have had positive experiences with their mentors, effective mentor principals are able to articulate and define their own leadership journeys and engage interns in conversations to develop their own. It is very important to model the mental model that leadership is a way of thinking and being rather than a process of accomplishing tasks. Mentors can do this by sharing their thinking and defining leadership. Mary stressed to her interns that it was not leadership if no one followed. This definition allowed the interns to develop an internal monitoring system to "know I was learning to lead when I saw the values and strategies that I care about being used throughout the school in new and different ways than I had even imagined" (B. Jones, personal communication, May 24, 2012).

Effective mentor principals use nonjudgmental and neutral language to encourage interns not to place value on what they do, but to unpack their decision-making process and identify new thinking. The reflective process was "so ubiquitous that it was not even formalized" (B. Jones, personal communication, May 24, 2012); it became a way of being that the intern was able to internalize. Effective mentors are also transparent with their own learning and thought processes so both mentor and intern go through a reflective process together. The mentor's actions should model consistent and constant learning as the way to lead. Questions like, "why did I do that" or "maybe I was up the ladder of inference on this issue because ..." are used rather than telling the intern what he/she should do. Some other examples of typical language to frame conversations are:

- So help me understand what you were thinking when you did ...
- What leadership successes have you had this week? How do you know? What data do you have?
- How do you think you might have contributed to these teacher or student actions?
- What leadership challenges have you had in moving students or teachers toward the vision or goals this week? How do you know? What data do you have?
- What do we want to see happen and what levers of change are available to us?
- What perceptions will the teachers bring to this situation and how might that affect our communication?
- What key values are we communicating by ...

The integration of thought, action, and value is evident in each of these questions. Mentors who are effective with these conversations allow themselves to be challenged and are able to confront mental models and actions. These questions often promote emotional responses and ground leadership within the integration of thought, action, and values toward the desired impact of improved teaching and learning.

LESSONS LEARNED

The full-time internship model of the Ritchie Program for School Leaders embraces Shulman's (2005) definition of professional education "to link ideas, practices, and values under conditions of inherent uncertainty that necessitate not only judgment in order to act, but also cognizance of the consequences of one's action" (p. 19). The generative nature of this work requires a balance between defining explicit processes and expectations and monitoring with flexibility and trust to allow the mentor principals and interns to customize their work to fit the needs of the intern, mentor, and the school. The experiences over the four years of implementation and evaluation of the full-time internship component of the Ritchie Program for School leaders have taught us that it is essential to continually clarify the mentor principal mental model and share best practices for releasing authority, engaging in reflective practice, and building a school culture that embraces adult learning. The Ritchie Compact emanated from our learning from program evaluation, perceptions of interns, and the practices of effective mentor principals. Our ongoing data collection through sharing practices among Ritchie interns and mentor principals, documenting authentic cases of exemplary mentor and intern interactions, and receiving feedback from interns, mentors, and facilitators are contributing to a compilation of best practices for mentor principals.

The success of the full-time internship is contingent upon the capabilities of the interns, mentors, and facilitators to collaborate and learn from each other. To obtain the third stage of the transformative process (Bloom et al., 2005), "we see the world differently, our learning is fully integrated" (p. 85), the impact of all leadership actions need to be explicitly and honestly articulated and interpreted by the intern and mentor principal. Transparent leadership practice fosters reciprocal growth where the intern, mentor principal, and program facilitator are able to integrate the cognitive, practical, and moral apprenticeships and learn from the consequences of actions. A comment on one of the intern's final projects revealed the value in engaging in the work of developing leaders as they are engaged in authentic practice:

> What I learned is that this is exactly the process of true collaboration, and it is often messy, frustrating, complex, overwhelming, and unruly. Being able to manage this mess of a process with dissenting opinions and shifting directions are exactly the skills we need to be successful leaders in an adaptive school. It is easy to pick a theory of action and then hold to it even when the walls are crumbling around us. It is harder and much more essential to be able to redirect, adapt, refocus, gauge where you are and

what you still need to do, and sometimes to totally shift directions when things are not working well. (J. Fields, personal communication, May 15)

This description of an intern's experience within the program reflects the personal impact and organic nature of this work.

The existence of a common goal with shared values, continual evaluation that guides program improvement, and collaboration that promotes triple loop learning (Hargrove, 2003) and transcends institutional boundaries have promoted the development of this full-time internship model. The authors hope that the description of our implementation and lessons learned clearly illuminates the need to help existing principals unlearn their experiences within their own internships and acquire a mental model of an internship that offers real-time leadership experiences to help interns engage in a process of transformative leadership to become effective principals. The evolution of the Ritchie Program for School Leaders and the features and initial impact of the addition of full-time internships can inform generative program development and promote reflective conversations among professionals engaged in the work of preparing effective school leaders for 21st century schools.

REFERENCES

Anderson, A. B., & DeCesare, D. (2008). *Profiles of success: Eight Colorado schools that are closing the achievement gap.* Denver: Colorado Children's Campaign.

Argyris, C., & Schön, D. A. (1978). *Organizational learning: A theory of action perspective.* Reading, MA: Addison-Wesley Publishing Company.

Bloom, G., Castagna, C., Moir, E., & Warren, B. (2005). *Blended coaching: Skills and strategies to support principal development.* Thousand Oaks, CA: Corwin Press.

Bottoms, G., O'Neill, K., Fry, B., & Hill, D. (2003). *Good principals are the key to successful schools: Six strategies to prepare more good principals.* Atlanta, GA: Southern Regional Education Board.

Braun, D., Gable, R., & Kite, S. (2008) Relationship among essential leadership preparation practices and leader, school, and student outcomes in K-8 schools. *Teacher Education.* Retrieved from http://scholarsarchive.jwu.edu/teacher_ed/1

Cochran-Smith, M., & Lytle, S. L. (2009). *Inquiry as stance: Practitioner research for the next generation.* New York: Teachers College Press.

Darling-Hammond, L., Meyerson, D., La Pointe, M. M., & Orr, M. T. (2009). *Preparing principals for a changing world.* San Francisco, CA: Jossey-Bass.

Davis, S., Darling-Hammond, L., LaPointe, M., & Meyerson, D. (2005). *School leadership study: Developing successful principals.* Stanford, CA: Stanford Educational Leadership Institute.

Deal, T. E., & Peterson, K. D. (1999). *Shaping school culture: The heart of leadership.* San Francisco, CA: Jossey-Bass.

Franke, M. L., Carpenter, T., Levi, L., & Fennema, E. (2001). Capturing teachers' generative change: A follow-up study of professional development in mathematics. *American Educational Research Journal, 38*(3), 653–689.
Freire, P. (1972). *Pedagogy of the oppressed.* Harmondsworth: Penguin.
Fry, B., Bottoms, G., & O'Neill, K. (2005). *The principal internship: How can we get it right?* Atlanta, GA: Southern Regional Education Board.
Fullan, M. (2001). *Leading in a culture of change.* San Francisco: Jossey-Bass.
Garmston, R., & Wellman., B. (1999). *The adaptive school: A sourcebook for developing collaborative groups.* Norwood, MA: Christopher-Gordon Publishers.
Gray, C., Fry, B., Bottoms, G., & O'Neill, K. (2007). *Good principals aren't born — they're mentored: Are we investing enough to get the school leaders we need?* Atlanta, GA: Southern Regional Education Board.
Guskey, T. R. (2000). *Evaluating professional development.* Thousand Oaks, CA: Corwin Press.
Hargrove, R. (2003). *Masterful coaching.* San Francisco, CA: Jossey-Bass/Pfeiffer.
Harri-Augstein, S., & Thomas, L. (1991). *Learning conversations: The self-organised learning way to personal and organizational growth.* London: Routledge.
Hess, R. (2003). *A license to lead? A new leadership agenda for American's Schools.* Los Angeles, CA: Progressive Policy Institute.
JVA Consulting. (2012). *Ritchie program for school leaders: Mentor—mentee survey results.* Denver, CO: Author.
Korach, S. (2011). Keeping the fire burning: The evolution of a university–district collaboration to develop leaders for second-order change. *Journal of School Leadership, 21*(5), 659–683.
Levine, A. (2005, March). *Educating school leaders.* New York, NY: Columbia University.
Malone, J. (2002). *Principal mentoring: An update* (Vol. 18, Issue 2). Eugene, OR: ERIC Clearinghouse on Educational Policy and Management.
Martin, W. M., Ford, S. M., Murphy, M. J., & Muth, R. (1998). Partnerships: Possibilities, potential, and practicalities in preparing school leaders. In R. Muth & M. Martin (Eds.), *Toward the year 2000: Leadership for quality schools* (pp. 238–247). Sixth Annual Yearbook of the National Council of Professors of Educational Administration. Lancaster, PA: Technomic.
Martorell, F., Heaton, P., Gates, S., & Hamilton, L. (2010). *Preliminary findings from the new leaders for new schools evaluation.* RAND.
McCarthy, M. M. (1999). The evolution of educational leadership preparation programs. In J. Murphy & K. S. Louis (Eds.), *Handbook of research on educational administration: A project of the American Educational Research Association* (pp. 110–139). San Francisco, CA: Jossey-Bass Publishers.
McCarthy, M. M., & Forsyth, P. B. (2009). An historical review of research and development activities pertaining to the preparation of school leaders. In M. D. Young, G. M. Crow, J. Murphy & R. T. Ogawa (Eds.), *Handbook of research on the education of school leaders* (pp. 86–128). New York, NY: Routledge.
Murphy, J. (1992). *The landscape of leadership preparation: Reframing the education of school administrators.* Newbury Park, CA: Corwin.
Murphy, J. (2002). Re-culturing the profession of educational leadership: New blueprints. *Educational Administration Quarterly, 38*(2), 178–191.

Murphy, J., & Forsyth, P. B. (Eds.). (1999). *Educational administration: A decade of reform.* Thousand Oaks, CA: Corwin Press.

Murphy, J., & Vriesenga, M. (2004). *Research on preparation programs in educational administration: An analysis.* Columbia, MO: University Council for Educational Administration.

Orr, M. (2010). Pipeline to preparation to advancement: Graduates' experiences in, through and beyond leadership preparation. *Educational Administration Quarterly, 47*(1), 114–172.

Orr, M. T., & Orphanos, S. (2011). How preparation impacts school leaders and their school improvement: Comparing exemplary and conventionally prepared principals. *Educational Administration Quarterly, 47*(1), 18–70.

Palaich, R., Kramer-Wine, J., Anthes, K., & Walker, C. (2008). *Evaluation of the ritchie program for school leaders.* Denver, CO: Augenblick, Palaich & Associates & Third Mile Group.

Senge, P. M. (1990). *The fifth discipline: The art and practice of the learning organization.* New York: Doubleday.

Shulman, L. S. (2005). The signature pedagogies of the professions of law, medicine, engineering, and the clergy: Potential lessons for the education of teachers. Paper delivered at the Math Science Partnerships (MSP) Workshop: "Teacher Education for Effective Teaching and Learning," National Research Council's Center for Education, February 6–8, 2005, Irvine, CA. Retrieved from http://www.taylorprograms.com/images/Shulman_Signature_Pedagogies.pdf. Accessed on October 10, 2010.

Southern Regional Education Board. (2006a). *Developing internship programs for school leaders: A how-to guide for university and school district partners* (Leadership Curriculum Training Module). Atlanta, GA: Author.

Southern Regional Education Board. (2006b). *Mentoring school leaders in competency-based internships* (Leadership Curriculum Training Module). Atlanta, GA: Author.

Spiro, J., Mattis, M. C., & Mitgang, L. D. (2007). *Getting principal mentoring right: Lessons from the field.* New York, NY: Wallace Foundation. Online http://www.wallacefoundation.org/KnowledgeCenter/KnowledgeTopics/EducationLeadership/GettingPrincipalMentoringRight.htm

Stein, S., & Gewirtzman, L. (2003). *Principal training on the ground: Ensuring highly qualified leadership.* Portsmouth, NH: Heinemann.

Strong, M., Barrett, A., & Bloom, G. (April 24, 2003). Supporting the new principal: managerial and instructional leadership in a principal induction program. Paper presented at the Annual Meeting of the American Educational Research Association, Chicago.

Wheatley, M. J. (2001). *Leadership and the new science: discovering order in a chaotic world.* San Francisco, CA: Berrett-Koehler Publishers.

APPENDIX A

Full-Time Internship Application

Ritchie Program for School Leaders and Denver Public Schools

The Ritchie Internship is an opportunity to serve as a full-time intern with the support of one of the district's strongest principals. Ritchie Program candidates are expected to leave the full-time internship prepared to step into the role of principal after 10 months of experiences. Full-Time Ritchie Interns leave their current positions and possibly leave their current school. To facilitate the best placement for you, please fill out the information below:

Name:_____ Current School:_____

Current Position:_____ Years Teaching

Experience:_____(Other)_____

Bilingual   Yes   No   (Circle One)

Describe any positions you have held within the DPS and the years of experience in each:

Describe the positions you have held external to the DPS and the years of experience in each:

Please rank order your preference of region with "1" being your first choice, "2" your second, etc. for possible placement (We may not always be able to honor your preference, but will take it in to consideration)

___Northwest   ___Far Northeast
___Southwest   ___Southeast
___Near Northeast

School Type Preference: (Check all those that interest you the most)

___Elementary   ___Innovation   Other:_____
___Middle School   ___Turn Around
___K-8   ___Charter
___High School   ___Multiple Pathways

If possible, would you prefer to stay at your current school as an intern?
Yes No (Circle One)
Why or Why Not?

Rationale for your desired level of work and school type:

Describe the skill set you would bring to the internship (Describe in detail using descriptive evidence that you would share in an interview for a principal position):

Indicate your areas of weakness and those areas you need to grow the most (Provide descriptive evidence):

Describe the "ideal" principal mentor that would challenge you and support your learning:

_____   _____
Intern Signature   **Date**

I understand that completion of this application is not a guarantee of being selected as an intern. I also understand if selected as an intern I must give up my current position.

APPENDIX B

Ritchie Program for School Leaders and Denver Public Schools

Mentor Principal Application

Name _____ School _____

Years of Service Principal ____years Assistant Principal _____years

Describe any prior mentoring experience and the results of these experiences.

List the names of those individuals whom you have mentored and their current position in the district.

Describe any formal mentor training you have received.

Explain your interest in becoming a mentor for a Ritchie Intern and describe what you expect to gain from this mentoring experience.

Describe how you will engage your intern as a leader in the school and provide detail about the varied opportunities you will provide for your intern to experience the principalship.

Please identify the competency on the DPS Leadership Framework that you are best equipped to teach/model and provide relevant experiences. Please provide specific reasons for your selection.

Please describe a difficult conversation you have had with a mentee or a staff member if you have not been a mentor. Include the outcome of this conversation.

Describe the elements of good feedback. Describe a situation in which feedback has informed your personal or professional growth. What made the feedback effective?

APPENDIX C

THE RITCHIE PROGRAM *for* SCHOOL LEADERS
putting vision into action

Ritchie Compact

The purpose of the Ritchie Compact is to outline the Ritchie Program's expectations for Mentor Principals, Ritchie Interns, and Ritchie Facilitators. It is our expectation that the mentor principals, interns, and facilitators will collaborate to achieve rich leadership learning opportunities, effective feedback resulting in improved leadership skill, and school improvement.

The following are expectations for the full-time internship:

- Interns are actively involved in all aspects of the principals' work (DPS Leadership Framework and work with students, staff, teachers, families, community members, and resources)
- Interns and facilitators attend the weekly Ritchie seminar
- Mentors, interns, and facilitators support the development and execution of a leadership project that is based on the leadership needs of the intern and the UIP
- Mentors, interns, and facilitators support the design and development of quarterly projects to advance the mission and goals of the UIP
- Mentors and interns commit to intensive weekly debriefs utilizing data and reflection journal
- Mentors, interns, and facilitators attend the Ritchie Mentor and Intern meetings
- Interns receive honest, open, and supportive critical feedback that further develops the intern as an effective DPS principal
- Mentors receive honest, open, and supportive critical feedback that further develops the mentor as an effective leadership mentor

- Facilitators receive honest, open, and supportive critical feedback for the improvement of the Ritchie Program for School Leaders
- Mentors, interns, and facilitators create a climate of trust and mutual support

Mentor Principals will

- Allow the intern to attend weekly Ritchie seminars
- Allow the intern to learn by making mistakes and offering supportive feedback
- Allow intern to take risks and lead others
- Introduce and define the role of the intern as a principal in training
- Support the decision-making authority of the intern
- Assess the performance of the intern against the DPS Leadership Framework for Aspiring Principals and the NYCLA Aspiring Principal Evaluation (quarterly)

Ritchie Interns will

- Maintain a reflective journal with a minimum of weekly entries
- Fully engage in all program requirements at a high level of quality
- Be punctual, present, and engaged at all school and class events
- Take responsibility for learning by articulating needs and collaborating with mentor and facilitator to differentiate work
- Self-assess their performance against the DPS Leadership Framework for Aspiring Principals and the NYCLA Aspiring Principal Evaluation (quarterly)
- Seek the assessment of their performance against the DPS Leadership Framework for Aspiring Principals and the NYCLA Aspiring Principal Evaluation by a colleague/teacher (quarterly)

Ritchie Facilitators will

- Review reflections on journals (monthly)
- Meet with the mentor and intern to discuss projects and leadership opportunities and learning (quarterly)
- Meet on site with each intern to observe the intern engaging others in the work of the school (quarterly)

- Critically analyze, provide narrative feedback, and evaluate all projects against rubrics for content, critical thinking, and communication
- Facilitate the analysis of a 360° feedback about performance against the DPS Leadership Framework for Aspiring Principals and the NYCLA Aspiring Principal Evaluation (quarterly)
- Actively contribute to planning meetings and cofacilitate class meetings

_____   _____   _____
Mentor Principal   Ritchie Intern   Ritchie Facilitator

ABOUT THE AUTHORS

Josh Bendickson is a Ph.D. student at Louisiana State University in the E. J. Ourso College of Business. He teaches principles of management in the Rucks Department of Management and is also involved in the Stephenson Entrepreneurship Institute. His research interests include strategy, entrepreneurship, and management history.

Al Bertani, Ed.D., currently works as an independent consultant focusing on leadership development; organization development; professional learning; large-scale change; and strategic planning. Dr. Bertani spent the last third of his career working on urban school reform in support of the Chicago Public Schools having served as senior researcher for the Urban School Leadership Program with the University of Illinois at Chicago; chief officer for Professional Development with the Chicago Public Schools; senior executive director for Chicago Leadership Academies for Supporting Success; and codirector of School and Leadership Development with the Center for School Improvement at the University of Chicago. During his 40 years in education, he divided his career between working in public schools and higher education having served as a classroom teacher, principal, assistant superintendent, college professor, university administrator, and senior research associate.

Kathy Blanc is program manager for the Alaska Staff Development Network (ASDN). She has eight years of experience organizing and facilitating distance delivered and face-to-face professional learning opportunities in Alaska.

David Collins is currently the lead practice coach for the Florida Turnaround Leaders Program. He was an elementary principal and senior director of planning and accountability for Orange County Public Schools in Orlando, Florida. He and his wife, Ann, have authored several publications, including the National Staff Development Council's 1998 Book of the Year. David now works as a consultant to school districts and small businesses in Florida and the Southern Regional Education Board.

Van E. Cooley was interim dean of the College of Education and Human Development, Western Michigan University. He had served as a Faculty

Member and Chair of the Department of Educational Leadership, Research and Technology. Dr. Cooley had published or copublished over 60 articles. Prior to his university appointment, Dr. Cooley was assistant principal, assistant superintendent, and superintendent.

Jeanne Cowan is an education specialist with Technology and Innovation in Education (TIE) in Rapid City, SD. She earned a Bachelor of Science in elementary education from Northern State University and a Master of Education in education administration from South Dakota State University. Jeanne has worked many years in the field of education: 20 years as a teacher, 15 years as an elementary principal, and most recently as a consultant. Jeanne has focused on improvement of teaching and learning by providing professional development and support to educators, especially in the rural areas of South Dakota.

Stephen H. Davis is professor of educational leadership at California State Polytechnic University, Pomona, *where he directs* the Great Leaders for Great Schools Academy. He has held faculty positions at the Stanford University School of Education and the Benerd School of Education at the University of the Pacific, and is a former school district superintendent, personnel director, high school principal, high school dean, and high school teacher. He is the author of *Research and Practice in Education: The Search for Common Ground* (Rowman & Littlefield, 2008), *The Intuitive Dimensions of Administrative Decision Making* (Scarecrow Press, 2003), and numerous articles and reports on educational leadership, principal preparation, administrative evaluation, and decision-making. Dr. Davis earned his doctorate in administration and policy analysis from Stanford University.

Lexie Domaradzki is an independent consultant. She has been working extensively in Alaska with the Department of Education and Early Development and several school districts around the state. Ms. Domaradzki worked for RMC Research as research associate with the Reading First Technical Assistance contract for the previous two years. Prior to that she served as assistant superintendent of teaching and learning in the Washington State Office of Superintendent of Public Instruction. Ms. Domaradzki was the Washington State Reading First director for almost 5 years. She has years of experience serving in rural Alaska as a consultant for increasing reading achievement.

Tierney Temple Fairchild is consultant and writer specializing in executive leadership and policy, turnarounds, public/private partnerships, and race and equity issues in education. She is the coauthor of *The Turnaround*

Mindset: Aligning Leadership for Student Success (Rowman & Littlefield, 2011) with former Virginia state superintendent Dr. Jo Lynne DeMary. As president of Socratic Solutions, Inc., Tierney consults with national and regional organizations, state agencies, private foundations, and leading nonprofits.

Dr. Fairchild was the founding executive director of the Darden/Curry Partnership for Leaders in Education at University of Virginia, where she led the design and delivery of a portfolio of executive development programs for educators, including Governor Mark Warner's Virginia School Turnaround Specialist Program. She also has over 10 years of private sector experience in human resources, executive development, corporate contributions, and community relations. Her cross-sector work began at United Technologies Corporation, where she designed and implemented a strategic K-12 education reform initiative for the CEO and Board of Directors. Dr. Fairchild has extensive media experience and her writing has been published in leading newspapers.

Tierney earned her Ph.D. in education leadership and policy studies at the Curry School, University of Virginia; her MBA from the Darden School, University of Virginia; and her BA in English from the University of Pennsylvania. She lives in Charlottesville, Virginia with her husband Greg and three children.

Betty V. Fry serves as director, Florida Leadership Academy and codirector, Florida Turnaround Leaders Program at the Southern Regional Education Board (SREB) in Atlanta, Georgia. She received her Ph.D. from the University of South Florida and has more than forty years of experience at all levels of education, including elementary and high school teacher, school principal, district supervisor of elementary education, state agency bureau chief of teacher education and professional development, deputy director of a regional educational laboratory, leadership program director at the university level, and director of several projects funded by the US Department of Education.

Dr. Fry specializes in teacher and principal preparation and development, educator performance evaluation, and development of strategies and training for school improvement. She has directed numerous state and regional projects focused on enhancing the capacities of schools, districts and universities to provide quality professional development and make the changes needed to increase student achievement. Consultancies include assisting more than 25 states to implement their initiatives in these areas. Recent publications authored by Betty and disseminated nationally and internationally by SREB include biennial reports that benchmark the southern states' progress in reforming principal preparation and the following special topic reports: *The District Challenge: Empowering Principals to Improve Teaching and Learning*; *Schools Can't Wait: Accelerating the Redesign of University Leadership Preparation Programs*; *Good Principals Aren't Born – They're Mentored; Principal Internships: How Can We Get It Right?* Betty has served on national task forces and presented at many state, national and regional conferences. She is married to Dr. Charles Ahearn and her family includes two daughters who are medical practitioners and parents of five young grandsons.

Miriam L. Fultz is president and senior consultant of Desertfrost Consulting Group, Inc., a consulting practice specializing in educational assessment and program evaluation. Currently, Dr. Fultz serves as external evaluator for various educational institutions and programs, including the Great Leaders for Great Schools Academy, a partnership between Cal Poly Pomona and the Pomona Unified School District. Dr. Fultz also serves as grant proposal development consultant to several public universities, bringing a unique evaluation-based approach to such efforts.

Dr. Fultz has more than 20 years of internal and external assessment and evaluation consulting experience gained through positions based in public postsecondary education and in the business sector. In her career, she has served in a range of internal assessment and program evaluation consulting positions (e.g., Director of Assessment and Instructional Research, Director of Institutional Research, Survey Research Director). As an external consultant, Dr. Fultz has served as external evaluator for more than 38 different projects funded by various private, state, and federal entities. The foci of the projects, among others, includes aspiring principal preparation, teacher quality enhancement, administrator and faculty professional development, quantitative literacy skill enhancement, preservice teacher education reform, student retention, and campus diversity enhancement.

Susan Garton is associate professor of educational leadership at the University of Alaska Anchorage (UAA). She is a former teacher, principal, director of schools and superintendent. She has 14 years experience in higher education devoted exclusively to the training of principals and superintendents for public school districts. Dr. Garton is now in her eighth year at UAA, where she currently focuses on the needs of rural Alaska school districts through her coordination of the Rural Alaska Principal Preparation and Support (RAPPS) program.

About the Authors

Richard Gonzales is an assistant professor in Educational Leadership at the University of Connecticut. He is a former teacher, principal and district-level administrator. His research interests include leadership, school improvement, urban education and schools as organizations.

Mark A. Gooden, Ph.D., serves as associate professor in the Educational Administration Department. He is also Director of The University of Texas at Austin Principalship Program (UTAPP). His research interests include the principalship, antiracist leadership, urban educational leadership and legal issues in education. His research has appeared in *Brigham Young University Education and Law Journal, Education and Urban Society, The Journal of Negro Education, Educational Administration Quarterly, The Sage Handbook of African-American Education*, and *The Principal's Legal Handbook*. He currently serves on the Executive Committee for UCEA, and has served on various committees for the American Educational Research Association. Mark also serves as PI on The University of Texas Collaborative Urban Leadership Project (UTCULP), a $3.3 million grant to develop 120 effective urban secondary school leaders.

Kristy Hebert is the CEO of advance innovative education in Louisiana. She is the project director of *Redesigning Lessons, Re-envisioning Principals*, a principal development program and alternative certification pathway in Louisiana. She has a Ph.D. in educational leadership from Louisiana State University. Her areas of focus include educational entrepreneurship, school leadership, and charter school development.

Janet Hensley is an education specialist with Technology and Innovation in Education (TIE) in Rapid City, SD. She holds a bachelors' degree from Black Hills State University and a master's degree in education administration from South Dakota State University. She has coordinated work with principals, mentors and aspiring leaders in high-need South Dakota schools through the PIRLL (Partnership for Improvement in Rural Leadership and Learning) grant. Janet taught for 17 years and was an elementary principal for 17 years. She has also worked as a grant evaluator and an adjunct professor for Black Hills State University in South Dakota.

Antonia Issa Lahera is assistant professor of educational administration and codirector of the Charter and Autonomous School Leadership Academy (CASLA) and Urban School Leaders (USL) Program at California State University Dominguez Hills. Dr. Issa Lahera has taught a variety of courses in the educational administration program. Working with the Leadership Learning Community Executive team she has been instrumental in developing and coordinating professional development opportunities that continue the growth of program graduates. During her 20 years in public education, Dr. Issa Lahera served as a teacher, staff developer, and principal with the Long Beach Unified School District in Southern California. Currently she works as a mentor with the National Urban Alliance and in that capacity she consults with teachers and school leaders around issues of instruction, the achievement gap and leadership development. Additionally, she works with a cadre of Teacher Leaders who serve in a variety of districts in Minneapolis, Minnesota around culturally responsive education and leadership. Dr. Issa Lahera is a Thinking Maps trainer and consults with districts nationally on a variety of issues surrounding literacy, leadership and issues surrounding the achievement gap. She has presented research at various national conferences including *University Council of Educational Administration (UCEA), American Educational Research Association (AERA), California Charter School Conference*, and *National Charter School Conference*.

Edward Iwanicki is professor Emeritus of educational leadership in the Neag School of Education at the University of Connecticut. While at University of Connecticut he spent 30 years working with national and state groups on the development of meaningful and productive approaches for the preparation, evaluation, and professional growth of learning-focused school leaders. As department head, he led the development of the University of Connecticut Administrator Preparation Program (UCAPP). UCAPP was selected as one of the eight quality programs for the preparation of principals included in the Stanford University study funded by The Wallace Foundation – *Preparing School Leaders for a Changing World: Lessons from Exemplary Leadership Development Programs*. Recently, he has served as consultant to the Arkansas Leadership Academy, the Florida Council for Educational Change, the Illinois Principals Association, and the Southern Regional Education Board.

Carol Kane, M.Ed. – Carol G. Kane has been an educator for 46 years. Her educational experience includes various capacities from early childhood, K-12, adult education, executive director of the Alaska Association of Secondary School Principals as well as the Communities In Schools Alaska, Inc. – state director. While working for the Matanuska-Susitna Borough School District she held positions as assistant principal, principal, director of instruction, associate superintendent, and EEO officer. For the last six years, she has been a coach for the Alaska Administrator Coaching Project, currently serving as a lead coach and the liaison for the Rural Alaska Principal Preparation and Support Grant.

Susan Korach is associate professor and program coordinator for educational leadership and policy studies at the Morgridge College of Education at the University of Denver (DU) in the Educational Research, Practice and Policy Domain. She co-created the Ritchie Program for School Leaders in partnership with Denver Public Schools. This program received a United States Department of Education School Leadership Program grant in 2008 and Wallace Foundation grant in 2011. She is an active participant with the UCEA/LTEL Taskforce on Evaluating Leadership Preparation Programs and a Research Associate with The National Center for the Evaluation of Educational Leadership Preparation and Practice. Her research areas are leadership preparation, learning transfer, university/district partnerships and institutional change.

Ronald J. Leon's first career was in K-12 education as a regular and special education teacher, assistant principal and principal, director, assistant superintendent of 15 elementary schools, assistant superintendent of personnel services, and 11 years as superintendent of the Rowland Unified School District in Los Angeles County. He served as president of the Superintendents' Group for the Association of California School Administrators in the Region and was awarded the National Superintendent of the Year Award from the Kennedy Foundation and Eunice Kennedy Shriver for his work in Character Education. His schools received numerous distinguished, blue ribbon, achieving and other state and national awards for excellence, innovation, and student achievement. The district was known as an outlier with its unprecedented student achievement. In addition to teaching future administrators at Cal Poly Pomona these past seven years, Dr. Leon has served as assistant director of the Great Leaders for Great Schools Program, coached leading superintendents in the area through Pivot Learning Partners and is currently serving as doctoral program director.

Eric W. Liguori is assistant professor of entrepreneurship in the Craig School of Business at California State University, Fresno. Dr. Liguori's research interests include entrepreneurial self-efficacy, entrepreneurial ecosystems, and entrepreneurship education.

Steve Myran is assistant professor of educational leadership in the Department of Educational Foundations and Leadership at Old Dominion

University. His work focuses on the gaps between theory and practice in the areas of instructional leadership, formative assessment and evidence based decision-making, and university/school collaboration. As a veteran of urban public schools and an experienced principal investigator on 20 some grant funded school improvement collaborations, Myran is committed to helping better utilize the tremendous knowledge base in higher education in applied settings. To these ends Myran's work is heavily invested in applied and design based research principals that address both school personnel's pragmatic and applied needs and facilitates rigorous scholarship.

Anthony H. Normore is professor and department chair of educational leadership in the Graduate School of Education at California Lutheran University located in southern California. He has 20 years as a former public school teacher, school-site, and district office administrator. He has worked with educational leaders in the Himalayan Kingdom of Nepal and more recently as a visiting scholar at Seoul National University in South Korea. Dr. Normore's research focuses on leadership development, preparation and socialization of urban school leaders in the context of ethics and social justice. His two most recent books include *Discretionary Behavior and Performance in Educational Organizations: The Missing Link in Educational Leadership and Management* (Emerald Publishing Group, and coedited with Ibrahim Duyar, 2012); *Leadership in Education, Corrections, and Law Enforcement: A Commitment to Ethics, Equity, and Excellence* (Emerald Group Publishing Limited, coedited with Brian D. Fitch, 2011). He is the author of 100 + pieces of scholarly research and has presented 150 + papers at national and international professional conferences. His research has appeared in *Journal of School Leadership, Journal of Educational Administration, Values and Ethics in Educational Administration, Leadership and Organizational Development Journal, Canadian Journal of Education Administration and Policy, International Journal of Urban Educational Leadership, Educational Policy*, and *Journal of Research on Leadership Education*.

Ann O'Doherty, Ed.D., is senior lecturer at the University of Washington where she develops school and district-level leaders through the Danforth Educational Leadership Program and the Center for Educational Leadership. In her previous role as clinical assistant professor at The University of Texas at Austin, she directed the University of Texas Collaborative Urban Leadership Project designed to prepare 120 effective secondary school leaders for Dallas, Houston, Harlandale and Austin area school districts.

Supported by a $3.3 million grant by the US Department of Education's School Leadership Project. Along with Mark A. Gooden, Ph.D., she has developed antiracist leadership curriculum modules for UCEA's Leaders Supporting Diverse Learners FIPSE grant. She devoted eighteen years to PreK-12 public schools including 12 years as a school administrator at elementary, middle, and high school levels. Her research interests include program evaluation, coaching, leadership development, and district-level influence on school success. She regularly contributes to research and scholarship efforts and currently serves as a member of the editorial board for Educational Administration Quarterly.

Margaret Terry Orr (Ph.D., Columbia) is faculty member of Bank Street College of Education (NY) and directs its Future School Leaders Academy, a two-year school and district leadership preparation program in partnership with 30+ suburban and small city districts. She has been a professor of leadership preparation for over 20 years, preparing school and district leaders, and developing several preparation and post-preparation programs for aspiring leaders and superintendents. She conducted numerous regional and national studies over the last 30 years on leadership preparation approaches and school and district reform initiatives, and published numerous books and articles on leadership preparation and its impact, including (with Linda Darling-Hammond and others) *Preparing Principals for a Changing World: Lessons from Effective School Leadership Programs* (Jossey-Bass, 2009). She is currently Division A vice president of the American Educational Research Association.

Maureen Sanders was the executive director of leadership development for the Denver Public Schools, Denver, Colorado. She was recruited to Denver 10 years ago from Los Angeles where she was serving as director of the California School Leadership Academy, Los Angeles County, where she worked to provide principal preparation and school leadership professional development for 81 school districts.

In her role in Denver, she was instrumental in the co-creation of the Ritchie Fellow Aspiring Principal Preparation Program in partnership with the University of Denver that has now been nationally recognized in several recently published research articles as being one of the top principal preparation programs across a number of other university programs throughout the country. Most recently, the DPS was one of 26 school districts invited to apply to the Wallace Foundation to extend this work. The DPS was selected as one of six winners across the country of a $12.5 million per year pipeline grant award from Wallace for five years as a result of the Partnership Principal Preparation program developed between the University of Denver and Denver Public Schools.

Maureen's other responsibilities in DPS included ongoing coaching of principals and principal professional development support for all sitting principals and assistant principals in the district.

Maureen was invited to join the New York City Leadership Academy National Initiatives Team in June. She began this new position with the New York City Leadership Academy in August of this year.

Karen L. Sanzo is associate professor in the Department of Educational Foundations and Leadership in the College of Education at Old Dominion University located in Norfolk, Virginia. She spent eight years in the public schools, serving as a middle school mathematics teacher and a school administrator. She has been principle investigator for several grants, including a USDE SLP grant funded in 2008. She is also the director of the USDE SLP Communication Hub. Her research has appeared in *Journal of School Leadership*, *Journal of Educational Administration*, *Journal of Research on Leadership Education*, *International Journal of Urban Educational Leadership*, *Educational Planning*, and *International Journal of Educational Reform*.

Jianping Shen is the John E. Sandberg Professor of Education in the Department of Educational Leadership, Research and Technology, Western Michigan University. He publishes widely in the area of educational leadership, policy analysis, and research methods.

Charles Teddlie is distinguished professor (Emeritus) in the College of Education at Louisiana State University. Professor Teddlie has taught research methods courses for over 25 years, including statistics, qualitative methods, and mixed methods. His major writing interests are in mixed methods research and educational effectiveness research. He is the author of numerous chapters and articles and the coauthor or coeditor of 12 books including: *The International Handbook of School Effectiveness Research* (2000), the *The SAGE Handbook of Mixed Methods in Social and Behavioral Research* (2003, 2010), and *Foundations of Mixed Methods Research* (2009).

J. Kelly Tonsmeire is director of the Alaska Staff Development Network (ASDN). ASDN is Alaska's largest provider of professional development and has built an extensive distance-delivery infrastructure that brings scores of highly qualified, national-level instructors to very isolated schools. In 2011, more than 4,000 educators statewide enrolled in ASDN-sponsored events. ASDN has an extensive grants management track record with large, distance-delivered rural school improvement projects. Tonsmeire received the national service award from the National Rural Education Association.

K. Mark Weaver is the Ben May chair of entrepreneurship in the Mitchell College of Business at the University of South Alabama. Dr. Weaver is a past president and fellow of both the United States Association of Small Business and Entrepreneurship and the International Council of Small Business. His research focuses primarily on international strategic alliance formation, though he is widely published in many related areas including entrepreneurship education.

Gary Whiteley, Ed.D. has been an educator for 32 years. He has served in numerous roles at the school level and district level; including classroom teacher, school principal, and assistant superintendent. Gary was a research associate with the Center for Research and Evaluation at the University of Maine. Gary has served in numerous capacities that focus on school improvement for the Alaska Department of Education and Early Development. Dr. Whiteley has been the director of the Alaska Administrator Coaching Project for the past eight years and is currently a leadership consultant for The Education Commission of the States.

AUTHOR INDEX

Adams, O., 115
Aiken, J. A., 56
Ajzen, I., 160, 162
Alford, B., 3, 5
Alle, B. A., 119
Allen, L. A., 5
Allen, L. W., 139
Allensworth, E., 119
Anderson, A. B., 243
Anderson, S., 76, 98, 118, 210
Andrews, R., 53, 168–169
Anthes, K., 242–243
Argyris, C., 240

Baker, B. D., 4
Baker, M. E., 168
Ballenger, J., 3
Bandura, A., 178
Banks, P., 118
Barber, M. E., 2–3, 13, 78
Barlin, D., 218
Barnett, B. G., 5, 54–56
Barney, J., 158
Barrett, A., 245
Barth, R., 58
Basom, M., 55
Basom, M. R., 55
Bates, M., 60
Beaty, D. A., 52–56, 67, 167
Benson, D. A., 138
Bernd, M., 176
Bielaczyc, K., 170
Bizzell, B. E., 146
Black, P., 230

Bloom, G., 218, 244–245, 247, 252, 254
Blumenfeld, P., 170–171
Borthwick, A. C., 169
Bosker, R. J., 115
Bossert, S., 118
Bottoms, G., 3, 13, 22, 47, 51, 59, 95, 99, 243–244, 246
Boudreau, S., 177
Boyatzis, R. E., 60
Boykin, A. W., 116, 119
Brahier, B., 61
Braun, D., 239
Brazil, N., 211
Bredeson, P. V., 167
Brent, B. O., 4, 52
Brooks, J. S., 50, 52–53, 55–56, 59, 61, 67
Brown, K. M., 5, 99
Browne-Ferrigno, T., 51, 55, 62, 66, 67, 78, 139, 168
Bruner, D. Y., 50, 52, 53, 55, 67, 68
Bryk, A. S., 115, 117, 119
Burkhauser, S., 212, 230
Burn, J., 218
Burt, W., 132

Caldwell, K., 50
Capper, C. A., 5
Carpenter, T., 238
Carsrud, A., 161
Carter, L., 50
Castagna, C., 218, 244, 247, 252, 254

AUTHOR INDEX

Celio, M. B., 118–119
Cheney, G. R., 47, 212
Chenoweth, K., 211
Clark, D. C., 54, 56
Clark, D. L., 52
Clark, S. N., 54, 56
Clarken, R. H., 168
Clayton, J. K., 168, 175
Cochran-Smith, M., 250
Codding, J., 50
Coffin, G., 3, 55
Cohen, C., 46, 76, 78, 98, 100, 141, 144, 191
Collins, A., 170
Cook, D. L., 169
Cooley, V. E., 118, 132
Copland, M. A., 5, 176
Corcoran, S., 215
Cornwall, J. R., 154–155, 158
Cosner, S., 117, 119
Cotton, K., 115, 117, 119
Cox, H., 177
Crawford, J., 98
Crow, G. M., 68, 167
Crum, K. S., 168, 175
Cunningham, R. T., 116, 119
Cunningham, W. G., 142

Daly, A. J., 119
Darling-Hammond, L., 3, 46, 47, 58, 76, 78, 97, 98, 99, 100, 120, 141, 144, 191, 239, 241, 242, 243
Davis, J., 47, 212
Davis, S. H., 47, 76, 97, 99–100, 242–243
Day, C., 177
De Groot, E. V., 178
Deal, T. E., 240
DeArmond, M., 167
DeCesare, D., 243

DeVita, C., 174
Diamond, J. B., 117
Dikkers, A. G., 61
Dill, E. M., 116, 119
Dill, V., 98
Diller, P. F., 55
Donaldson, G., 191
Drucker, P., 157
Duffett, A., 69
DuFour, R., 31, 62
Dwyer, D., 118

Edelson, D. C., 170
Edens, R., 169
Elmore, R. F., 175, 212, 230

Farkas, S., 69
Feldman, N., 118–119
Fennema, E., 238
Fenwick, T. J., 28
Fishman, B., 170–171
Foleno, T., 69
Folley, P., 69
Ford, S. M., 238
Forsyth, P. B., 51, 239
Franke, M. L., 238
Freeman, H. E., 13
Freire, P., 240
French, J., 58
Frieler, J., 50
Fry, B., 47, 51, 59, 95, 99, 243–244, 246
Frye, B., 3, 13, 22
Fullan, M., 51, 212, 240
Fuller, E., 4
Fulmer, R., 50

Gable, R., 239
Garcia-Lopez, S. P., 58
Garmston, R., 250

Author Index

Garrett, K., 47, 212
Gates, S., 212, 230, 239
Gerstl-Pepin, C., 5
Gewirtzman, L., 244
Giber, D., 50
Gilsinan, J., 169
Glaser, R., 177
Glasman, N. S., 50
Goddard, R. D., 116, 119
Goldrick, L., 218
Goldring, E., 54–56, 79–80, 118
Goldsmith, M., 50
Goleman, D., 60
Gooden, M. A., 6
Goodlad, J. I., 122
Goodnough, K., 168
Goodnow, E. J., 6
Gordon, M., 210
Gray, C., 244
Green, R. L., 61, 141
Greenlee, B. J., 50, 52–53, 55, 67–68
Grogan, M., 52–56, 67, 167–169
Gronsky, B., 5
Guarino, A., 115
Gundlach, L., 167
Guskey, T. R., 1, 3, 241

Haas, W., 5
Haberman, M., 98
Haertel, E., 211
Hafner, M., 169
Hale, E. L., 76
Haller, E. J., 4, 52
Hallinger, P., 115–119, 210
Halverson, R., 103–104, 117
Hamilton, L., 212, 230, 239
Hancock, J., 217
Hanushek, E. A., 154
Hargrove, R., 249, 255
Harri-Augstein, S., 240

Harris, A., 98, 211
Harris, S., 5
Harvey, J., 118, 119
Hasazi, S., 5
Hassenpflug, A., 98
Havard, T., 50, 53, 55–56, 59, 61, 67
Heaton, P., 239
Hebert, K., 154, 155
Heck, R. H., 115–119, 210
Herrity, V. A., 50
Hess, F. M., 54, 58, 191
Hess, R., 239
Hewitson, M. T., 3
Hicks, M., 216
Hill, D., 243, 244
Hix, B., 50
Holdgreve-Resendez, R. T., 119
Holleran, J., 47, 212
Hopkins, D., 98, 211
Horn, R. A., 55
Hoy, A. W., 116, 119
Hoy, W. K., 116, 119
Hughes, J. E., 61
Hughes, R. C., 54
Hughes, S., 177
Hurley, E. A., 116, 119

Iacona, C. M., 52
Ikemoto, G., 212, 230
Isenberg, D. J., 155

Jackson, B. L., 3, 5, 51, 53–56, 59, 61–62
Jackson, K., 4
Jacobson, S. L., 52
Jakubowski, T. G., 58
Jamison, M. G., 55
Jantzi, D., 3, 4, 55, 115–116, 118–119, 210
Jean-Marie, G., 52–53, 55

Johnson, J., 69
Johnson, S. M., 60
Joseph, D., 170

Kaplan, L. S., 118
Kardos, S. M., 60
Kauffman, D., 60
Kearney, K., 60
Keirsey, D., 60
Kelley, C., 3, 5, 51, 53–56, 59, 61–62
Kelly, A. P., 54, 58, 191
Killeen, K., 5
King, C., 77, 79
King, R., 56
Kingsbury, A., 160
Kingston, S., 118
Kirby, E., 118
Kirkpatrick, D. L., 1–3
Kirst, M., 211
Kite, S., 239
Kitsantas, A., 116, 119
Knowles, M. S., 42
Knuth, R., 118
Kolb, D. A., 28–29
Korach, S., 3, 240
Kottkamp, R. B., 18
Kozol, J., 58
Krajcik, J., 170–171
Kramer-Wine, J., 242–243
Krovetz, M., 34
Krueger, J. A., 54, 56
Krueger, N., 161
Kruger, M. L., 115
Kruse, S. D., 119
Kuh, G. D., 52

La Pointe, M. M., 3, 239, 241
Ladson-Billings, G., 116, 119
LaMagdeleine, D., 167

LaPointe, M., 46, 76–79, 97–100, 141, 144, 191, 242–243
Larson, T., 118
Lawson, L., 50
Leary., 3
Lee, G., 118
Lee, V., 116, 119
Leidner, D., 58
Leithwood, K. A., 3–5, 55, 76, 98–100, 115–116, 118–119, 210–211
LePage, P., 177
Levi, L., 238
Levine, A., 50, 52, 167, 191, 239, 243
Levine, R., 211
Lieberman, A., 177
Lies, A., 138
Liguori, E. W., 154–155
Lindsey, D. B., 58
Lindsey, R. B., 58
Lipsey, M. W., 13
Little, J. W., 175
Liu, E., 60
Lortie, D., 61–62
Louis, K. S., 98, 116–119
Lytle, S. L., 250

Ma, X., 132
Maier, S., 177
Malone, J., 243
Manthey, G., 116, 119
Marcoulides, G. A., 115–118
Marks, H. M., 115–119
Martin, W. M., 238
Martorell, F., 239
Marx, G., 118
Marx, R. W., 170–171
Marzano, R. J., 44, 51, 114, 118, 119, 141, 145, 197, 212
Matthews, L. J., 68

Mattis, M. C., 244
Maxcy, B. D., 167
McCabe, D. H., 55
McCarthy, M. M., 13, 52, 54, 239
McCauley, C., 217
McGee, J. E., 160
McKee, A., 60
McKenzie, K., 99
McLaughlin, M., 177
McLeod, S., 61
McNamera, J. H., 4, 52
McNulty, B. A., 44, 51, 114, 118, 141, 145, 197, 212
Meyerson, D., 3, 46, 76, 78, 97–100, 141, 144, 191, 239, 241–243
Mezirow, J., 28, 31
Michlin, M., 210
Miller, L., 50
Miller, P., 169
Milstein, M. M., 51, 54, 56, 81
Mintrop, H., 174
Mitgang, L. D., 244
Moir, E., 218, 244, 247, 252, 254
Moolenaar, N. M., 116, 119
Moore, S., 210
Moorman, H. N., 76
Moxley, R., 217
Mueller, S. L., 160
Munoz, M., 4, 169, 179
Munro, R., 177
Murphy, M. J., 51–53, 58, 167, 238–239
Muse, I. D., 54, 55
Muth, R., 55, 168, 238
Myran, S., 168, 175, 176

Nathan, J., 191
Nauman, A. D., 169
Newell, L. J., 52

Newmann, F. E., 117, 119
Nicholson, B., 3
Normore, A. H., 50, 52–53, 55
Norris, C., 55
Norris, C. J., 55
Norton, J., 143
Nunnery, J., 118
Nuri-Robins, K., 58

O'Doherty, A., 6
O'Donnell, R. J., 116
Okunade, A. A., 138
O'Neill, K., 3, 13, 22, 47, 51, 59, 95, 99, 243, 244, 246
Orphanos, S., 3–4, 239
Orr, M. T., 1–4, 7–8, 13–14, 46, 76–79, 98, 100, 141, 144, 191, 239, 241, 243
Osta, D., 218
Owings, W. A., 118

Palaich, R., 242–243
Papa, F. Jr., 98
Pasternak, R., 118
Patrick, L., 50, 53, 55–56, 59, 61, 67
Payne, F., 177
Peel, B. B., 168
Peel, H. A., 168
Perry, M., 211
Peske, H. G., 60
Peterson, D., 216
Peterson, K. D., 51, 240
Peterson, M., 155, 160
Pfeffer, J., 158
Pintrich, P. R., 178
Plotz, J., 191
Popp, T., 159
Portin, B., 167
Pounder, D. G., 3, 116, 167

Preiss, S., 52–56, 67, 167
Printy, S. M., 115–119

Qian, H., 119, 167

Rainey, J. M., 132
Reed, C. J., 167
Reeves, P., 132
Restine, L. N., 3
Ricciardi, D., 55, 169
Roberson, S., 56
Robinson, J., 177
Rodosky, R. J., 4
Ronstadt, R., 160
Rorrer, A., 1–2, 4
Rossi, P. H., 13
Rowan, B., 118
Ruiz, R. d. J., 5
Rusch, E. A., 18

Salancik, G., 158
Salloum, S., 116, 119
Sanzo, K. L., 168
Sawyer, D., 138
Schechter, C., 118–119
Schneider, P., 167
Schunk, D. H., 178
Schwartz, A., 215
Scott, L., 222
Seashore Louis, K., 76, 210
Sebastian, J., 5
Sebring, B., 115, 117, 119
Senge, P. M., 240
Sequeira, J. M., 160
Shen, J., 118–119, 122, 127, 132
Sherman, W. H., 52–56, 67, 167–168
Shulman, L. S., 238–239, 244
Simmons, J., 50, 169, 179

Simpson, M., 177
Sims, P., 54–56, 79–80
Slater, C. L., 4
Sleegers, P. C., 119
Smith, J. B., 116, 119
Smith, W., 115
Solansky, S. T., 5
Soloway, E., 170–171
Somers Hill, M., 50, 52, 53, 55, 67, 68
Speck, M., 34
Spillane, J. P., 58, 117, 118
Spiro, J., 244
Stake, R. E., 11
Stein, S., 244
Steinbach, R., 5
Stirling, T., 169
Streshly, W., 176
Strom, P., 115
Strong, M., 245
Studier, C., 211

Tatum, K., 50, 53–56, 59, 61, 67
Teitel, L., 177
Terrell, R. D., 58
Theoharis, G., 5, 58
Theokas, C., 211
Thomas, E., 210
Thomas, L., 240
Thompson, E. R., 160
Tierney, W. G., 50
Trujillo, T., 174
Tucker, M., 50

Vanderhaar, J. E., 4
Velsor, E., 217
Vogel, L. R., 56
Vozikis, G. S., 154–155
Vriesenga, M., 239

Wahlstrom, K. L., 76, 98, 116–119, 210
Walker, A., 167
Walker, C., 242–243
Wall, S., 50
Ware, H., 116, 119
Warren, B., 218, 244, 247, 252, 254
Wasylyshyn, K. R., 5
Waters, T., 44, 51, 114, 118, 131, 141, 145, 197, 212
Weaver, K. M., 154–155
Weber, K., 154
Weinstein, M., 215
Weiss, C. H., 4
Wellman, B., 250
Wenger, E., 68
Whale, D. E., 118

Wheatley, M. J., 80, 240
Whitaker, K. S., 54, 56, 76
White, G. P., 116
Whiteside, A., 61
William, D., 230
Williams, T., 211
Wilson, P., 3
Winter, P., 169
Witziers, B., 115–118
Wolk, R. A., 155
Wunnava, P. V., 138

Yerkes, D., 55
Yerkes, D. M., 55
Young, M. D., 1, 2, 4, 6, 11, 97, 99
Youngs, P., 60, 117, 119
Yuan, W., 132

SUBJECT INDEX

Accountability, 13, 64, 68, 76–77, 100, 105, 123, 125, 140, 212, 214, 225, 230, 249
Adult Learning, 42–43, 120, 130, 196, 213, 254
Aspiring leaders, 6, 17, 57–59, 62–65, 99, 132, 139, 147, 166, 168, 177–178, 183, 188, 214, 238–240, 246

Best practices, 59, 83, 119, 124, 154, 156–157, 199, 202, 242–243, 254
Building relationships, 145, 148
Buy-in, 35, 37, 39–40, 45, 86, 171

Change agents, 160, 210
Coaching, 2, 5–7, 11–12, 17, 27–28, 31, 33–35, 38, 42, 44, 63, 65, 80–82, 87–88, 145, 159, 179, 184–185, 188–192, 194–195, 209–230, 245, 249, 252
Cohorts, 11–12, 17, 26, 32, 34, 42, 46, 54, 139, 162, 186–187, 190, 199
Collaboration, 5–6, 26, 30, 32, 37, 41, 45–47, 56–57, 62, 75–77, 79, 88, 138–140, 142–143, 147, 162, 167–168, 170–171, 176, 184, 193, 197–198, 207, 220, 238, 240, 254–255
Communication, 14–15, 32, 41, 45–46, 50, 88, 90–91, 115, 139–140, 142, 146–148, 174, 176–177, 179–180, 188, 193–194, 205, 224–225, 250–253, 255
Community of professional practice, 49–50, 68
Competency-based Coaching, 219
Competency-based Support, 221
Competitive advantage, 153, 158
Context, 1–2, 4, 6, 28–29, 34, 38, 47, 52, 56, 99, 131, 138, 144, 155, 166, 175, 178–179, 190, 202, 211, 213, 219, 223, 226, 230, 238–239, 241, 244
Context-specific Programming, 213
Continuous Support, 220
Culturally responsive, 137, 187
Customer needs, 153
Customized principal preparation, 137–138

Data analysis, 104–106, 154, 218, 227
Design team, 78, 81, 85–89, 185, 188, 195–199, 201–202
Distance learning, 171, 184
District/university partnership, 74, 82–83
Diverse learners, 27

Education reform, 50, 154, 159
Effective leadership behaviors, 27
Effective leadership practice, 3, 209, 244, 252
Effective school leaders, 51, 56, 80, 97–99, 210, 255

Engagement, 40, 45, 86, 124, 168, 176, 193, 199, 219, 223, 226, 229, 247
Entrepreneurial school leadership, 153, 160
Experiential learning, 28–30, 38, 42–43, 212–213

Facilitating, 46, 193, 230
Facilitative coaching, 225
Facilitative Learning, 219
Feedback, 2, 5, 28, 43, 46, 66–67, 81, 105, 117, 123, 140, 160, 172–173, 192–194, 214, 216, 218–220, 223, 225, 227–230, 242, 246, 248–249, 251–252, 254
Field Observation, 227
Financial outcomes, 153

Goal setting, 193
Growing your own leaders, 139

Hard-to-staff schools, 139

Institutional partnership, 25, 27, 29, 31, 33, 35, 37, 39–41, 43, 45, 47
Instructional leadership, 17, 38, 54, 61, 115–117, 119, 178, 187, 193–194, 212, 222, 239
Instructional practices, 73, 82, 178, 184, 197, 231
Interagency collaborations, 26
Internship, 9–10, 16, 61, 83, 139, 141–143, 147, 149, 176, 186, 188, 190, 217, 237, 239, 241, 243–249, 254–255
Intervisitations, 218, 227–228
ISLLC standards, 141, 147, 193
Iterative, 39, 91, 165, 170, 175, 196–197, 230

Job-embedded, 124, 131, 149, 214, 219, 222, 226, 243

Leadership development, 13, 17, 26–28, 43–44, 46, 49–52, 67, 83, 97, 99, 113–114, 118–120, 122, 129, 132, 140, 183–184, 191–193, 210–211, 213–216, 219–220, 224, 239–240, 248–250, 252
Leadership performance, 44, 209, 211, 213–214, 218–219, 221, 228–231
Leadership potential, 17, 32, 102–103, 107
Leadership preparation, 1–5, 7–9, 11, 13, 15, 17, 25–26, 49, 51–56, 66–68, 73, 77, 97, 99, 113, 137, 145, 153, 165–168, 178, 183, 209–210, 212–213, 237, 239, 242–243
Leadership Standards, 67, 86, 213
learning outcomes, 8–11, 17
Learning-Centered Leadership, 113–115, 117–123, 125, 127, 129, 131–132
Low performing schools, 25, 27, 38, 41, 83

Management strategies, 27
Market-based approaches, 153
Market-driven organizations, 153
Memorandum of understanding (MOU), 84–85, 87, 139–140, 144
Mentoring, 28–29, 44, 80, 121, 137–138, 143–145, 147–149, 159, 190, 212, 217, 231, 238, 243, 246–250, 252
Mission statements, 148

Subject Index

Motivation, 38, 50, 55, 60, 62, 211
Mutual Accountability, 214

National Council for Accreditation of Teacher Education (NCATE), 61, 66–67, 98, 141
Network, 59, 62, 78–79, 92, 145, 149, 157, 175, 185, 188–190, 193, 195–196, 205, 207, 230
Nominate, 101, 186, 202

Observations, , 127, 145
On-site mentoring, 137–138, 147–148
Ongoing Improvement, 214
Ongoing planning, 49
Organization building, 153
Organizational capacity, 153, 172, 179
Organizational reform, 26

Planning, 1, 8, 12, 14–16, 27, 29–30, 35–36, 39–45, 49–51, 53, 55, 57, 59, 61, 63, 65, 67, 73–76, 78, 80, 83–87, 89, 91, 115, 125, 127–128, 141, 146, 160, 176, 188, 194–195, 198–199, 202, 204–205, 221, 223
Planning Team, 27, 29–30, 39–45
Practice-ready school leaders, 25–26, 42, 46
Problem-based curriculum, 28–30
Problems of practice, 16, 29–30, 165, 169, 198–202
Professional cultures, 74
Professional Development, 37–39, 42–43, 46, 53, 59, 79–82, 86, 114, 117, 120, 125, 127, 129, 137–138, 141, 144–147, 149, 166, 171–173, 175–176, 178, 185, 188, 192–195, 198, 207, 217, 220, 224, 227, 241, 245–246, 251
Professional learning communities, 146, 148, 197
Program evaluation, 1–5, 7–9, 11, 13–17, 33, 44, 178, 196, 227–228, 241–243, 254
Project budget, 92
Project management, 85, 91, 93, 185

Quality education delivery, 140

Re-envisioning principals, 153, 155, 157, 159, 161
Recruitment, 32, 44, 52, 84, 97–101, 103, 105, 107, 137–139, 177, 188
Reflection, 2, 5–6, 29–30, 33, 58, 64, 66, 76, 120, 145–146, 165–166, 170, 179, 197, 202, 205, 219, 222, 226, 228, 230, 247
Relationships, 13, 15, 17, 26–27, 29, 44–45, 48, 55, 59, 77, 79, 88, 123, 145–146, 148, 174, 179, 192, 200, 205, 214, 219, 231, 241, 250
Resource allocation, 78, 140
Responsive to District Needs, 220
Retention of school leaders, 67, 166, 178
Rigorous, 3, 16–17, 28, 32, 43, 57, 67, 81–82, 97–101, 103, 105, 107, 122, 209, 213
Rigorous candidate nomination and selection process., 28
Risk assessment, 85, 92
Rural Leadership, 137

Schedule, 55, 63, 65, 84–85, 91–92
School coaching, 209

SUBJECT INDEX

School culture, 82, 116, 124, 156, 166, 178, 180, 214, 249–251, 254

School improvement, 4, 7, 27, 29, 81–83, 85, 97–99, 114–115, 117, 121, 125–126, 128, 132, 141, 145–146, 170, 173–176, 179, 185, 191, 199, 202, 207, 210, 212–213, 218, 220, 224, 229, 245, 250

School-wide improvement planning, 146

Shadowing, 61, 142, 247

Social entrepreneurs, 153–155, 160, 162

Social solutions, 153

Socioeconomic needs, 138

Southern Regional Education Board (SREB), 51, 59, 79–83, 93, 212, 244, 246

Staff development, 50, 58, 65, 185, 188–190, 195–196, 205, 207

Stakeholders, 18, 34, 39–41, 43–44, 46–47, 53, 68, 81, 85, 88–92, 120–121, 123, 125–127, 129–130, 172, 179, 230

Standards for principal preparation, 25

Student achievement, 26–27, 35–36, 38, 50, 56, 58–59, 61, 64–65, 74, 79–82, 90, 113–116, 118–119, 121–122, 124–127, 129–130, 132, 140, 144, 146, 157, 190, 210–212, 219, 221–222, 228–229, 239–240

Student achievement gains, 50, 58

Support, 6, 8, 11, 13, 16, 27–28, 31–32, 35–37, 39–40, 42–43, 45–46, 50, 55, 57–60, 62, 64–65, 67–68, 78, 80–82, 99, 106, 115, 117, 121, 128–129, 137, 140, 144–149, 154, 157, 162, 168–169, 171, 175–176, 178–179, 183–191, 193, 195–197, 199, 201, 203–205, 207, 209–221, 223–224, 226–231, 241–245, 247–248, 250–251

Sustainability, 158, 199

Sustainable business models, 153

Tailored Support, 220

Teaming, 213–214

Thematically Integrated curriculum, 43

Time estimates, 92

Timeframe, 83, 85

Timing, 37, 45

Training, 12, 29, 32, 52, 58–59, 62–65, 67, 81–82, 84–86, 92, 106, 121, 131, 137, 145–146, 148, 156, 161–162, 171, 175, 179, 185–186, 189, 194, 197, 209, 215–216, 220, 243, 245–246, 249

Trust, 26, 31, 39–40, 55, 117, 119, 171–172, 218, 221, 250–251, 254

Turnover, 89, 184, 190, 230

Underperforming schools, 26, 34, 56, 58–59, 184, 212–213

Urban schools, 6, 27, 47, 66–67